THE
TROUBLE
WITH
DOCTORS

THE TROUBLE WITH DOCTORS

Fashions, Motives and Mistakes

Ann Dally

ROBSON BOOKS

First published in Great Britain in 2003 by Robson Books,
The Chrysalis Building, Bramley Road, London W10 6SP

An imprint of Chysalis Books Group plc

Copyright © 2003 Ann Dally

The right of Ann Dally to be identified as author of this work
has been asserted by her in accordance with the Copyright,
Designs and Patents Act 1988.

British Library Cataloguing in Publication Data
A catalogue record for this title is available from the British
Library.

ISBN 1 86105 373 8

Typeset by SX Composing DTP, Essex
Printed in Great Britain by Creative Print & Design (Wales),
Ebbw Vale

Contents

Preface and Acknowledgements

This book has been in my mind for at least ten years. I have watched the increasing criticism of doctors, hospitals and the beliefs on which much of modern medicine is based, the increasing public resentment about these and the hysterical outbursts that occur whenever it is revealed that mistakes have been made. Then, just as I was planning the book seriously, the subject became immensely topical and of so much interest to the general public that every newspaper and news bulletin seemed to be filled with criticism of doctors.

The question that concerned me was this: What is wrong with modern medicine? Why, when it has advanced so much, does it attract so much criticism? Why do so many patients seek alternative or complementary practitioners? When these hostile critics of medicine become genuinely or seriously ill themselves, why do they so often revert to conventional medicine? Medicine has 'progressed' enormously during the last half-century, yet why is it now increasingly criticised and derided? What is the relationship between progress and discontent in medicine?

The present state of affairs clearly has wider and deeper causes than arrogant doctors, posturing politicians or bureaucratic managers in a cumbersome, underfunded National Health Service. The roots of the trouble can be better seen and understood in the history of medicine and the medical profession, in the widespread ignorance of this history among both professionals and laity, and in the obsessional pursuit of the future with little or no consideration of the past. The aim of this book is to explore these roots further.

I should like to thank members of the former Wellcome Institute for the History of Medicine (now the Wellcome Trust Centre for the History of

vii

Medicine at University College, London, and the Wellcome Library), and the many friends with whom, over the years, I have discussed subjects relevant to this book.

Unfortunately, when the preparation of the text was nearly finished, I became ill. During this illness I suffered a small stroke which left my memory and powers of concentration impaired, and since then I have also had difficulty in using my computer. I should like to thank my publishers for their tolerance and assistance in this situation. In particular I thank my long-suffering editor, Jennifer Lansbury, who made several visits to my home in the country to help me. Without her the book would never have appeared.

Introduction

Medicine is in trouble. Doctors and the medical profession in general are being criticised as never before. Their mistakes and misdeeds – or at least some of them – are being exposed and examined instead of being carefully concealed by the profession or ignored by the media and public as happened in the past, when doctors seemed to be above criticism. They are now often blamed when things go wrong and may even be tried by the General Medical Council for being incompetent. As the *Daily Mail* put it, in a statement typical of British national newspapers in the early twenty-first century:

> These are bleak days for the practice of medicine. Suddenly a profession that has always enjoyed universal trust and respect is plunged into a nightmare succession of scandals. (Editorial, 14 June 2000, p. 12)

Increasingly, patients, potential patients and journalists criticise not only doctors and hospitals but also the beliefs on which much modern medicine is based. Often aided by the Internet, patients question their diagnoses and treatments, demand explanations and discussions and are sometimes quick to sue doctors and hospitals, often for reasons that, only a generation ago, would have been unthinkable or regarded as ungrateful.

Dirty hospitals, uncaring doctors and nurses, mistakes, hurry and hustle, fraud in research and elsewhere, doctors interested only in one part of the body or in making money, side-effects, unnecessary treatment, long waiting lists, uneven 'postcode' treatment – these are some of the things that now anger patients and lower their respect for doctors.

Fifty years ago, few lay people were even aware that such issues existed. We now live in a society that is increasingly contemptuous of authority and suspicious of the motives of professionals, be they doctors, lawyers or politicians. As a result, the failings of these professionals are revealed more readily and are ever more difficult to cover up.

Nonetheless, it is my belief that a greater public understanding of the background of medicine and how it works would alter unattainable expectations and reduce discontent and complaints. This requires a different outlook from members of the public, greater understanding of history and less idealisation of health care. My aim is to start to achieve such a change through this book.

Among recent medical scandals in the UK, many, such as health professionals missing evidence of growth malignancy or the retaining of body parts for research purposes, would not even have been regarded as wrong in the past. Some of these practices continued for many years, often with the knowledge of people in positions of authority. The cult of secrecy has always been strong in the medical profession. No one likes to admit mistakes if they can conceal them, and the results of doctors' mistakes can be so devastating and distressing that there have always been particularly strong incentives to hide them – with the support of the entire medical profession and its institutions.

With society's increasing scepticism, however, secrecy is now more difficult to achieve, and many scandals have come to light. Dr Harold Shipman murdered his patients, perhaps hundreds of them; surgeons in Bristol continued to operate on babies when they knew that many more of them died than was the case in other hospitals; pathologists in Bristol and Liverpool kept the organs of dead babies on false pretences and without the parents' permission; other pathologists made wrong diagnoses that led to unnecessary operations; gynaecologists botched operations and left patients with permanent pain or disability; other gynaecologists assaulted or even raped their patients, who did not dare, until recently, to expose them; medical researchers collected, and sometimes published, fraudulent figures to enhance their reputations and careers. Many people either knew or suspected that these things were going on, but they either did nothing or tried to cover up the details, conforming to the culture of secrecy, even when it was their job to supervise what was going on. The whole nation has been shocked.

This book is not primarily about hidden scandals, lack of funds, unimaginative administration, understaffing or poor medical ethics.

These topics are widely discussed elsewhere. It is more concerned with our basic approach to medicine; how it is regarded by doctors, by patients, and by the scientists who make the advances and discoveries. I shall examine the nature of modern medicine and the powerful forces that contribute to its idealisation, how attitudes and beliefs influence practice, and how society's attitude towards medicine has long been unrealistic and largely the cause of the trouble it is in today.

It is fair to say that we are in a state of some self-contradiction in our attitudes to the medical profession today. We are shocked, angry and appalled by the revelations and scandals of recent years; we are increasingly sceptical of doctors' authority, and more willing to complain when mistakes occur. And yet it is also clear that many doctors, patients and members of the general public still cling to previously idealised beliefs concerning the medical profession. Incompetent, sadistic or murderous doctors are dismissed as being 'just a few rotten apples in the barrel'. We are assured, and many of us believe it to be true, that medicine makes constant and irreversible progress, and that progress is always good. Alongside reports of the latest scandal in our newspapers, we often find naïve accounts of 'breakthrough' or 'wonder' drugs. Even when dangerous side-effects are known about, they tend to be ignored amid the wonders of the new.

A typical example of this occurred in the middle of some intense criticism of doctors, the NHS and the GMC. On 27 June 2000 it was announced that scientists had unravelled the human genome, a feat described by *The Times* as 'opening the book of life'. President Clinton told Tony Blair that they were 'learning the language in which God created life'. Mike Dexter, chairman and director of the Wellcome Trust which partly funded the research, announced in *The Times'* article that the achievement was more important than the invention of the wheel. The *Times* columnist Simon Jenkins wrote that he was talking 'gibberish', but Dexter was only stating the traditional view of medical 'advances'. Although little benefit had as yet emerged from the human genome, Dexter foresaw the end of cancer, old age, stupidity and the failure of most people to run a four-minute mile. He spoke on BBC radio of the possibilities and limitations of the new revelations. He said nothing, however, of the possible disadvantages, despite the fact that there are very real concerns in some circles about such mattters as the likely creation of a new form of eugenics, the emergence of new genetic errors, the probable difficulties in obtaining insurance cover that may be experienced by those with 'tainted' genes, and the inevitable fashion for striving after 'superior' babies. The result is a mixed message, and increasing confusion. What is the truth? Who should we believe? Is progress inevitably for the better?

Surely medicine has never been more successful. Nowadays it can actually achieve much of what it intends to do. Every year there seems to be more success, more progress. Yet there is also more trouble. Doctors are no longer seen as the gods they once seemed to be. Like politicians, they are increasingly perceived as arrogant, self-seeking, untruthful, deliberately deceptive, masters of the cover-up and even sadistic. When scandals and problems come to light, the main criticism is aimed at 'the system' (i.e. the administrative system), or the need for more cash in the NHS, or the arrogance of consultants, or the occasional evil doctor. Interestingly, however, there is little or no criticism of the subject of medicine itself. Despite misgivings about the system, or about individuals within it, the public and the media seem to display an undiminished faith in the marvels and progress of medicine. This faith, unfortunately, often seems incapable of discriminating between fact and fiction, common sense and wild speculation. Confusion and frustration are inevitable. Newspaper headlines scream often contradictory news. A new 'breakthrough', a cure for that incurable disease, new hope for sufferers, a new drug that will be a revolution in disease/old age/pain. Chocolate is good for you; chocolate induces heart attacks. Red wine protects you against heart attacks; red wine gives you heart attacks. Vitamin supplements promote health and prolong life; vitamin supplements accelerate death.

During the past fifty years, health and disease have become topics of huge interest to the public. Formerly, knowledge of these subjects was held to be largely confidential, the sole prerogative of 'medical people'. Newspapers cautiously published a few column inches a week on the subject of medicine or health, and this was often written anonymously by 'A Doctor' or 'A Specialist' and tucked into the inside pages. Nowadays the subject is often given several prominent pages each day, and much of the information is misleading or out of context. Often it is clear that the writer does not understand the subject or has a distorted view of it. There is often little awareness that readers need not only accurate information but also a valid framework in which to view it and a suitable mindset with which to judge it. Today, too, the Internet houses ever-multiplying medical websites, many of dubious origin.

Bombarded with 'knowledge', patients are challenging their doctors, often with more information about their ailments than the professionals can deal with.

In this book I hope to reconcile some of these apparent discrepancies and show how they have arisen. Those who suggest solutions to the problems of modern medicine have usually advocated a return to former, more 'human' values and practices, or to past medical standards apparently forgotten. There is, understandably, much discussion of topics such as 'the patient as a person' and 'the caring professions'. These approaches are fine in their own way, but I suggest that what is needed first and foremost is a completely different outlook, a different way of looking at the whole subject of modern medicine which makes it more understandable and less mysterious, and in which its practitioners are regarded as more human and vulnerable.

My aim is not to denigrate progress, undermine the advances of medicine or fuel discontent, but to throw light on the current difficulties by looking at modern medicine not only as *progress* but also as *fashion*, or as multiple series of fashions. Progress triumphs in fashion, but fashion is not necessarily part of progress. Progress can be seen as fashion that has not been discarded.

Our problem is that we tend to think too much about the progress of medicine and too little about its fashions, too much about its avowed and perceptible aims and too little about its contexts and realities. We concentrate on diseases and their possible cures rather than on the people who suffer from them. We tend to assume that 'the doctor' is a certain type of person, practising in a standard way for the benefit of the patient. We pay too little attention to variety in doctors and their individual beliefs, motives and desires. We give no thought to the various needs that can be met in practising medicine, or to its many different satisfactions.

We mislead ourselves partly because we tend to look first for the latest discovery, the new, fashionable treatment, the most recent breakthrough. In this we are strongly encouraged by the media and the pharmaceutical industry. We often concentrate on what is new without examining it carefully. What has been discredited is pushed to one side; what is outmoded is dropped and ignored; what is new fills the headlines and often, soon afterwards, the textbooks. A different approach would take history and background into account, and would allow both journalists and medical professionals to assess new situations more efficiently.

By looking at medicine as largely a series of fashions, a few of which remain valid and useful for many years or even centuries, we can introduce a new perspective that places medical progress into a more realistic context. Such an approach is, I believe, more helpful than many of the attitudes that have developed in the modern Western world.

Part I is devoted to influences in Western medicine, including some not normally considered. (Readers who are already well acquainted with modern ideas in the history of medicine may prefer to skim over Chapter 1 and begin with Chapter 2.) There is a chapter on the motives of doctors, some of which are seldom discussed or even mentioned. A chapter on progress discusses the part that this plays and has played in medicine, and a chapter on fashion introduces this concept as a way of understanding modern medicine. A final chapter concerns the way in which medicine has gradually taken over parts of life where before it had no place. Part II concerns individual medical fashions of the past. Accounts of these fashions reveal their wide variety and the huge range of influences that form them, and put into perspective their relation to progress.

PART I
Doctors

CHAPTER 1

Western Medicine

Western medicine, sometimes known as biomedicine, is the medicine that has been developed and practised both generally and officially during the last two hundred years in those industrial nations collectively known as 'the West', chiefly Western Europe, North America, Australia and South Africa. This chapter concerns Britain principally but not exclusively.

Background

Modern Western attitudes towards science took several centuries to take over the theory and practice of medicine, which had long been dominated by the doctrine of 'humours'. This held that the Earth is composed of four elements, earth, air, fire and water, which are reflected in the four major substances of the body, blood, phlegm, yellow bile and black bile. Temperament was believed to depend on the dominance of one of these humours, and illness was due to an imbalance between them. The aim of treatment was to restore the balance. This system prevailed at least until the late eighteenth century and is also found much later. There are traces of it even today, especially in 'folk' medicine. For example, many people today believe that health is often a question of taking a 'tonic' (or a vitamin or food supplement) or of ridding the body of 'toxins'. There is also a widespread idea that some disorders, such as depression, are due to 'chemical imbalance'. Humoralism is also enjoying a strong comeback through the development of 'complementary' medicine, with its concentration on the whole person and its acceptance of the unity of body and mind.

Under the humoral system, the doctor did not have the professional authority enjoyed by later doctors and he did not receive the same respect. He was more the patient's equal in knowledge and opinion. Patients had their own theories about how their bodies worked. There were thought to be two kinds of medical problems: those requiring the immediate evacuation of poisons, and those requiring 'tonic' restoration of the body's forces. The patient judged the competence of the doctor and the suitability of the treatment.

Giving a name to a patient's disorder did not define it in the specific way it did later. A diagnosis might go no further than 'fever' or 'flux'. A sick person's condition was thought to follow from a series of errors, many of which were held to be the result of self-neglect. What mattered was not the diagnosis but the symptoms peculiar to the sufferer and the unique disturbance of the humours thought to have produced them. Furthermore, a disease was not regarded as constant or specific, but as a malady that could turn into another condition. For example, the 'matter' causing pneumonia might shift to produce liver disease, or arthritis could become a disease of the stomach.

The physician was expected to maintain the balance of his patron's body, to regulate the fluids, to restore harmony and to keep a balance between the patient's body and the outside world. For this a detailed knowledge of the sufferer's lifestyle was necessary, as well as theoretical knowledge of nature's healing powers, of drugs and of physical remedies such as purging and bleeding. Learning the patient's history was a lengthy business essential to the process by which the physician came to know the individual and his or her way of life. Physical examination was much less important than it became later, and was confined to external observation and attention to general appearance, pulse, tongue, urine and faeces. There was no such thing as the thorough clinical examination that developed in the nineteenth century, increasingly supported, even to the point of replacement, by the laboratory, the x-ray, the CAT scan and other scientific machines and methods.

What brought about the change? Medicine reflects its historical and social context and the dominant views and beliefs of the time. The development of Western scientific medicine can be viewed as a result of the Enlightenment and the Industrial Revolution, an era of extraordinary change and invention. The change in medical practices came gradually, prompted also by new influences in society and religion. As trade and industry developed, more and more people moved into cities, which grew immensely in size. Life in large cities was quite different from life in the country and it also brought its own diseases, demanding different standards of hygiene and health care, making the development of hospitals possible and providing the means of studying and understanding disease.

Some sort of scientific medicine, as opposed to pre-scientific medicine, dominated the medical scene from about the beginning of the nineteenth century. The new influences in society and religion clearly affected attitudes towards both medicine and the medical profession. Urbanisation was just one of those influences. Others included increasing scientific knowledge and technological sophistication, progressive secularisation with loss of Christian faith and developing materialism, changing beliefs about death, new doubts about the afterlife, and greater involvement of doctors, who were increasingly expected to make a diagnosis of the illness based on demonstrable pathology. There was also greater expectation of treatment or cure, or at least alleviation of symptoms and distress.

This weight of expectation brought its own problems. The Western world has now been through a period of at least one hundred and fifty years in which we have idolised doctors and the medical profession. Whereas in the eighteenth century they were regarded with some suspicion as tradesmen on the make, during the nineteenth century doctors gradually came to be regarded and portrayed as selfless healers who aimed to treat illness, appease suffering, fight disease and make progress in discovering new cures. The fact that they could in reality do little to cure their patients made it all the more important for them to *appear* to be selfless and omnipotent. As 'scientific' medicine developed, breakthroughs, new cures (both current and potential) and the latest wonder drug gained coverage in the media, and are now ubiquitous. Much progress has been made since the early days of scientific medicine, but fantasy and reality are often still poles apart.

Characteristics of modern Western medicine

Modern Western medicine consists of whatever its practitioners and patients regard as scientific. This usually aims – at least in theory – to be what is objective, demonstrable, measurable, self-evident and, increasingly, the result of personal observation or high-tech practice.

The concept of what is scientific changes over time and varies between individuals and institutions. Scientific medicine values accurate observation and, still more, measurement. It has a single-minded, materialistic approach that effectively reduces all bodily function and dysfunction to material causes, physical mechanisms and structural flaws that can be thought of and studied in isolation from the sufferer. Medical practitioners have often emphasised (particularly in recent years) that patients are people and should be treated as such, but at the same time many modern doctors make it clear that they are interested in the disease or the part of the body rather than in the people who have the problem. They can make their patients feel valued only as walking stomachs, blood sugars, heart valves, etc. Though the great physician William Osler said, 'It is much more important to know what sort of patient has the disease than to know what sort of disease the patient has,' this is not the way of modern Western medicine. The emphasis on the 'lesion' (the anatomical abnormality) and the disease became more conspicuous as investigation and treatment became more objective, complicated and 'scientific'. This is an important reason why so many people are now turning to other forms of medicine for relief of their symptoms and suffering.

The scientific attitude has many advantages and disadvantages. As long as the patient's illness can be successfully accommodated within the boundaries of scientific medicine, it has a good chance of cure or at least of alleviation. If it cannot be fitted within those boundaries, scientific medicine has little to offer and may even do harm. Scientific medicine rejects all concepts of 'vitalism', the use of immaterial spiritual or vital forces to explain natural phenomena. It has no place for 'life forces' or vital principles distinct from physical and chemical processes. In this it differs from other major medical systems, such as Ayurveda, the traditional Hindu system based on ideas of balance in the bodily systems, emphasising diet, herbal treatments and yogic breathing.

Scientific medicine is strongly geared to progress and encourages this belief in society by producing and marketing spectacular advances in knowledge and practice in specific areas, with dramatic discoveries and cures. These phenomena, sometimes genuine, sometimes disappointing, are often glamorised by media hype that goes far beyond the claims of the physicians and medical scientists responsible for them. This hype encourages patients to demand the latest treatment and incites doctors to use it. Sometimes these discoveries and cures save people from death or greatly improve the lives of sufferers, but they can also cause disappointment or even devastation. Hype within the profession encourages a tendency to apply a reportedly new or successful method of treatment to many more patients than will benefit from it. As a result hopes are unfairly raised and doctors become busy and skilled at the expense of some of their patients.

Another problem is the number of operations that are carried out on people who are subsequently found not to need them. The doctors fear the consequences of missing a real illness, so decide to operate 'just in case'. The life of anyone who has an abdominal catastrophe such as acute appendicitis or peritonitis is more likely to be saved by modern surgery than by any other kind of medicine, and many cases would undoubtedly die without such surgery. However, not every operation is necessary or successful – it is not unknown for appendices to be removed and found to be normal – and every operation carries a risk of complications and death. Sometimes the mere suggestion that an operation might be needed can dramatically affect a person's life. Responsible surgeons are aware that the history of their subject covers many operations, once regarded as valuable and even vital, that eventually turned out to be useless or harmful. (Some of these will be explored in Part II.)

There are many other examples of scientific medicine's tunnel vision. Anyone who develops 'heart block' (a failure of the electric circuitry in the heart) is, if untreated, likely to be disabled and in constant danger of sudden death. He or she will gain benefit, and probably a longer life, from the insertion of a modern cardiac pacemaker, a triumph of medical engineering. But someone whose aberrant heart rhythm reflects anxiety or inner conflict may find no relief from modern science and may even be labelled contemptuously by a modern cardiologist as 'NAD' (Nothing Abnormal Discovered), then dismissed with the problem unsolved. Thus someone who suffers from pain but has no detectable lesion may be harmed by the attitudes and treatments of scientific medicine. Having undergone an unnecessary operation, or having been dismissed as not needing one, they find that scientific medicine cannot help them, though they still have the pain or other symptoms.

Undeniably, scientific medicine has many means of saving and improving life, and these are constantly increasing in number and efficiency. No other system of medicine can perform such feats. Sometimes, however, they are unsuccessful or there are serious obstacles or side-effects. Moreover, those who practise Western medicine seldom confront the fact that many of its advances are developed at the cost of numerous lives and that, even when they are outstandingly successful in general, they do not always succeed in individual cases. For instance, the uncomfortable life of a person with arthritic hips may become much worse if the hip replacement operation is unsuccessful. Or a person whose heart is faulty may deteriorate or even die as a result of the operation or treatment rather than the disease itself. Conversely, forms of 'miracle' treatment may save or transform the lives of individuals, which makes these treatments seem generally attractive, but their effect on mortality rates is seldom impressive and there may well be long-term side-effects and disadvantages.

It is general knowledge that more lives are saved by improvements in diet, hygiene and living conditions than by scientific medicine. For most doctors, though, actively treating patients, saving lives, solving problems and pushing forward the frontiers of knowledge are more attractive than persuading people to change their diet, lose weight and stop smoking. Much of the attraction and power of scientific medicine is for the individual who falls seriously ill, when scientific medicine may be the only salvation.

There are many health problems that scientific medicine does not begin to tackle, because they are, unsuitably, regarded as not belonging to accepted beliefs about medicine. This often means they are treated without success. Much chronic (i.e. long-term) disease comes into this category. Scientific medicine is, on the whole, more efficient in dealing with acute illness. Furthermore, those who practise it sometimes enhance their power and reputation by claiming a wider success than is justified by the evidence, and by failing to curb excessive or dangerous extensions of genuine advances in scientific knowledge.

In capitalist societies medicine is linked with a profit-seeking pharmaceutical industry. Both have done much to create a population that is dependent on drugs. Pharmaceutical companies invent and develop drugs that are increasingly specific and powerful and save

many lives, but they also extol and exaggerate the benefits, often
without acknowledging, and sometimes even concealing, the side-
effects. Some doctors go along with this and prescribe drugs freely with
little indication of risks. A high percentage of patients in hospital are
there because they have been damaged or poisoned by scientific
treatment. For example, a recent study in a large hospital in the United
States – typical of hospitals across the Western world – found that
errors (euphemistically called 'adverse events') occurred in the care
of more than 45 per cent of patients. More than one in six patients
suffered serious consequences, ranging from temporary physical
disability to death.

Western medicine tends to emphasise its successes and to bury its
failures, metaphorically and often also literally. It is capable of effective
onslaught on many common and fatal diseases, but it tends to concentrate on those diseases that are common in rich countries and to pay
less attention to those that are common in poor countries, where a little
scientific medicine, applied very cheaply, could save millions of people
from lifelong infirmity and death. It trains doctors from poor countries,
but often only for them to stay in the West or else to return home and
practise sophisticated and expensive medicine for the rich.

In constructing its myths and images and in contemplating its many
and impressive successes, scientific medicine tends to ignore its blind
spots and failures. It also avoids dialectical modes of thought. It has
been suggested that Western medical thought has been shaped by
Western monotheism, concentrating on a single, underlying truth, with
little tolerance for alternative ideas. The development of such 'subversive' alternative ideas could be compared with the history of heresies
in Christianity.

One area in which Western medicine has been outstandingly successful is in the prevention of disease, particularly infectious and nutritional
but also cancerous and degenerative. Sometimes the knowledge is
theoretical only, but even when the methods are not carried out, often
for reasons of cost, it has at least shown the way. Among the best
examples of successful prevention are vaccines for diseases such as
smallpox (eradicated globally in 1980 through Western medicine),
poliomyelitis (which *could* now be eliminated), diphtheria and many
others. Other triumphs, at least in theory, are the treatments of cholera
and tetanus. It is not possible to cure these diseases directly, but Western
medicine has shown how and why they spread and how they could be

prevented. It has also devised ways of keeping sufferers alive until the acute phase of the disease is over. This can be done cheaply in cholera through rehydration, and more expensively in tetanus through continuous anaesthesia. Similar techniques have recently been devised for meningitis. The discovery of vitamins (in 1912) made many diseases treatable and preventable, often simply and cheaply. These included scurvy, rickets, pellagra, beri-beri, kwashiorkor and many anaemias. Since then, a whole vitamin industry has developed, and many people in the West who have adequate diets are convinced that they require extra vitamins and food supplements in order to be healthy. The pharmaceutical industry benefits greatly from such beliefs.

Western medicine is not always interventional. It has shown that many cancers can be avoided, for example by not smoking, or by avoiding radiation and some chemicals. Medical research has also produced evidence that degenerative diseases such as some forms of arthritis, diabetes and heart disease can be improved or prevented by certain lifestyles.

Western medicine prides itself on being scientific, but is necessarily based on medical judgment and interventionist skills as well as on scientific evidence. This raises a number of questions. Can the doctor's personal and clinical experience be 'scientific'? Is the doctor–patient relationship 'scientific', and how does it influence the 'science' – for example, how effective the prescribed treatment is, given the relationship? What is the relationship between medicine and science, and how has it been influenced by the way in which it developed?

Medicine in the sixteenth to nineteenth centuries

Western medical science can be conveniently dated from the time of the Scientific Revolution (*c*. 1550–1700), the transformation of thought about nature or the physical world in which the traditions of the ancient Greeks and Islam were replaced by modern science. This coincided with the political dominance of Europe in the world and the development of capitalism, strongly influenced by Protestantism. At first the revolution was most powerful in mathematics and physical sciences, emphasising mathematical analysis based on systematic experiments and challenging the idea that humankind was the centre of the universe.

Initially it also retained the idea of a Christian God as creator and judge, but later there was discussion and dispute about this. At least until the mid-nineteenth century, however, the majority of scientists and doctors were practising Christians and used theological arguments alongside their scientific reasoning.

The earliest application of the Scientific Revolution to medicine is usually associated with the physician William Harvey (1578–1657), who discovered the circulation of the blood, and with the philosopher René Descartes (1596–1650). Descartes regarded the human body as a machine. Since his time the division between mind and body has been one of the mainstays of Western medicine – and to this day is both a strength and a weakness of the system. Unlike most other medical systems, scientific medicine is strongly linked with many inventions, customs and advances that depend on the idea of the body as a machine. Most modern drugs, major surgery and prostheses (such as artificial limbs and joints, cardiac pacemakers and plastic eye lenses) that have eased and prolonged so many lives have developed as a result of this hypothesis, and so its disadvantages tend to be overlooked or ignored.

One main disadvantage is that the theory is associated with a contempt for symptoms that originate in the mind. Many who believe in it refuse to take psychological factors into account and develop an attitude that sees people as merely an aggregation of human parts. This is becoming increasingly pronounced as medicine divides into ever more specialities and subspecialities. It suits some patients who like to feel that they are in control and are content to be relieved of a symptom or to have a painful or damaging part excised or replaced. However, if their disorder is less specific or is connected with wider aspects of their lives or personalities, the mechanistic approach of Western medicine becomes unsatisfactory, even for its most ardent supporters, and can be dangerous. Such danger may include a failure to reach correct conclusions, or the performance of unnecessary surgery. The tendency of many doctors to concentrate on the disease rather than on the sufferer has led many people to seek other kinds of medicine.

The nineteenth century saw the firm establishment of what we think of as scientific medicine. From about the middle of the century, the textbooks and the attitudes they reveal are recognisable as not so different from modern ones. Before that they were clearly written with a different mindset. Science and the scientific attitude were developing alongside ideas about evolution, and were often seen to conflict with religion.

Medicine became more scientific, seeking causes for illness in morbid anatomy and specific diseases, and beginning to apply statistics to medical situations. Doctors were becoming more involved in illness and death, especially among the middle classes. Death became less associated with sin, divine judgment and hell. People increasingly regarded it as a medical matter, of concern to the doctor, who was expected to make a diagnosis of the illness based on physical examination, physical signs and demonstrable pathology – and, preferably, to treat the condition before death occurred. As expectation of treatment or cure increased, so did the doctor's prestige, and the profession felt a growing need to be seen as effective. An increasing market economy contributed to this trend.

Traditionally, the medical profession in the West has concentrated on diagnosis and treatment rather than on promoting health and preventing disease. This was the rationale behind the rise of the family doctor as a trusted friend and helper (largely to the middle classes). Even though he was not much good at preventing death, he was expected to help in some way. Knowledge of anatomy and, to a lesser extent, physiology, had increased enormously. Pathology was expected to reveal why a person had died, and new laws insisted that this must be recorded. In addition, new techniques (such as anaesthesia and radical surgery) brought new dangers, including sudden death. Doctors were increasingly expected and obliged to give reasons for what happened. Registration of deaths was introduced in England and Wales in 1837; giving the cause of death became compulsory in 1872. Such labelling gave a semblance of control even in uncontrolled situations.

FOUCAULT

The French philosopher Michel Foucault (1926–83) thought long and hard about the development of scientific medicine. His book *The Birth of the Clinic: An archaeology of medical perception* (first published in 1963) has had considerable influence on medical historians, though many have disagreed with him. He used what he saw as the mechanisms of power which have developed in Western society since the end of the eighteenth century to explain the development of modern Western medicine. He presented his idea of 'the clinic', by which he meant not only hospitals but also the clinical medicine that developed in them after the late eighteenth century. Earlier medicine had relied largely on the authority of printed books. Part of the rejection of the past that was typical of the French Revolution (1789–99) was the rejection of this tradition in favour of direct observation of patients, which Foucault called *le regard*, cleverly translated as 'the gaze'. The gaze is reductionist, analytical and progressively more intense. It develops continuously with new scientific evidence and invention and thereby becomes progressively more penetrating in ever more varied ways. New inventions (e.g. x-rays, CAT scans, electrocardiographs and methods of genetic analysis) continually reveal new ways of 'seeing', analysing and judging the human body.

The main features of Foucault's 'clinic' which have most influenced the early development of medical science are hospitals, the postmortem examination and clinical examination.

HOSPITALS

The development of modern hospitals was a fundamental change that initiated, promoted and supported the development of scientific medicine. The hospital, once a charitable Christian refuge largely for the urban poor, without much medical action or significance, gradually became central to the practice of medicine. This hospital movement began in Paris. In Britain, with the expansion of the middle classes in the eighteenth century, many general hospitals were established. Then, in the middle of the century, specialist hospitals also began to be founded.

The development of modern hospitals was closely bound to changing ideas about disease. The system developed based on observation, physical examination, pathological anatomy, statistics and the concept of the lesion. A lesion is a morbid change in the body, which was (and still is) thought to be the cause of disease, and became the object of search in diagnosis. By the middle of the nineteenth century investigations had extended beyond the bedside and the mortuary to the laboratory. In modern times the hospital has become a high-tech institution where illness is investigated and treated, accidents and emergencies are dealt with, and invasive and dangerous life-saving procedures are carried out under conditions made as safe as possible. It is also the place where doctors, nurses and other professions associated with medicine are trained, where the élite of the medical profession work and where status in the profession is acquired. At the top of the tree are the teaching hospitals, which are associated with universities and have medical schools attached to them for the training of doctors.

To be elected to a prestigious consultancy at one of these is the aim of most doctors who are ambitious for 'success'.

The growth of the hospital movement influenced the fundamental examination of medical knowledge. Interest shifted from the patient who had the disease to the disease itself, and that disease could be studied in isolation, with the aid of inventions such as the microscope and special stains for examining slides and clinical instruments. The anatomy of the diseased body became increasingly important, while the individual patient received less attention. Instead of learning by talking to patients, doctors were increasingly likely to learn by concentrating on their bodies, alive or dead. Much important medical examination now took place in the postmortem room.

Such increasingly detailed analysis of patients' bodies and the differences between them allowed the gradual delineation of separate diseases. Diseases became afflictions that were common to all who suffered from them rather than something unique to each individual. When many ill people were gathered together, the similarities between certain groups became apparent. Doctors began to describe, measure and count them. Their study was based on 'bedside' medicine, which entailed physical examination by hand, eye and ear and, increasingly, with instruments. It also depended on pathological anatomy, statistics and an understanding of the lesion. When patients died, their bodies were dissected for more information. The delineation of diseases according to lesion rather than as general and humoral phenomena made it possible to locate them in specific places and organs where they could be studied and treated separately.

It was gradually realised that big surgical operations, like other complicated scientific procedures, were safer when they were carrried out in institutions organised for them and with a range of skilled people available. The introduction of anaesthesia in the late 1840s was a huge advance. Hospitals became the institutional basis of professional power, status and prestige. Some doctors who could not gain a foothold in the big hospitals set up their own, often specialist hospitals for eyes, ears, gynaecology and so on. By 1860 London alone had 66 special hospitals. At first such hospitals were criticised and opposed by the élite doctors in the big general hospitals, but by the end of the century these doctors were keen to have appointments in the specialist clinics.

Medicine practised in an institutional setting had many possibilities not open to those practising in isolation. Greater numbers of patients to be grouped and classified, colleagues with different skills and experience available for co-operation and discussion, and the stimulus of organised teaching were just a few of the obvious advantages. There were also many disadvantages, however, of which the most prominent was infection. Some diseases seemed to arise in the hospitals themselves. These 'hospital diseases' were often fatal and were particularly common in the surgical wards. By the middle of the nineteenth century, strenuous efforts were being made to overcome them. Scientific medicine in the form of logical thinking by a Hungarian obstetrician, Ignaz Semmelweiss (1818–65), eventually revealed that puerperal fever, a particularly virulent form of hospital disease, was spread by staff and students who had visited the dissecting rooms. Semmelweiss came to this conclusion by close observation in a maternity hospital, comparing wards run by doctors and medical students, who attended postmortems, with those run by midwives, who did not. Later work by Louis Pasteur (1822–95) established the existence of germs that caused disease, and Joseph Lister (1827–1912) introduced the concept of antisepsis, which gradually gave way to asepsis, still the basis of germ control in surgery today (see page 25). Its practice has enabled surgeons to develop much more complex operations and to perform them much more frequently. Yet infection has remained one of the great dangers of surgery and has recently become even more of a menace. In July 2002, patients at a Teeside hospital were put at risk of contracting the fatal brain disease sporadic CJD when it was found that surgical instruments used earlier on a patient diagnosed with CJD had not been properly decontaminated (or disposed of). Sometimes even the most advanced units have to be closed because of infection.

A greater understanding of infection was just one of the discoveries to come out of the flourishing hospital movement. The development of hospitals undoubtedly influenced the fundamental examination of medical knowledge in many ways. Some of the most significant revelations came in the postmortem room.

POSTMORTEM EXAMINATIONS
The story of the postmortem is complicated. Regular or routine dissection of corpses began in the eighteenth century in Italy, where it was sometimes done as part of a public demonstration to raise the status of medicine and to establish it as a true body of learning and a suitable

subject for university study – and not the manual trade that many thought it to be. The postmortem became a central part of medical enquiry and important medical ideas emerged from it. It demonstrated that disease alters the body in ways that can be seen, described and used for the benefit of the living. Physicians improved their skills in both diagnosis and prognosis by doing postmortem examinations and correlating the results with their patients' previous illnesses, comparing the lesions they found in death with the symptoms and signs they had observed in life.

Examination of the dead body was developed in particular by the Italian Giovanni Battista Morgagni (1692–1771) and was made more available to practising physicians by the Scot Matthew Baillie (1761–1823), who published *The Morbid Anatomy of Some of the Most Important Parts of the Human Body* in 1793. In 1801 the French physician Marie-François-Xavier Bichat (1771–1802) published his *General Anatomy, Applied to Physiology and Medicine*, which introduced the new concept of different types of body tissues (as opposed to body organs) as the basic units of the body. This became one of the foundations of medical science. Bichat emphasised, 'You may take notes for twenty years … and all will be to you only a confusion of symptoms [and] incoherent phenomena. Open a few bodies, this obscurity will soon disappear.' This theory of the anatomical localisation of pathology, together with the correlation of clinical findings with structural changes in the body, was an outlook previously confined to surgeons. It became the basis of a new medicine and was enhanced by the development of clinical examination skills, by the physicians' increasing use of a hands-on approach, and by the new instruments invented for them.

CLINICAL EXAMINATION

Western medical science developed on the basis of clinical examination of the patient by the doctor. Previously, direct examination had been purely external. From the beginning of the nineteenth century, however, the 'gaze' began to turn inwards, aided by scientific techniques and inventions, the most important of which are explored below.

SOUND AND THE STETHOSCOPE

The first clinical method to develop was the detection of pathology by the use of sound. This was first suggested by the Viennese physician

Leopold Auenbrugger (1722–1809). In 1761 he published his *Inventum novum*, in which he described a method of examination he called 'percussion', producing sounds indicating the vitality of the internal organs. He believed that his method would revolutionise the diagnosis of chest disease. Like Morgagni, he thought that the key to medicine was the link between structural change and disease. He maintained that this should be achieved by objective means – by physical examination, and not by talking to the patient.

Auenbrugger's work did not catch on. It remained for a young French physician, René-Théophile-Hyacinthe Laënnec (1781–1826), to change the scene. In 1819 he published *On Mediate Auscultation*, which described in detail pathological lesions found in the chest at autopsy and showed how they correlated with disease detected in living patients.

Laënnec, rather than place his ear against the patient's chest, rolled paper into a cylinder, then improved it with an instrument made from wood, and named it the 'stethoscope' (from the Greek words for 'chest' and 'to view'). The technique was not excessively difficult to learn, the stethoscope was comfortable to use (as opposed to twisting the body into awkward positions in order to listen directly) and was a compromise with the sense of indelicacy associated with close physical contact between doctor and patient. Doctors adopted it enthusiastically and seem to have regarded it as a form of 'seeing' into the body, an extension of the 'gaze'. Since then, almost every doctor has worn a stethoscope round his or her neck, and the technique has been refined, developed and widely applied in diagnosis, assessment and treatment. The instruments have become increasingly sophisticated and sensitive. It is now possible, for instance, to 'look' at every cell in the body and to operate by remote control, often far inside the body, perhaps on a heart or blood vessel or on an unborn child.

THE EYE AND THE EXTENSION OF THE 'GAZE'

Another important scientific invention for clinical examination was the ophthalmoscope. Until the early nineteenth century it was impossible to see into the blackness of the eye. Then the Czech scientist Jan Purkynje (1787–1869) discovered how to reflect light into the eye using a source of light and a lens. His work had little direct influence, but others followed in the field, most notably the German physician Hermann

Helmholtz (1821–94), who invented the ophthalmoscope and published an account of it in 1851.

The ophthalmoscope rapidly became popular with physicians, who gradually realised that the condition of the eye and what can be seen in it often reflects disease elsewhere in the body. To this day a popular examination question for student doctors is: 'Describe and discuss how general disease in the body may be revealed in the eye.'

The next organ to be submitted to the new scientific 'gaze' was the larynx. In 1806 Philippe Bozzini (1775–1809) made an instrument involving a light source and a series of tubes containing mirrors, which made it possible to see into the body. The immense theoretical possibilities of this were recognised but not thought to be practical. Eventually a Polish professor, Johann Czermak (1828–73), designed the first laryngoscope, which made disorders of the larynx visible rather than merely audible, as they had been previously through hoarseness, coughing, noisy breathing, and so on.

By that time the importance of being able to see into the body was being widely recognised. There were still some strict limitations, however. Sometimes moral considerations intervened – there was much hostility to the vaginal speculum, for example, on the grounds that it offended female delicacy. Sometimes physicians, hostile to novelty, objected to the new custom of using the eye, for instance in detecting bladder stones by visual methods instead of the traditional method of probing and feeling.

Instrument design improved markedly in the 1870s, when it became possible to have sources of light powered by electricity. In 1881 Thomas Edison invented the carbon-filament lamp, which greatly increased brightness.

Another visual technique that emerged was photography, which began to be used to provide objective records of patients. This culminated in 1895 with the discovery of x-rays by Wilhelm Roentgen (1845–1923). At first this discovery met with little interest and some ridicule, but the technique soon became popular and ever since x-rays have been one of the most powerful tools in the medical armamentarium. Refinements of the technique soon followed, including the fluoroscope and the use of bismuth to explore the gut on x-ray. During the twentieth century other visual techniques were developed, such as ultrasound, imaging and scanning.

THE MICROSCOPE

The microscope has played an important part in medical science, and still does. Its techniques developed through several centuries as the quality of lenses improved. In 1681 the Dutchman Antoni van Leeuwenhoek (1632–1723) discovered that protozoa and bacteria inhabited the human body, but he did not associate them with disease. One of the problems with using the microscope in medicine in those early days was that of optical defects, including the distortion of images and spherical and chromatic aberrations. These were so great that no one knew what was true, but after the improvements in lenses introduced by Joseph Jackson Lister (1786–1869; father of Lord Lister), the microscope was used increasingly to study body fluids and diseases. Blood, urine, pus, phlegm and mother's milk were some of the first fluids to be studied.

In 1843 Guy's Hospital in London established a department of microscopy and doctors began to take a serious interest in alterations in body tissues in disease. Gradually the idea developed that examination of postmortem material with the naked eye alone was no longer sufficient. Ideas about the basic structure of the human body also changed. The existence of cells had been known about since the seventeenth century, but the new microscopes meant that knowledge of them could be greatly extended. In 1839 Theodor Schwann (1810–82) showed that tissues were composed of cells, and in 1858 the German pathologist Rudolf Virchow (1821–1902) published his famous book *Cellular Pathology*. He insisted that cells arose from other cells and not from undifferentiated fluid as had previously been thought. He also demonstrated that health depended on the orderly function of cells and that disease was caused by disruption of cellular function.

The adoption of the microscope as a tool of medicine led to the development of bacteriology, which became one of the most important laboratory supports of Western medicine. In 1840 Jakob Henle (1809–85) published his essay 'On miasmata and contagia', in which he tried to show that tiny living creatures in the human body caused infectious diseases. The idea of 'germs' began to challenge the prevailing theory that diseases were caused by 'miasmata', pathological states of the atmosphere. Discussion about these opposing theories remained lively and contentious until the 1860s and the work of Louis Pasteur and Joseph Lister. Pasteur showed that putrefaction of organic matter did not occur in the absence of micro-organisms. Lister, worried by the appalling rate of mortality from compound fractures (in which the broken bone penetrates the skin), devised methods of destroying bacteria in wounds during surgery. His method, a carbolic spray, became known as antisepsis. A few years later it was superseded by asepsis, which attempts to keep infection out altogether. This has been practised with increasing refinement ever since.

The German physician Robert Koch (1843–1910) took bacteriology further with his work first on anthrax, then on tuberculosis. He developed complex microscopic and chemical techniques and advanced the important sciences of culturing bacteria and staining microscope slides for examination. In 1882 he announced his finding of the tubercle bacillus. He set out his ideas in what became known as 'Koch's postulates': that the organism must be present constantly in diseased parts, that it must be cultivated outside the body, and that it must be produced in a susceptible animal which had been inoculated with the cultivated micro-organism.

Ever since then, medical students have been taught the importance of Koch's postulates. It was long held that if they could not be demonstrated, the source of the illness could not be determined. It is impossible, however, to adhere to these rules in many diseases, such as AIDS, and the criteria are now not so strict. This detracts from the value of some research because it is less stringent, but it is the only way of doing it.

Bacteriology developed rapidly after Koch. During the 21 years between 1879 and 1900, the specific organisms of at least 21 serious diseases were discovered. These included gonorrhoea, typhoid, erysipelas, cholera, diphtheria, tetanus, pneumonia, meningitis, plague, syphilis and whooping-cough.

PHYSIOLOGY AND BODY FUNCTIONS

The basic sciences on which modern Western medicine is based – microscopic anatomy or histology, physiology, pathology and pharmacy – all developed rapidly during the first half of the nineteenth century and gradually came to be applied to medicine. During the eighteenth century and earlier, scientists had been either practising physicians or amateurs, often working in their own homes. Now there developed a new sort of scientist, full-time and professional, who worked for medicine but did so in laboratories rather than at the bedside.

The movement began in Germany, where the reformed universities offered a suitable environment. German universities were more important in medicine at that time than were universities in the Anglo-Saxon world, where medicine remained more individual and pragmatic. Germany was also more attuned to research and had little of Britain's anti-vivisection and anti-dissection feelings, or its grave-robbing scandals. Thus Germany came to lead the world in medicine in the second half of the nineteenth century.

The development of the basic sciences had a profound influence on Western medicine. There was now an unprecedented knowledge of the structure and functions of the human body. Pathological signs could be correlated with changes of structure. Deviations from the normal could be measured and assessed in a way that was previously impossible. New methods of treatment could be devised and predicted.

To the idea that illness was due to defects in body architecture was added the idea that measurements in illness should be of changes in body function, such as temperature, breathing, heartbeat and blood circulation. Unless changes in these functions were long-standing, they did not change the structure of the body and so did not show at postmortem. This study of function was the beginning of the medical science of physiology.

Instruments began to appear that could portray functions by measuring them in numbers or transcribing them onto graphs, often on rotating drums covered with smoked paper and marked by an indicator arm. This transformed subjective monitoring (e.g. of the nature of muscle contraction or the nature of the pulse) into objective data that could be seen by all. It became possible to construct many of the body functions as objective transcriptions that could be compared with other measurements taken at different times.

One of the best known of these instruments was the thermometer. Attempts had been made to construct one for several centuries and such a machine had been invented by Galileo late in the sixteenth century, though he had not applied it to disease. There had been many technical hitches in developing the thermometer, but from the 1840s onwards the interest of physicians was roused. In 1868 Carl Wunderlich (1815–77) published *On the Temperature in Disease* and thereby brought thermometry into prominence in medical diagnosis. He showed that the temperature of a healthy human being was constant apart from small diurnal swings, and that certain variations in temperature were characteristic of certain diseases.

Other instruments soon followed. The spirometer, which measured various aspects of breathing, began to rival the stethoscope. The sphygmomanometer measured blood pressure against a column of mercury, and the sphygmograph recorded movements of the pulse onto paper and converted them into graph form. By the end of the nineteenth century there were also machines that tracked the path of the electric currents of the heart. This developed into the electrocardiograph, or ECG, which became an essential part of the examination of the heart.

Thus physiological functions were made scientific and brought under the all-embracing 'gaze'. Medical diagnosis, along with monitoring a patient's progress, became increasingly mechanical. Nevertheless, the opinion of talented and experienced physicians, especially in Britain, where the tradition of the personal doctor has remained strong, if slowly declining, is still greatly valued.

LABORATORY MEDICINE

Many physicians were dissatisfied by the limitations of trying to correlate disease with structural changes at postmortem, because such correlations could often not be found. Another line of thought developed in response to this. In 1848 a new medicine, 'laboratory medicine', made its appearance in Paris under the leadership of Louis Pasteur, Claude Bernard and the Société de Biologie. The various factions of the preceding half-century had all been devoted to pathological anatomy, but laboratory medicine was different.

Chemistry had been used in medical diagnosis since the sixteenth century, a time when physicians attached great importance to visual examination of the urine. The Swiss doctor Paracelsus (1493–1541) recommended chemical analysis rather than mere visual inspection. During the eighteenth century various chemical properties of urine in disease were discovered, especially in diabetes, but few physicians took a serious interest until Richard Bright (1789–1858), in his *Reports of Medical Cases*, showed that dropsy, a common disease with accumulation of fluid in the tissues, was often accompanied by shrivelled kidneys and large amounts of albumin in the urine. From then on, the use of chemistry to evaluate disease increased – though not without some opposition from doctors who believed that little could be gained from laboratory examination, because it was so far removed from the realities of health and disease. Other tests were devised for finding abnormal chemicals in the blood, protein, sugar, bacteria, products of infection, and so on. Some of the tests could be done at the bedside, albeit often with cumbersome equipment, while others required a fully equipped laboratory.

At the same time, the microscope was being used to examine the blood and its cells. In 1877 William Gowers (1845–1915), in his 'On the Numeration of the Blood-Corpuscles', showed how examination with the microscope could make certain tentative and difficult diagnoses certain. Soon afterwards his method was used to make the hitherto difficult distinction between anaemia (then a popular and often mis-guided diagnosis) and hysteria (also a common diagnosis at the time), in which the blood cells are normal. These techniques were supple-mented by others, such as the alternative counting technique of using centrifugal force to pack the cells together in a haematocrit and then measuring the quantity of haemoglobin in the cells.

The discovery of bacteria as causal in disease led to the establishment of publicly funded laboratories to identify widespread and epidemic infectious disease. Gradually there grew up a profession of those adept at laboratory techniques and doctors began to specialise in various forms of pathology, including bacteriology, chemical pathology and haematology. These doctors were largely divorced from patients and spent most of their time working in laboratories.

How Western medical science developed

The German model of medical science, closely linking universities and hospitals, were copied in the United States at Johns Hopkins University, Baltimore, which became and has remained a leader in the field. The surgeon William Halsted (1852–1922), who had studied in Germany, began to perform radical surgery there which had a considerable influence on his colleagues and on the direction that medicine would take. In Britain at this time, medicine still tended to be less scientific and conducted more at the bedside, relying on individual clinical experience and judgment rather than on scientific tests and assessments. This was thought to be more agreeable for patients, and it was said, 'On the continent and in America they have the best *science*: in Britain we have the best *practice*.'

SPECIALISATION

The development of specialists in the medical profession was slow and was initially associated with 'quacks' such as bonesetters and cataract-extractors – despised by the grand physicians and viewed as threatening by the burgeoning general practitioners. Originally, the early medical specialities such as urology, ophthalmology and obstetrics were not part of medicine at all, but were the province of lay people and the itinerant quacks. From the late eighteenth century onwards, however, these fields were encroached on by ambitious individuals who were in some important respects marginal to the medical profession. A century later (in an article on 6 January 1900) *The General Practitioner* said of specialists, 'Their minds are narrowed, judgment biased and unbalanced by disproportionate knowledge of one subject.' In the end, it said, the patient suffers, for unlike the patient's family doctor, the specialist 'knows nothing of the constitutional idiosyncrasies of the individual, which are essential to correct diagnosis and treatment'. This was a typical opinion of the time.

Nevertheless, specialism developed inevitably as medical knowledge and medical science advanced beyond the scope of any individual. The first effective specialities were ophthalmology and gynaecology, and specialist hospitals began to appear from the late eighteenth century onwards. Between 1800 and 1890, 88 specialist hospitals were founded in London, 22 of them in the 1860s alone. Even distinguished specialists, such as Abraham Jacobi, complained that specialisation tended to degrade the general practitioner, but these specialist hospitals – essentially a direct product of the development of medical science – were mostly set up independently by medical men who were ambitious but could not gain entry into the élite corps of physicians that formed the medical establishment.

Whatever the initial hostility, specialism was an inevitable development with the growth of scientific knowledge, and the trend has continued to the present day. There are now subdivisions of sub-specialities, such as paediatric cardiology, colorectal surgery and neuroendocrinology. In one sense, specialism means knowing more and more about less and less, so, while it is safer to be operated on by someone who does that operation all the time, sometimes the general situation is sadly lost in the detail.

MEDICAL SOCIETIES AND JOURNALS

The growth and development of medical science demanded new methods of spreading information about the latest techniques and discoveries. The first British medical society of note was the Medical Society of London, founded in 1773, which, along with several other societies, became the present-day Royal Society of Medicine. The nineteenth century was a period of proliferation of medical journals of all types – most notably the *Lancet*, first published in 1823, and the *British Medical Journal*, or *BMJ*, established in 1840 – and the trend has continued. New journals are constantly being founded as one speciality or subspeciality breaks away from its parent subject.

MINORITY GROUPS

The way in which medicine supports social inequalities such as those of class, race and sex shows how much it reflects the beliefs and prejudices of the day, even to the extent of doctors diagnosing diseases according to these categories. For instance, a single mother living in a high-rise flat is likely to be diagnosed as suffering from depression, whereas a successful executive overworking in the City is said to be suffering from stress.

Much nineteenth-century literature attempted to demonstrate the inferiority of non-white races. A black skin was sometimes regarded as a disease in itself, and was often seen as a source of disease on 'scientific' grounds. An example of this was drapetomania, a so-called disease which consisted of the strong desire of a slave to be free. There was much measuring of skulls, often of only a few carefully chosen subjects, to demonstrate that blacks and women had smaller skulls and were therefore inferior. In 1792 Benjamin Rush (1745–1813) introduced the idea that all negroes suffered from a mild form of congenital leprosy whose only symptom was blackness. Such ideas helped to maintain the status quo of society. They were also part of the process of 'medicalisation', by which medical theory and the medical profession gradually took over various aspects of living (see Chapter 5). In the twentieth century, the belief that blood types differed according to race was linked to widespread prejudice against receiving blood transfusions from non-white donors, a belief which was later disproved.

Of wider concern in the nineteenth century than the 'diseases' of black people were those of women, who were also perceived to be an inferior, minority group. As the power of religion declined and medicine became more authoritative and powerful, medical ideas came to embody, both explicitly and implicitly, current social ideas about women. These included ideas about their nature, their role in society, their abilities and limitations. In this, doctors gradually took over a moral role, supporting the established order and justifying the control of women through medical authority. Middle-class women were regarded as pure, indolent and sickly. Working-class women were regarded as polluting and a potential hazard from infection. Much of the medical literature concerned middle-class women, who had the time and money to visit doctors. Popular literature existed on the subject of female health in general, but it revealed little, for doctors disapproved of 'popular' health. Scientific medicine was essentially the preserve of the profession, with the patient as passive recipient.

Scientific medical theory said first that women were ill because they were women, and second that they became ill if they tried to do anything outside their female roles – a catch-22 situation. The 'illness' almost always related to the reproductive system, which, it was thought, limited their activities and required the constant attendance of a medical practitioner. To be female was to be pathological. Puberty was viewed as a period of stress and crisis: girls must be treated as invalids during this period. Menstruation was also pathological. The Victorian physician Dr Edward Tilt, writing in the *Lancet*, claimed that 'for thirty years the [uterus and ovaries] are thrown into a state of haemorrhagic and other orgasm every month'.

Pregnancy was also regarded as an illness and was even thought to involve a form of epilepsy. Expectant mothers needed to stay in bed as much as possible, it was said. The responsibility for care during pregnancy was moved from traditional women to male medical practitioners. The menopause was likewise seen as pathological, a condition in which, as Dr Tilt described in his book *The Change of Life in Health and Disease* (1857, 1883), 'the nervous force, no longer finding useful function, goes astray in every direction'. It was thought that the functions of ovulation, gestation, labour, lactation and the menopause in turn dominated the entire organism of women.

Ideas such as these concerning the inferiority of black people and women were still prominent in the twentieth century, and can even be detected in our society today.

Scientific medicine in the twentieth century

Scientific medicine made huge advances during the twentieth century. It is difficult to decide which have been the most important developments.

CONTROLLED TRIALS

Perhaps one of the most significant developments is the concept of controlled trials and their gradual adoption as a standard in research. During the nineteenth century it was regarded as acceptable and scientific to question a patient as he left the ward and tick him as a 'success' if he was grateful or trying to please the doctor. Many statistics were published triumphantly to 'prove' that certain treatments were valuable, and many of these were later shown to be useless or dangerous. Then came the idea that patients who were being studied should be matched by 'controls' and compared with them. It became important to plan the trial prospectively, not retrospectively, to compare like with like and, where possible, to study both groups in a 'double-blind' manner in which neither the patient nor the doctor was aware of who was being treated and who was a control. The practice was not always strictly followed, but it was understood that only by this method, properly carried out, was it possible to be certain about the results.

The first famous trial of this kind was carried out soon after World War II, on the use of steptomycin in the treatment of tuberculosis. The results were spectacular in favour of the drug. Nonetheless, the double-blind controlled trial is not an infallible method. Sometimes, even when efforts have been made to carry out the practice, the results have been labelled 'the double-blind leading the double-blind'.

Moreover, in some cases it is impossible to devise a double-blind controlled trial, even a prospective one. Then every attempt has to be made to match like with like, and to correct for the influence of age, sex, class, race and so on. And whatever their validity, the results of scientific trials tend to be believed, rejected or shelved according to whether or not they suit the current beliefs and prejudices of the profession and/or the public. For instance, in the mid-twentieth century the Royal College of Physicians published the results of a well-constructed study into cigarette smoking and showed beyond reasonable doubt that it led to cancer. It was not what the public, and still less the tobacco industry, wished to hear and it was only after many years and many more trials that the results were widely accepted. Even today, in spite of a vast amount of supportive evidence, the conclusions are resisted by the tobacco industry and by some hardened tobacco addicts.

The overall standard of statistical research still leaves much to be desired, but it has improved enormously during the last hundred years. Editors of medical journals are also now much more aware of the importance of such research, and many now hire statistical experts and others to 'peer review' articles before they accept them.

CLINICAL RESEARCH AND PRACTICE

Clinical research in Britain developed rather later than in the United States or Germany. In 1905 the famous physician Sir William Osler went from Johns Hopkins University in the USA to Oxford as Professor of Medicine. He was dismayed at 'the medical educational desert' he found there and criticised it repeatedly. He founded the Association of Physicians of Great Britain and Ireland, but this differed from the United States in that it did not include basic scientists, pathologists, physiologists or bacteriologists, nor those working in public health. Also, unlike the association in the USA, the meetings were closed, limited to physicians and their guests. It was 'an intimate club of mainly academic physicians' and had little contact with individuals in other scientific disciplines. It therefore never had the same national impact on medical science as the American equivalents did.

Nevertheless, by 1910 there had been a number of outstanding Britons whose contributions to clinical research had been internationally recognised. Sir James Mackenzie pioneered the polygraph, Sir Thomas Lewis the electrocardiogram (ECG). Sir Archibald Garrod of Bart's Hospital published the influential *Inborn Errors of Metabolism*. There was much research going on into the understanding of thyroid disease. Surgeons were improving their knowledge and inventing new operations. Sir Victor Horsley was making major contributions to the new speciality of neurosurgery.

In 1913 The Royal Commission on University Education in London under Lord Haldane emphasised the importance of scientific research in clinical medicine, but its findings were opposed by many and were shelved during World War I. Nevertheless, it laid the foundation for the establishment in British medical schools of modern academic departments in clinical subjects, where research would be emphasised. During the 1920s and '30s such positions began to be created in British, as well as American, universities. In Britain the most influential person in this movement was Sir Thomas Lewis. Although many people disliked him, his department at University College Hospital, London, has been described as 'the Mecca for all aspiring clinical research workers'. But in spite of his efforts, the Medical Research Council (founded in 1913 as the Medical Research Committee and renamed in 1920) did not open its own Clinical Research Centre at Northwick Park until 1970, long after Lewis's death.

By 1925 there were five chairs of medicine among twelve medical schools in London, but their background tended to be in medical politics rather than academic medicine, and they had curious rules: for instance, professors needed little or no experience of research, but had to come from the same hospital. Thus some of them were inept and on the whole they were not as powerful or as able as their American counterparts.

Clinical research as we now know it emerged after World War II with the advent of the National Health Service, when funds became available to support substantial numbers of professional clinical scientists paid with university salaries and provided with laboratories. Sir John McMichael (1904–93), one of the most distinguished, had a vision of 'a profession increasingly led by scientifically trained medical academics cascading their knowledge throughout clinical practice in the UK and abroad'. Nevertheless, Britain has never produced a Nobel prizewinner in clinical science, whereas the United States has produced many.

Research, of course, is not the be-all and end-all. In order to be effective, it has to be applied, and that is where the trouble seems to lie. It may seem ironic that now, when medicine is more effective than ever before, it should attract so much discontent that many thousands of people are rejecting it, at least in part, in favour of other systems. One of the reasons for this is that many modern treatments, however well researched and scientific they may be, are applied inappropriately or excessively. This is particularly true of drugs and surgery. As mentioned earlier, the number of people damaged rather than helped (and sometimes damaged as well as helped) is enormous. In 1974 a Senate investigation reported that 2.4 million unnecessary operations were performed in the US per year and that they caused 11,900 deaths and cost about $3.9 billion. The situation has not improved since. More deaths are caused annually by surgery in the US than the annual number of deaths during the wars in Korea and Vietnam. 'Iatrogenic disease',

disease caused by doctors, is common. In the West, estimates for patients admitted to hospital because of poisoning by prescribed drugs have varied from 10 to 40 per cent. Through the idealisation of scientific medical progress, our society has created a situation in which people tend to assume that there is 'a pill for every ill', and it suffers as a result, often without realising it. Naturally the situation is concealed as much as possible by those concerned.

MEDICALISATION IN MODERN TIMES
Doctors have always had power. They have known secrets, both about poisons and remedies and about their individual patients. They have let it be thought that they know what they are doing even when they do not. Perhaps they have always liked to 'medicalise' as a means of establishing themselves, of giving their profession importance. Many have used their power wisely, but some have abused it. Doctors have great power over their patients, and the abuse of that power is a serious danger to society. Ultimately, they can be controlled only by their patients, by what those patients demand to know, and by what they allow to be done to them in the name of treatment. The balance seems to be disturbingly wrong at present. We are a society increasingly preoccupied by bodily and medical matters, more often than not in a negative way.

While judging candidates for the Best of Young British Novelists promotion in 1993, the author A S Byatt complained about the recurrent preoccupations which she encountered in many of the entries: 'We seemed to be in a world of human bodies seen as objects of desire and violation, a world in which most of the action was penetration by the penis or the knife or the needle, where everything dripped with blood and other fluids.'

She pointed out that British fiction is remarkably body-obsessed, and the bodies with which it is obsessed are invariably sick or damaged.

Fiction, like medicine, reflects the society in which it grows. In his 'The Scientific Doctor', D H Lawrence wrote:

> When I went to the scientific doctor
> I realised what lust there was in him to
>   wreak his so-called science on me
>   and reduce me to the level of a thing.
> So I said: Good morning! And left him.

Many feel like this sometimes, but few would choose to die by refusing to have their acute appendix removed, or would wish to deny life-saving antibiotics to a child suffering from the otherwise fatal tuberculous meningitis. Few would refuse a hip or knee replacement for an intolerably painful joint. Scientific medicine benefits us all. It is all of our excesses and follies that sometimes spoil its potential benefits.

CHAPTER 2

Doctors' Motives

It has been generally assumed that a doctor works primarily to help patients, alleviate symptoms and cure disease. Doctors are known to have special knowledge and skills that enable and encourage them to do these things. Most people still take this for granted when visiting a doctor. Especially when ill, we are likely to assume that doctors are selfless – and even omnipotent. We seldom question their motives. A search of existing literature reveals almost nothing on the subject of doctors' motives. Conversely, doctors may explore the motives of their patients, being aware, for example, of the gain that some people seek through illness. Such studies do not, however, cover the doctors' own motives. For the past two hundred years, doctors' practices have been questioned quite regularly, but their motives have seldom been put under the microscope. Even when this has happened, the evidence has usually been ignored.

Today that situation is changing. People are increasingly wary and critical. It is now acknowledged that some doctors cheat, neglect, assault, abuse or even murder their patients. This is not as surprising as it seems. After all, someone with a desire to do such things will, if suitably qualified, be quite likely to apply to join the medical profession as a means to an end. This negative undercurrent has emerged only recently, but public confidence has been considerably shaken. The subsequent criticism in the media has made many people anxious about both the medical profession and the NHS in general, though not, usually, about their personal doctors.

Hidden Motives

I believe that, like other people, doctors act in their own interests and that, luckily, these are usually enlightened or at least coincide with the interests of their patients. Society in general, however, assumes that doctors act *only* in their patients' interests. As a result of this assumption, any underlying motives tend to be difficult to perceive and largely overlooked.

In truth, doctors' interests and motives, just like those of other people, may or may not be enlightened. People who have suffered at the hands of arrogant or money-grasping consultants, or indifferent general practitioners, or who have been damaged by inefficient or inhuman (let alone murderous) medical procedures will easily agree with this statement, but there is more to it than these obvious failings. What about the 'dedicated' doctor whose patients' needs always seem to be foremost in his mind, who works long hours and will put himself out for his patients to an extreme degree? We can assume that he too is actually behaving in his own interests. He may get his satisfaction from helping people, from doing a professional and skilled job well, from gaining the admiration and gratitude of patients, from being too busy to confront his own furies, or from having a reason to avoid his family or the things he dislikes doing. His conscience may tell him how he is to behave, with the result that, if he is not helping his patients in every possible way, he feels uncomfortable or anxious and therefore will act to avoid such feelings. In a few cases the conscientious doctor may be deliberately concealing quite different motives, as did Dr Harold Shipman, who was regarded by his patients as caring and dedicated.

Doctors whose motives – if we knew about them – we might regard as dubious or even sinister are often difficult to identify. Some of those whose hidden motives have been exposed turn out to have been in trouble or under suspicion before, sometimes in another country. They have usually been given the benefit of the doubt and allowed to continue practising. The disciplinary authorities of the medical profession have sometimes chosen to keep the evidence secret or to hide behind regulations absolving them from considering certain evidence. The General Medical Council (GMC) – the official disciplinary body of the British medical profession – has argued that it has no machinery for taking foreign evidence into consideration, yet it has made no effort to get these regulations changed. Moreover, whistleblowing in the medical profession has usually been rewarded with disapproval and often dismissal. When a medical scandal occurs, it often emerges that many people knew about it long before but were scared to mention it or were actively discouraged from bringing it into the open. A typical example of this occurred in the mid-1950s, involving an anaesthetist who was addicted to the gases he administered to his patients. During operations he would sit at the patient's head, quietly inhaling the anaesthetic. One day, when he was woozy from this habit, a child died in the middle of an operation. It turned out that surgeons, nurses and even porters had long known about the anaesthetist's addiction, but no one had done anything about it.

A standard question to a candidate who has applied to a medical school is, 'Why do you want to be a doctor?' The applicant is unlikely to say that he seeks power or money, let alone that he enjoys controlling or hurting people or that he wishes to damage them. The examiner, aware of the brief time available, is unlikely even to try to explore possible underlying motives, and would probably get nowhere if he did. Probably no one will ask or even consider the question again. It is not a top priority. A search through HISTLINE, a comprehensive index of medical references on the Internet, produced only three entries on 'motives of doctors', none of them relevant to modern practice. Yet it seems likely that a young person with a sexual perversion such as sadism or necrophilia, or with a strong desire to kill, injure or cause pain would, if he or she could, choose the medical profession as a suitable environment for the realisation of these motives. Easy access, an inherent possession of power, lack of public suspicion and a universal assumption of goodwill and skill must make it irresistible to such people – who are, fortunately, extremely rare. Much commoner are those who seek power, prestige or security, or who have a desire to solve problems or to experiment.

Thus doctors, like other people, have multiple motives and the extent to which these influence their professional behaviour is itself influenced by issues such as their individual personalities and the customs, pressures and standards of their places of work. In most places and under most conditions, whatever underlying motives may exist, it is surely true that the strongest motive of a doctor is to help the patient. Other motives may be noticed and sometimes discouraged, but are generally tolerated. However, truly destructive motives such as sadism, financial exploitation, indifference to patients or a self-seeking desire for new knowledge are mostly regarded as 'unthinkable' and, for that reason, are unsought and overlooked.

Thinking the unthinkable

There is one group of doctors whose motives and behaviour have been questioned and brought under the spotlight: the Nazi doctors who worked in the concentration camps in World War II. Because they seem remote from us and because the Holocaust and all its horrors has become a respectable field of study, the evidence against these doctors ceased to be unthinkable and much has now been written about them. We can acknowledge openly that their motives were not benign and that they were wicked men. We are 'allowed' to think and write about them because they have been separated in our minds from other Western doctors, even from those who are also shown to have behaved badly.

Twenty-three Nazi doctors were tried at Nüremberg. There is evidence that doctors in the Third Reich became Nazified more thoroughly and much sooner than any other profession, and as Nazis they did more in the service of the nefarious regime than people in other professions. An extreme manifestation of this occurred in the euthanasia wards, the concentration camps and on the selection ramp at Auschwitz. Michael H Kater, who wrote on the subject in his book *Doctors under Hitler* (1989), believed that at one end of the medical spectrum was the doctor who gave his life for his vocation, and at the other end was the doctor who killed in the name of it. In the middle stood the regular practitioner. Kater thought that this midpoint was not the same in 1942 as it had been in 1932. The norms had changed under a brutalising regime, making crimes more ordinary. Daily doctoring took place against a background of crime, and this gradually changed the professional ethos motivating all doctors in Germany.

Other writers believed that no profession demonstrated greater power for evil under the Nazis than was seen in the medical profession. According to *The Martyrdom of Jewish Physicians in Poland* (1963), edited by Louis Falstein, 'The Nazis prostituted law, perverted education and corrupted the civil service, but they made killers out of physicians.' In *Medicalised Killing: Auschwitz Physchiatry* (1982), Robert Jay Lifton wrote:

As a profession German physicians offered themselves to the regime. So did most other professions; but with doctors, that gift included using their intellectual authority to justify and carry out medicalised killing.

Some doctors in the camps were obsessed with human experimentation. Those who criticised were penalised, even many years later. A young biogeneticist, Dr Harmut Hanauske-Abel, published a critical article on the subject in the *Lancet* as late as 1986. As a result he was dismissed from his post and destroyed professionally.

The phrase 'the banality of evil' has been much used since Hannah Arendt wrote about the trial of Adolf Eichmann in *Between Past and Future* (1963). The idea suggests that ordinary people in certain environments are capable of the worst kinds of evil deed. This idea has seldom been applied to doctors other than those directly involved in Nazism and it was resisted by the German medical establishment, as it has been by other medical establishments, who all prefer the aberration theory, blaming the 'few rotten apples in the barrel'. This absolves the profession as a whole from blame, and encourages silence, secrecy, indifference and inactivity. Until recently medical crime and mis-behaviour have usually been dismissed as rare phenomena and nothing to do with the profession in general. It was unthinkable to suggest otherwise.

The situation is changing now. A number of cases of unethical behaviour have drawn attention to the existence of harmful motives in some doctors, such as financial or pornographic motives, research rather than healing, laziness, sadism or even necrophilia. A consultant physician stole blood prepared for transfusions and sold it. A surgeon left the operating theatre and hospital in the middle of an operation and the patient died. Another doctor failed to wash his hands between seeing patients and infected some of them with hepatitis. Others performed dangerous experiments on patients who could not in any way benefit from them. There are doctors who have used patients as a source of pornographic material or have seduced, assaulted or even raped their patients. The discovery that Dr Harold Shipman of Manchester had been killing patients for his own gratification shocked and appalled so many people that the story was prominent in the media for many weeks.

Shipman's behaviour was often described as 'unthinkable'. Why was that? It was because such things are not supposed to happen in our society and, when they do, they are regarded as so outlandish and horrendous that people turn away and cannot face them. Dr Shipman was unchallenged for some time even when he *was* suspected, and he was able to continue to murder his patients and become a record serial killer. He was killing patients during the time when the nurse Beverly Allitt was found guilty of murdering babies in her charge, in 1999. Her case was also treated as 'unthinkable' and was regarded, probably correctly, as a rare case unrelated to common practice. Yet in various countries other doctors and nurses have been found doing similar things, and more many have been found to be acting against the interests of their patients.

It is only recently, however, that wider questions have been asked about underlying motives in a previously idealised profession. It is a subject that deserves far more attention. After the Shipman case I was asked several times, 'Do you think there are other Dr Shipmans in practice?' Yet the questions were largely in jest, delivered with the black humour that comes from anxiety, and were not followed up. The true answer would have been 'Yes'. Other shocking cases following Shipman soon had people asking questions in earnest. In 1998 the gynaecologist Rodney Ledward was found guilty of 'butchering' his patients. In 1999 at Alder Hey Children's Hospital in Liverpool, pathologists were found to have kept and stored the organs of dead babies without the proper consent of their parents. The media and the public became less convinced by the theory of the 'few rotten apples', and began to lose faith in the medical profession and to question seriously some of its motives.

Understanding motivation

Killing patients for pleasure or relief of tension is probably extremely rare in doctors, though even as I write another suspected case in New York is described in the newspapers; and nurses in several countries, including the UK, have been charged with murdering their patients. The desire to kill may be rare, but motives other than the desire to help patients are surely common. Yet any less desirable fantasies and motives are generally easy to hide under a layer of professional behaviour, and in any case patients visiting a doctor are not likely to have that doctor's personal motives uppermost in their minds.

Society demands that doctors *appear* to be acting in their patients' interests, so much so that they hide underlying motives, often unconsciously suppressing them or converting them into more acceptable forms. This conforming behaviour derives from social and professional pressures and training, perhaps supported by conscience or an internal code of religion or morals. Motives are generally revealed only when they are regarded as 'suitable'. In that doctors are just like everyone else.

Do motives matter? Yes, of course they do, but perhaps not as they might appear at first sight. Different motives are needed for different aspects of medicine. No one would wish to be treated by a doctor whose motives are murderous, but what about a doctor whose motive is to display his skills, increase his knowledge, make money, or simply to go home? And what about the doctor with sadistic tendencies who actually enjoys controlling, inflicting pain or creating anxiety amongst his patients? At first it might seem that these people are also unfitted for the job, but this is not always so. Most patients would rather have a difficult and delicate operation done by a highly skilled surgeon, even if he is badly behaved, cares nothing for the patient as a person, or is trying to show off or improve his operating record, than be operated on by a surgeon who seriously 'cares' about the patient but is incompetent at surgery. Horses for courses.

How are we to get to grips with this tricky question of motivation? A distinguished medical sociologist suggested to me that the reason why doctors' motives are largely unexplored may be because they are difficult to ascertain and even more difficult to measure – but I do not see why this should apply to the motives of doctors more than to those of other people. Why should higher motives be ascribed to them than to others? Why should they not be subject to scrutiny? The idealisation of the medical profession that developed over the last one and a half centuries may have been damaged, but it still lingers, even among those who might be thought to be sophisticated.

George Bernard Shaw expressed a definite view of doctors' motives in the preface to his play *The Doctor's Dilemma* (1906) when he wrote: 'As to the honour and conscience of doctors, they have as much as any other class of men, no more and no less.' If this was the general view, Western medicine and the lives of its doctors and patients would be very different.

As it is, the idea that doctors always act in their patients' interests has become somewhat tarnished but is still strong and enthusiastically supported by the profession itself. As we saw in Chapter 1, this idealisation really arose during the nineteenth century, when science, progress, the 'conquest of disease' and the development of professional behaviour and standards all combined to create a strong belief in medical science and a respectful trust in its practitioners. Before that time, though, there was little science in medicine, little trust in science and little confidence in doctors, even famous ones. Few ascribed high motives to doctors then. John Aubrey (1626–97) recorded that Dr Ridgley, himself a medical doctor, wrote, 'If the world knew the villainy and knavery (beside ignorance) of the physicians and apothecaries, the people would throw stones at 'em as they walked in the streets.' Coleridge wrote of doctors, 'They are *shallow* Animals: having always employed their minds about Body and Gut, they imagine that in the whole system of things, there is nothing but Gut and Body.' Doctors were thought to be out merely to fleece and then kill the public. 'When a Nation abounds in physicians,' commented the *Spectator*, 24 March 1711, 'it grows thin of people.' For William Blake, disease and doctors worked together. In 1800, Parson William Holland 'met Mr Forbes the surgeon going to kill a few patients.'

Our opinion of doctors' motivation today has not sunk back to such lows, nor should it. Recent revelations, however, have perhaps served to open our eyes and to take the edge off excessive idealisation. Perhaps we should take Shaw's more realistic view (from his preface to *The Doctor's Dilemma*, 1906):

Unless a man is led to medicine or surgery through a very exceptional technical aptitude, or because doctoring is a family tradition, or because he regards it unintelligently as a lucrative and gentlemanly profession, his motives in choosing the career of a healer are clearly generous. However actual practice may disillusion and corrupt him, his selection in the first instance is not a selection of a base character.

Doctors undeniably have special knowledge and skills which they have spent many years acquiring. Yet I would argue that this does not set them above others in terms of their motivation. Quite apart from a right and proper desire to use their skills professionally, other motives are almost certainly present in most individuals, and these may help or hinder their desire to heal, and may affect their judgment as to what is best for the patient. Lack of awareness of this mixed motivation by both doctors and their patients increases the difficulties of the medical treatment and is partly responsible for the growing tendency to criticise and vilify doctors. Some of the range of hidden motives – both negative and positive – are examined below.

Power and status

Power in medicine used to rest with those who treated royalty and members of high society. During the past century it has come to lie with those who never see patients and have no direct responsibility for them: the scientists, the pharmaceutical companies, the hospital boards. Nevertheless, the doctor who treats patients for a living acquires a great deal of power over them and it may be an important motive, particularly for the hospital doctor who may be gratified by a train of followers suggesting power and status. Many are delighted to achieve a position of power in their hospital because it means they can introduce improvements and rearrange things as they wish. Some simply enjoy exercising their power, using it as a tool to achieve further success, to display superiority or even to humiliate others. The doctor may insist that a patient is cured, or at least improved, until that patient, in thrall to the doctor (who has knowledge and therefore power), believes it. The doctor then records the case as a 'success' and may include it in his or her research. Many scientific publications have resulted from this technique.

A good example of this occurred after the discovery in 1926 that liver could cure pernicious anaemia. It was hailed as one of the great medical discoveries of the twentieth century, yet many chronic patients did not respond to the new treatment. A young physician, William Sargant (1907–88) who had a powerful personality and huge confidence in his own ability, thought that the health of these patients would be improved if they were given doses of iron far greater than anything previously recommended. He proceeded to administer this, and at the same time insisted to the patients that they were improved, saying, 'You *are* better, aren't you?' Few were brave enough to deny it. He published accounts of this treatment in the *Lancet* and the *British Medical Journal*. These were well received, until experts in blood diseases exposed the method as false. Sargant had a nervous breakdown, but then turned to other fields and became one of the most powerful and influential psychiatrists of the twentieth century. He became well known for 'imposing' cure on his patients through his dominating personality, which he clearly loved to exercise.

Status may be associated with power and the desire to control, or it may be largely separate from those considerations. The desire for status can be a significant motive for doctors, as for other people. Having status usually means being admired, a welcome sensation, whether the admiration comes from colleagues or from patients. For a junior hospital doctor, who may have been qualified for as long as fifteen years, the ultimate aim is to become a consultant. Some consultants like to enhance their status further by taking on administrative duties, doing research and publishing papers, reviewing books, or sitting on committees – whatever means they can find of gaining and exercising power.

A desire to climb the ladder to the highest echelons of the profession often lies behind slavish behaviour and an unwillingness to step out of line. Medicine is an ordered, conventional profession and those who wish to advance in it must impress powerful people. There is a great fear of offending or annoying those in power by putting one's head above the parapet. There have been many occasions on which doctors and other staff have turned a blind eye to undesirable and even dangerous practices in colleagues such as drunkenness, drug abuse or incompetent surgery, because they did not wish to be accused of 'sneaking' or 'whistleblowing'. As a result, patients have been damaged or even killed. The gynaecologist Rodney Ledward boasted that he was the 'fastest gynaecologist in the South-East' and botched many operations, leaving some patients maimed, incontinent or in pain. He had been doing this for 16 years and his arrogance and incompetence was well known to other doctors and nurses, who felt afraid or reluctant to blow the whistle in a climate of 'It's wrong to sneak'. His inadequacies had long been known to the General Medical Council, but they had other priorities and had long been notorious for paying more attention to sexual peccadillos and to guarding their own power than to dealing with dishonesty or incompetence in practice. Although faced with incontrovertible evidence, they responded with silence and inertia, behaviour that is common on the part of those whose job is to deal with misbehaviour. When challenged, they tend not only to talk of the 'few' who transgress but to assert that, since the events in question, things have improved or 'moved forward' so that little now needs to be done. This provides an opportunity for boasting about the new situations that they have initiated, rather than concentrating on their past behaviour, a favourite trick of politicians.

Seeking and using power is also psychologically related to sado-masochism. Some readers may be shocked or bewildered at the idea that doctors may be motivated by sado-masochism. It would seem, after all, to be diametrically opposed to the purpose of healing, which should be a doctor's primary concern. Also, of course, the subject of sado-masochism is usually discussed in a sexual context. Yet if we take the basic explanation of sadism as the desire to control or to hurt or to inflict pain, and masochism as the desire to be controlled, then it becomes more explicable. Some doctors are very controlling in their attitude and will not concern themselves with what the patient thinks or wishes, while some patients are very willing to be controlled; less common are doctors who allow themselves to be controlled by what the patient wishes, and patients who dominate the doctor.

The desire to heal

Most people assume that the primary motive of doctors is to heal their patients – surely the most straightforward and positive of motivations. Yet even this can be complicated by other considerations, other impulses. Even Dr Shipman seems to have possessed a desire to heal, when he was not actually killing anyone. Such a desire is probably nearly always present, though it may be subordinated, perhaps by a need to demonstrate power or conformity. There is plenty of satisfaction to be had from sewing up a wound, relieving pain, prescribing what one is pretty certain will solve the problem, or reassuring someone that the test was normal and they have not got cancer. Yet a doctor may be motivated to do all these things not just from a simple desire to heal but also from a desire to be seen to be doing the right thing, to conform to current beliefs, to please his or her superiors, not to step out of line. The motive may also be enhanced by fear of *not* healing the patient and the possible consequences of this.

No doctor wishes to be thought to be doing anything to a patient other than healing or helping, and this serves to reinforce the motive. The pleasure of exercising a skill for its own sake is another powerful motive. Performing a procedure that one has learned over the years, or in which one knows one is skilful is enormously satisfying – even to the extent that the doctor may do it for the pleasure of doing it, or to show off to others, rather than for the patient's benefit. This is especially obvious when the procedure is not strictly necessary: a surgeon may do an operation more because he likes doing it than because he thinks it is vital for the patient's healing. He may justify himself with an explanation that fits what society regards as an acceptable motive, perhaps saying that he operates 'to be on the safe side', or 'so that it won't give trouble later', or he may say, 'If I don't do it, someone else will, probably less skilfully.' Many operations have been done under such auspices, and many people have lost their appendices, wombs and other parts quite unnecessarily. Sometimes unnecessary procedures are carried out as 'defensive medicine', so called because it refers to medical tests, treatment and procedures done or not done purely to cover the doctor in case of future dispute or litigation, not out of a plain desire to heal. Common examples are ordering x-rays or scans, or performing tests or operations which the doctor knows are unnecessary. It is said that part of the huge increase in Caesarean section in recent years can be attributed to this motive. Even when an operation *is* necessary, the doctor may still be pleased at the opportunity to practise or display his skill, and the desire to show off may be stronger than the desire to heal the patient.

Showing off skills

A doctor may also obtain satisfaction by healing a patient successfully when other doctors have failed. This is the satisfaction of one-upmanship – showing that one is cleverer or more skilful than others. Some doctors may deliberately arrange their practice and reputations in order to achieve such an aim. Others, including elderly, retired doctors, love to boast of the clever diagnoses they have made in the past.

A correct diagnosis is much admired by colleagues, especially where others have failed, and of course is welcomed by the patient, but there may be little interest in what happens to that patient afterwards. Lord Horder (1871–1955), a famous doctor, believed that the most important thing in medicine is diagnosis, the second most important thing is diagnosis, and the third most important thing is diagnosis. Another saying among some doctors runs, 'What matters is the diagnosis. The treatment can be looked up in a book.' Some doctors go no further. They can gain much kudos for being good at diagnosis. Having made a difficult diagnosis, they may enjoy the glory but take no interest in helping the patient to get better. For example, a doctor may go to great lengths to make a precise diagnosis when it is of academic interest only, because the condition is untreatable – the patient endures many tests and procedures that in the end prove to be of no use to their treatment, and they would have benefitted more from palliative care.

It is, of course, true that unless the diagnosis is correct, the treatment is likely to be useless or inappropriate. Nonetheless, to say that diagnosis is all that matters surely degrades the activity of healing to something of secondary importance in which the patient is denied both individuality and special needs. Another famous doctor, John Ryle (1889–1950), took a different view. He defined diagnosis as 'thorough knowledge of our patients'. That is a lesson to take to heart.

Problem-solving

An enthusiasm for solving problems often lies behind the desire to make a difficult diagnosis, especially where others have failed. It is possible, however, to regard every patient as a problem to be solved rather than as a person with a problem, and the doctor's satisfaction may come from solving the puzzle rather than helping the patient. For such a doctor, the disease is more important and interesting than the patient – but he may be more likely than his humane colleague to make the correct diagnosis.

Research is an important part of problem-solving, and this is now a significant aspect of the medical profession. Research is undertaken by doctors interested chiefly in scientific or clinical progress, and often takes place in a rather rarefied atmosphere quite divorced from the realities experienced day to day by patients. Many university departments are now devoted to clinical science and, whereas some are run on humane lines and make sure that their staff regard the patients as people, in the past there have been scandals because this has not been the case. Doctors who are interested primarily in finding a solution to a problem and see individual patients only as 'research material' have sometimes performed damaging and dangerous experiments on patients who could not possibly benefit from them.

Some years ago, H K Beecher in America and Maurice Pappworth in Britain wrote seminal books that drew the world's attention to this worrying medical characteristic. Since then, scientific doctors have been more careful in designing experiments, and editors of medical journals have scrutinised more carefully the papers submitted to them for publication, keeping an eye out for evidence of unethical practices. Yet there is always a tendency for research-minded doctors and institutes to forget the ethical side of their work in their absorption with the push for progress. Humanity is maintained at the price of eternal vigilance.

Money

A financial motive is sometimes attributed to doctors, particularly private doctors. It is not generally acceptable for a doctor to proclaim that money is his chief interest. George Bernard Shaw thought that doctors were interested *only* in making money and that they were intent on agreeing with their patients so that they could do just that. This motive is suspected less in the National Health Service than in private practice and is particularly likely to surface when, for example, a private doctor advises a big operation or a prolonged course of expensive treatment. Those opposed to private medicine tend to agree with Shaw and to suspect a financial motive all the time. The rest of us probably do not, and simply try to avoid the charlatans in the profession. We recognise, of course, that most doctors who undertake private practice do it for the money, but this does not mean that they do not care just as much about being skilful and helping the patient. Some people believe that private medicine is superior to public medicine. The advertisements for private medical insurance support this idea, though they do not say so specifically. Their underlying message, however, is often that 'good medicine' resembles a five-star hotel.

Even in the NHS, money may be a motive. There have been scandalous accounts of doctors neglecting their NHS patients in favour of their private practices, and of surgeons who deliberately engineer long waiting lists for operations such as hip replacements in the hope that patients, tired of the pain and the waiting, will transfer to the private sector where the operation can be done without delay for a large fee, often in the same hospital by the same surgeon. The money motive may also be a consideration when a doctor in public service seeks money for research or to enhance his department.

Of course, it would not be right to paint an entirely black picture. Even when the chief motive for being in private practice is money, a doctor is likely to have other motives as well. He may have entered private practice in order to enhance his income, but it is likely to be just as important to him to do a good job, to practise his skills and to have more time for the patient. Some doctors reduce their fees readily if necessary, or only charge patients whom they feel can afford it. All in all, money influences most doctors as much as it does other people.

Self-interest

Apart from a passive interest in money, motives of personal convenience may also be strong. At a recent London conference a consultant obstetrician described how he delivered the babies of his private patients. He always delivered them on a Wednesday. He made the mothers come into hospital early, then 'started them off' (i.e. broke the waters) and put up a pitocin drip to ensure effective contractions. He then went off to do his NHS clinics and returned at 5 p.m. to deliver the babies, and was almost invariably 'home by teatime'. Several participants praised his honesty, but others were concerned at how little regard he had for the patients as people.

Silence in self-defence

Another motive might be described as 'keeping the silence' which is often part of the desire to maintain the status quo. Like most other things, medicine has its silences and taboos. At one time it was not done for a doctor to touch a patient's body. He had to be content with looking at what could be seen, such as the face and tongue, and examining the body products – urine, faeces and so on. Nowadays a doctor is expected to perform as full a physical examination as the condition requires and is at fault if, for example, he fails to perform a vaginal or rectal examination when this is indicted to be necessary.

Modern medical silences, however, are more concerned with communication and feelings. Efforts are made to encourage doctors to talk to their patients, to treat them as 'whole' people instead of just examining the offending part, but this exhortation is often ignored. Many doctors observe a silence over anything to do with psychiatry or the mind, and some are silent about anything that does not concern their speciality directly. An old joke in medical circles concerns a surgeon who referred his patient to another department to have his fingers counted. Even doctors who are aware of the strong relationship between body and mind may prefer to remain silent rather than discuss a patient's marriage, family and sexual relationships or inner fantasies, even though they may be aware that these lie behind the illness. It is easier to operate on whatever part of the body onto which the patient has displaced his or her personal problems. Still more, a doctor may be silent on the question of death and shy away from the subject. A few decades ago the subject of death was almost totally a zone of silence, even when the patient was clearly dying. Young doctors were instructed to inform the relatives, but never the patient.

Modern medical silences are often conditioned by the time available. If a doctor has only a few minutes to give to a patient, he cannot discuss fully the worries that may be in that patient's mind. He may regret this and be aware of the deficiency, or he may justify his avoidance of the issue on the grounds that he is concerned only with the scientific or medical aspects of the case and that the rest does not concern him.

Conclusion

We have looked at a variety of motives in this chapter, some positive, some negative, some a bit of both. Motivation among doctors is a very neglected field of study, but it is surely something we should learn to understand more fully. If we did, we would perhaps learn to view the medical professional in a less idealised way, and our criticisms would at least be better informed.

Healing patients, curing disease, exercising skill, keeping high professional standards, a desire for social standing, pleasing parents, teachers or superiors, impressing colleagues, exercising a sense of superiority, receiving the adoration of patients, power, control, status, money, narcissism, ambition, pleasure, achievement, curiosity, experimentation, identification, a sense of duty, guilt, sex, sadism, hurrying through the clinic as fast as possible, an overwhelming interest in finding rare diseases, avoiding effort, causing pain. Any of these can motivate doctors, and any of them may be combined with professional rectitude and doing a good job. Patients would do well to remember that, and view their doctors with a more realistic eye.

CHAPTER 3

Progress

The modern idea that progress is associated with improvement can be traced back to the Enlightenment of the eighteenth century. Before that there was little idea that humankind was improving either morally or scientifically. Gradually the idea of progress became linked with that of the ultimate perfectibility of human beings, and the concept of progress as improvement reached its greatest prominence in Victorian times. Few people today believe, as the Victorians did, that society, morals and human character are progressing and improving. The twentieth century, with all its horrors and disillusionment, effectively demolished the idea that we are moving towards perfection. Nonetheless, in relation to medicine there is still widespread belief in ultimate health and the conquest of all disease. This idea is championed continually by the media and the pharmaceutical industry, often supported by doctors and medical scientists. As patients, we want to believe them. No one wants to die and fewer of us now believe in an afterlife. More people are preoccupied by living to the full in this life, rather than preparing for the next. Every new medical discovery or drug is hailed as a mark of progress, usually without any suggestion that it might turn out to have effects that are far from progressive.

A mixture of attitudes

Medicine is generally thought to be 'advancing' in knowledge and power over disease. There has been much of this kind of progress in many medical fields especially during the last fifty years. People in the

West today are concerned with their health and try to preserve it to a degree unknown before. We all like to know that medical knowledge is advancing, especially in the fields of our own particular interests and problems. On most days the media give us dramatic accounts of new 'advances', as well as advertisements for products said to encourage 'healthy' living – though these are often contradictory. It is a curious paradox, therefore, that at the same time as it is receiving such trust in its inevitable progress, modern medicine is also attracting a degree of hostility and criticism unknown in previous years. Such an uncomfortable mixture of attitudes has led to a great deal of confusion and anxiety, as the general public becomes increasingly uncertain about who and what they should believe.

During the twentieth century, the idea of progress became linked with the profits of the pharmaceutical industry. The latest new drug was hailed repeatedly as 'the answer', and such was the power of advertising that even if a drug were shown eventually to be ineffective or even dangerous, many people (including doctors) would probably continue to use it. Each of us, medical or lay, tends to have faith in particular remedies, regardless of the scientific evidence. Notably, the exposure in the journal *Family Doctor*, published by the British Medical Association, of a particular drug as useless was followed by readers' letters asking where it could be obtained. Unfortunate incidents such as misuse of a drug by doctors or previously undetected side-effects have often been ignored. Doctors might be pressurised by the pharmaceutical companies into continuing with a potentially unsafe drug, or they might use it because it is cheaper than another, safer or more effective treatment. It is still happening today. Occasionally a scandal will arise, as happened most memorably with the drug thalidomide. Then, for a short time, we are shocked into a more measured attitude, but soon the next item on the conveyor belt of 'progress' comes along and we are taken in as before, with lessons apparently unlearned.

Changing concepts of 'progress'

What do we really mean by 'progress'? The *Oxford Dictionary of Current English* defines it as 'forward or onward movement: advance or development esp. to better state'. The word is derived from the

Latin *progredi*, meaning 'to step forward'. Originally its meaning was concrete, describing, for instance, the course of a journey or a disease. The ancients had little or no concept of progress in the sense of improvement. In 1605 Francis Bacon (1561–1626) wrote that progress in medicine was 'rather in a circle, than in progression'. During the eighteenth century, however, the word developed new meanings that reflected changing social conditions, and became associated with the idea of the perfectibility of man and with the now established scientific systems of Bacon and Newton. Many people began to think that increase in scientific knowledge led to moral improvement. The idea of *change* developed, especially in the sense of change for the better. Science in the modern sense began to be important in society and became a stimulus that has encouraged the idea of progress as improvement ever since. People looked forward as well as backward and saw the future and the people in it as changing for the better. As conditions and opportunities improved, at least for the well-to-do, the idea spread that humankind could be improved and even perfected. The idea of perfection through progress replaced the idea of heaven in the minds of many Victorians, in an age that was increasingly secular. It provided a kind of faith and a basis for hope.

Throughout the centuries, various influential commentators have written on the subject, reflecting the outlook of their particular era. In his *Decline and Fall of the Roman Empire* (1776–88) Edward Gibbon came to 'the pleasing conclusion ... that every age of the world has increased, and still increases, the real wealth, the happiness, the knowledge, and perhaps the virtue, of the human race.' The philosopher William Godwin (1756–1836) wrote, 'Perfectibility is one of the most unequivocal characteristics of the human species.' In 1793 he proclaimed, 'Man is perfectible, or in other words susceptible of perpetual improvement.' Godwin based this statement on his belief that people acted according to reason, that it was impossible to be rationally persuaded and not to act accordingly, because reason taught benevolence. This belief came outdated, but its remnants can still be seen today. In 1829 Thomas Carlyle (1795–1881) thought that the age was advancing because 'knowledge, education, are opening the eyes of the humblest, are increasing the number of thinking minds without limit'. Charles Darwin (1809–62) ended his *Origin of Species* (1859) with the argument that 'all corporal and mental environment will tend to progress towards perfection'. Tennyson (1809–92) expressed a common Victorian view in his poem 'Locksley Hall':

Yet I doubt not through the ages one increasing purpose runs,
And the thoughts of men are widened with the process of the suns.

These were just a few of the many intellectuals and social commentators who had an unshakable faith in progress.

This faith was inextricably linked to scientific progress. The rate of such progress greatly increased during the nineteenth century, and medicine was part of it. Gradually the discoveries of medicine and its associated sciences became absorbed into the ideas of inevitable progress and perfectibility.

In medicine, the idea of progress had, and still has, many meanings. It may refer to a transition from simple to complex, from bad to good, slow to fast, lower to higher, dangerous to safer, painful to less painful. It also embraces increasing knowledge, more efficient technology and greater control over the environment in terms of health and disease. It gradually came to represent increasing information about disease and the power to describe, understand and control it. Above all, it became associated with a steady stream of new treatments and cures.

The idea of progress in medicine has now become detached from the idea of progress in society or in human nature. The twentieth century produced much disillusion and its many human disasters revealed that humankind was no nearer perfection than it had been in the past. Today the idea that humans are perfectible is no longer fashionable. Many liberals think of progress partly in terms of humanitarianism, in which there have been some slow but undeniable advances – for instance, in the abolition of the death penalty in most developed countries, the conversion of slave-trading from a legitimate business to a crime, the more equal treatment of women, and the law in relation to children – but we all know that on the whole people are as vicious, untrustworthy, selfish and dishonest as they ever were and that many people, when permitted, need no persuasion to indulge in acts of dishonesty and sadistic misanthropy. This is brought home to us every day in media reports of crimes and atrocities, and in the way in which the audience enjoys them. It is increasingly difficult these days to cover up misbehaviour or bad practice.

It is now widely acknowledged that technical advances are a real and enduring form of progress – indeed, its only enduring form – and that these advances do not in themselves generate social or moral progress. It is also recognised by some that such advances may turn out to have effects that are far from progressive. Nonetheless, where medicine is concerned, a naïve belief in progress as improvement seems to linger on very strongly. The twentieth century, remarkably, saw the general public conduct a blossoming love affair with medicine at a time of increasing disillusion about moral and social progress and even about doctors.

Discoveries and dangers

Until comparatively recently, modern medicine has been almost universally accepted with little criticism – aided by an assumption of goodwill on the part of doctors and other health workers, and the suppression of failures, dangers and disadvantages. To some extent this mindset has continued into the twenty-first century. Idealisation of medical progress in general is still marked, but the public has a greater tendency to show scepticism, and even hostility, towards a particular doctor or medical custom or procedure. As individuals we naturally tend to see problems in specific situations before we start to look around us and recognise the general malaise. Thus admiration for progress still persists and we still expect advances to occur without undesirable effects. This outlook may change in time. As society becomes increasingly sceptical and critical, disappointment and disillusion are almost bound to set in, even where our faith in medical progress is concerned.

Until that outlook does change, however, we are caught in the trap of being willing victims, undergoing unknown dangers in the name of progress. Without complaint or doubt, many thousands of patients have undergone dangerous and inadequately tested treatments and have swallowed drugs whose side-effects are not fully known. People have permitted unnecessary investigations and operations, caught dangerous hospital infections and endured anything the doctor ordered – simply because they have believed unquestioningly that 'doctor knows best'. Although this belief has declined today, it is still powerful. Only a minority of new treatments and medical processes have survived over time, but the successes and failures are usually regarded not as false or dangerous phases but as steps in medical progress. As such they are seldom questioned, and we move on to the next discovery without looking back and taking stock of the wider implications.

In some ways medicine has become a kind of religion, worshipped as producing new perfections concerned with health and the conquest of serious disease. Medicine has changed so much during the last two hundred years. It has 'conquered' many diseases, introduced 'advances' and 'improvements' and changed the lives of so many people that it is difficult to think of it as anything other than progress. Few would willingly now live in a world without anaesthetics, asepsis, antibiotics, vaccines or the diagnostic and therapeutic technology of modern medicine. Just looking back at what ill-health and disease was like two hundred, one hundred or even fifty years ago, gives a powerful image of progress. Looking at the highly technological advances of the last fifty years merely enhances this view.

Nevertheless, many diseases are still enigmas and uncontrolled – but it is widely assumed that they will sooner or later be conquered. Some diseases could be conquered now, of course, including poliomyelitis, tuberculosis and many tropical diseases. We have the science necessary, but the opportunities are often ignored for political and economic reasons. Problems may also be ignored when doctors make bad mistakes, when the health services are inadequate or break down, when there is a serious epidemic or a shortage of nurses or doctors, when the health budget is used up by administration or there are serious lapses in public health. These matters are not popularly regarded as 'medicine', however. They are a side issue, and medical progress is seen to march on regardless, conquering diseases through diagnosis, treatment or prevention.

Medical progress is charted by what may be called the 'textbook mentality'. A textbook is a practical book dealing with the state of the subject at the time of writing and giving information and advice about practice. It often exalts its subject. At one time most medical textbooks began with a brief account of the history of the subject, but in recent years this custom has been largely discontinued, perhaps because of the amount of current information that needs to be included. Most modern textbooks therefore overlook the past – especially the less reputable or superseded past. Medical historians have often looked at modern textbooks and described the discoveries and fashions that still hold good, omitting, as do the textbooks themselves, those practices that went wrong or fell into disfavour. Past medical history is often judged only insofar as it is relevant to contemporary practice. To look at medical history more widely, one has to look at old textbooks, journals and records. These give a picture of the state of the art at the time they were written and they include, of course, what was later thought to be wrong, misguided or dangerous before it was cut from the text.

For example, two common treatments valued for centuries but later shown to be dangerous were mercury and bleeding. Another example is status lymphaticus, a disease once described as the most important problem in medicine, yet which few modern doctors or medical historians (except perhaps the most elderly) have even heard of. It was a worrying condition associated with sudden death in children and young people, and it had a death rate of virtually 100 per cent (see page 185). A century ago this disease was regarded by the prominent physician R E Humphry, writing in the *Lancet* (1908, ii) as 'one of the most important [diseases] we will have to contend with'. He asserted that 'there is no disease of greater medico-legal importance.' Despite the apparent importance of this disease, and the efforts made to treat or prevent it, it eventually became apparent that the condition had never even existed. If people today were more aware of these histories, they would probably be more critical of new 'advances' and less likely to develop a false and often dangerous view of medical progress.

It is a fact, too, that most of our successful operations were learned and worked out on patients who were killed by early experiments. Who thinks of that now? The mortality from surgery in the nineteenth century was appalling – even, or one might say especially, after the introduction of anaesthesia and asepsis, which led to wild operating in what has been called 'the adolescence of surgery'. Surgeons were learning their way round the abdomen, and acquiring various skills such as removing parts and learning what could be removed without actually killing the patient. Of course disasters happened. Sometimes they learned, often only after many decades, that their magnificent operations, so lovingly and care-fully learned and performed, were useless or worse than useless. One example of this was Battey's operation, or 'normal ovariotomy', the nineteenth-century operation to remove healthy ovaries to cure alleged disease elsewhere in the body, usually hysteria. Other examples that later proved to be pointless were colectomy (removing the large bowel) for constipation, tenotomy (cutting tendons) for clubfoot, and partial glossectomy (cutting out part of the tongue) for stammering. These are but a few of the 'discoveries' hailed as progress over the years, now all but forgotten, passed over as failures and buried in the mists of time. Many diseases have been described and many treatments have been prescribed which have turned out to be transitory, false 'advances'. They were fashions that came and went – an aspect of progress that still holds true today and that we ignore at our peril.

CHAPTER 4

Fashion

It could be said that most new treatments and cures in medicine are fashions – temporary and largely unproven, with any supporting evidence likely to be over-influenced by current beliefs or interests. Sooner or later these fashions disappear because they are found to be unhelpful or harmful, or because they are superseded by something better. Even some diseases turn out to be passing fashions. When a new fashion develops, it is often hailed as a permanent scientific advance, particularly by the media, who thrive on the idea of progress and the excitement of the new. Little attention is paid to the ephemeral nature of many of these 'advances'. Yet most of us automatically think of medicine as *progress* rather than *fashion*. Why is this?

The meaning of 'fashion'

The world 'fashion' is related to the Latin *facere*, meaning 'to make or do', and *factio*, meaning 'fact'. In Anglo-Saxon there was *fasun* and in Old French, *façon*. In its meaning of 'to make or shape', it entered the English language in the thirteenth century. In the fourteenth century it included the concepts of mode and manner, and during the fifteenth century it also came to imply established custom or conventional usage, sometimes also suggesting something that is current. In the sixteenth century came hints of the word's future use, especially in the sense of something superior. Edmund Spenser informed readers of *The Faerie Queen*, 'The general end of all the book is to fashion a gentleman or noble person in virtuous and gentle discipline.' Shakespeare referred to 'fashion' more than a hundred times and used the word in several senses – including, from *Cymbeline*, 'I am stale, a garment out of fashion', 'The glass of fashion, and the mould of form' and, from *As You Like It*:

> O good old man! how well in thee appears
> The good old service of the antique world,
> Thou art not for the fashion of these times,
> Where none will sweat but for promotion,
> And having that, do choke their service up
> Even with the having.

From *Twelfth Night* comes:

> He will come to her in yellow stockings, and 'tis a colour she abhors, and cross-gartered, a fashion she detests.

The word 'fashionable' first appeared in the seventeenth century. There is, perhaps, a hint of the modern meaning in the Authorised Version of the Bible (1611): 'The fashion of this world passeth away' (1 Corinthians 7:31). It seems to mean primarily 'how it is made', but one can see the way in which the meaning was changing.

In the eighteenth century, the word 'fashions' came into use in the sense in which we have used it ever since. During the late eighteenth century, the search for novelty grew alongside the idea of progress, probably as part of the middle classes' attempt to differentiate themselves from the mob with fashionable clothes, dolls, magazines, and so on. Increasing prosperity meant that a rising middle class could afford to be concerned with material nonessentials. No sooner had fashion invaded clothes, books and everyday life than it invaded medicine. Since that time, Western medicine has produced many diagnoses, diseases and treatments that quickly came into fashion, then declined and faded into oblivion.

The historian Roy Porter maintains that the modern concept of fashion, both in medicine and elsewhere, was a product of the Enlightenment and that it is inappropriate to apply it to events that occurred before the mid-eighteenth century. Its origins can, however, be discerned a little before that time. In some comments of the period we can recognise the later meaning of being up-to-date and somewhat superior. In 1696 the actor and dramatist Colley Cibber (1671–1757) wrote, 'One has as good be out of the world, as out of the fashion.' Bernard Mandeville (1670–1733), author of 'the first book on minor mental maladies', wrote in 1723, 'Experience has taught us that these Modes seldom last above Ten or Twelve years, and a Man of Threescore must have observ'd five or six Revolutions of 'em at least.' A few years later Lord Chesterfield wrote, 'If you are not in fashion, you are nobody.' Such sentiments are not uncommon today, and nowhere more strongly than in medicine or among those concerned with health.

What makes a fashion?

Readers older than about forty probably remember fashions in disease or treatment that were common in our own past or in our parents' time and which have since declined or disappeared. Experienced doctors can remember customs or fashions that once prevailed, such as a particular operation, drug or procedure that was believed to be essential for a particular condition, yet fell into disuse – sometimes because it was shown to be useless or even dangerous, but often simply because it fell from favour. No one nowadays diagnoses 'grumbling appendix', believes in 'rest cures' or routine tonsillectomy, prescribes thalidomide for morning sickness, or advises leucotomy (lobotomy) for schizophrenia. This list could include rest and dietary restrictions during menstruation, routine purging, the dangers of getting wet feet and many more ideas that have passed from current usage.

Where do these ideas come from? Why do they come and go? What distinguishes them from less transient diagnoses and treatments? Sometimes the answers may seem simple – medical progress, new discoveries, unexpected complications – but further enquiry is likely to show that the whole picture is more complicated. How did these diseases and treatments arise when they did? Why did they become so popular? Why did many become prominent or continue to exist despite evidence against them? How far do patients suffer or benefit from this? Why does Western medicine, in contrast to other systems of medicine, change so much and depend so much on fashion? Some diseases are seen as common and important for a time, then fade into obscurity and come to be regarded as irrelevant, trivial, a normal variation or nonexistent. Why is this? Why do some treatments seem to be effective, even essential, then become unpopular, dangerous, immoral or plain silly? Why do we continue to think of every part of this process as 'progress'?

To answer all these questions fully would require a long and detailed exploration of the whole history of medicine, but some of the answers are obvious. Some infections have become less worrying and therefore less prominent because we can now tackle them with antibiotics, or because the organisms associated with them have become less virulent (for example, the haemolytic streptococcus, scarlet fever). (However, some of these, such as tuberculosis, are becoming more dangerous again.) Venepuncture (bleeding or blood-letting), long used to treat virtually any serious disease and often for maintenance of health as well, was eventually shown to be dangerous and ineffective and is no longer used as a treatment. Blood-letting made a lot of people feel better, and healthy people would often have a regular bleeding, because it produced a slightly pleasurable light-headed sensation and often relieved immediate symptoms. Likewise mercury, once the fashionable treatment for many serious diseases, is poisonous, has been removed from the *British Pharmacopeia* and nowadays is not prescribed for anything. Yet for centuries it was the most effective treatment for syphilis and doctors were convinced of its benefits. Nor would any doctor now lance a teething baby's gums; or prescribe several hundred enemas to the same patient in one year. However, there is true evidence in favour of progress; for instance, smallpox no longer exists (except in laboratories) because medicine has conquered and eliminated it from the world. (This is the only major infectious disease where this has happened.)

Some medical fashions were passing phases, perhaps associated with the illness of a celebrity. For example, the diagnosis of 'appendicitis' became much commoner after King Edward VII's operation, and Nancy Reagan's mastectomy (rather than lumpectomy) for breast cancer led to a resurgence of that treatment in other women at a time when the fashion for it had actually been diminishing. Some fashions are associated with a particular drug. The fashions for Prozac and Viagra, for example, are now abating because they have been found to be less useful than was initially believed or suggested. Other drugs turn out to be dangerous: thalidomide deformed unborn babies, for instance. Yet these straightforward answers do not fully explain why certain diseases and treatment become fashionable and others do not.

'Fashion' is not a word much used specifically in relation to medicine, yet I would argue that it is possible and useful to think of medicine as a series of fashions – often judged by trial and error, and kept or discarded on that basis. The very word 'fashion' seems unsuitable, even frivolous, in the context of the serious subject of disease and death. Few of us would like to think that the diagnosis and treatment given to us by our medical advisers may be no more than the current fashion, perhaps due to fade in the near future. Nonetheless, not only is the idea of fashion relevant to modern medicine, but it is essential to appreciate this relevance if we are to understand enough about medicine not to be eventually disillusioned by dashed expectations. The need for such understanding has never been more acute than it is today.

So what is fashion in medicine? Surely it must be different from fashion in clothes and other material things? 'Fashion' is related to custom, habit, style, trend and fad, and also to taste, craze, enthusiasm and mindset. A fashion in medicine is an idea or practice, often a diagnosis or a treatment, that is not based on proven evidence but is believed in and practised by many doctors for an unspecified period of time. A fashion may last for a short time or for centuries, in which case we may decide to call it a custom. It may be more or less universal, or confined to a particular group of doctors or lay people, or to a particular country, district or hospital. The latest gas selected for surgical operations is a fashion, whereas anaesthesia is a custom – just as the miniskirt is a fashion in dress, whereas the skirt is a custom.

We can divide different kinds of fashion into a multitude of categories, not only fashion and custom, but also fad, tradition, mode, habit, style, taste, craze, mindset and even novelty or superstition. This applies in medicine also. The trouble is that it may be impossible, until history reveals it later, to see which is which. It is perhaps easier to retain the general word 'fashion' but remain aware of the big differences in meaning that it may carry.

A fashion may linger for generations or may be rejected quickly. Evidence may accumulate that proves the theory and enables a fashion to join the mass of scientific evidence and become part of a permanent or semi-permanent core of knowledge. On the other hand, it may become increasingly apparent that there is no supporting evidence, let along proof, and that the medical custom is merely the product of a fashion that will sooner or later pass out of use. For example, in 1987 the *New England Journal of Medicine* published an article that declared: 'In the areas of nutrition and physical fitness, fashion and fads run amok and almost completely dictate medical care.'

Most medical practice is to a greater or lesser extent a matter of fashion, the widespread, and often temporary, acceptance of an unproven idea. In spite of the modern emphasis on evidence, fashion is still the essence of medicine. Proof is not the same as evidence and, although much evidence supports the practices of Western medicine, relatively few of its ideas and methods are *proven*. Fashion still covers most medical practices and advances, both in the past and today.

A 'proven' idea can be defined as one that has been shown to work, such as Koch's demonstration that the tubercle bacillus is present in every case of tuberculosis and can be passed on to others (see page 26). 'Koch's postulates' were for many years considered to be necessary proof of the presence of a particular infectious disease, but the limitations of this for other infections later became apparent. Koch's postulates were neat and convincing in themselves, but it became impossible to demonstrate them convincingly in all cases. More recently and less convincingly, what is known as 'evidence-based medicine' has come to be regarded as the basis of proof. This is another fashion, and will eventually be shown to be so. Medical fashions are popular with doctors or patients, or both, but often have little more than anecdotal evidence and a particular belief or mindset to support them.

Fashion is all-pervasive in medicine as elsewhere in everyday life, and you cannot have medical progress without it; but being unaware of it leads to misunderstanding and can be dangerous.

CHAPTER 5

Medicalisation

Medicalisation is the process by which medicine, in theory and practice, becomes involved in matters that previously did not concern it. Medicalisation is an important means whereby medicine increases its power. For two hundred years medicine has been greatly expanding its influence. Increasingly, human problems are seen in medical terms and are defined accordingly. New diseases are discovered, constructed or invented and medical treatments are devised as solutions to those problems. Different kinds of behaviour and feelings are increasingly labelled as 'diseases' or 'medical conditions', and allotted to doctors to cure if they can. Many of these were previously judged to be part of the moral sphere, for example, kleptomania and hyperactivity, or else simply part of everyday life, for example, insomnia. Some of the new 'diseases' are closely associated with drugs that have recently been synthesised. A recent example is shyness (often now called 'social phobia'), and there is now pressure for us to regard this as a 'condition' requiring medical intervention.

We have a tendency to regard anything labelled as 'illness' or 'disease' as a misfortune that has arrived by chance, rather than as a responsibility of the sufferer. By contrast, the few conditions that are regarded as the patient's 'fault' are despised. Drug addiction, for example, has even acquired a label of low morals through being called 'drug abuse'. Nowadays the term 'medical condition' is often used to provide a vague explanation or excuse, often for a misdemeanour or a crime. If you cannot do anything about it, the doctor must treat it, and if you think that the doctor can treat it, there is no personal responsibility involved in its cause or cure. This includes conditions such as hyper-activity, bad behaviour, stealing, depression, anorexia, post-traumatic stress disorder and irritable bowels. The process clearly increases the power and perceived importance of doctors and is also strongly supported by the media and public. In a way, medicalisation seems to be in everyone's interest, even when it is misleading or deleterious. On the whole people like to think and be told they suffer from a medical condition rather than a personal fault.

The growth of medicalisation

Through the process of medicalisation, doctors have gradually taken over such matters as 'normal' childbirth, sex and sexuality – including homosexuality, contraception and abortion – dying and grieving, sleep, alcoholism, drugs and drug 'addiction' (a term devised to provide a medical context), criminal tendencies and some criminal behaviour (for example, stealing), and conditions or behaviour previously regarded as spiritual and religious, the province of the priest, such as loss of faith, bad behaviour and some sexual problems.

Medicalisation goes with urbanisation, industrialism and the free market economy. The growth of cities led to an increase in epidemics, the control of which required regulations involving matters such as quarantine, notification of disease and public health – all matters requiring greater involvement from medical experts rather than lay people and having a small but significant effect on people's everyday lives. At the same time there was a gradual decline in traditional religious faith and respect for the clergy, while respect for doctors was increasing. People were impressed by advances in medical science, and began to approve of and even to demand 'medicalisation'. This has continued to the present day. George Carey, Archbishop of Canterbury from 1991 to 2002, has said (in a lecture reported in *The Times*, 8 March 1996) that modern general practitioners are weighed down by a burden – the new confessional: 'All of life's ills at the personal level have apparently become medical ills which can be treated by medical means.'

Medicalisation has long had its critics. In 1711 Joseph Addison wrote in his *Spectator* that 'when a nation abounds in physicians, it grows thin of people'. Two centuries later George Bernard Shaw asked, in the preface to *The Doctor's Dilemma* (1906), 'Have we lost faith? Certainly not; but we have transferred it from God to the General Medical Council.' The forthright ex-priest Ivan Illich believed that medicalisation had gone so far that 'the medical establishment has become a major threat to health' (from his *Medical Nemesis: The Expropriation of Health*; 1976).

The process of medicalisation dates at least from the eighteenth century. The French philosopher Michel Foucault devoted much effort to trying to understand how it came about and what its consequences were. Discussing France (and the same would apply to other industrialising countries), he believed that the whole population slowly became integrated into 'a system of medical institutions and social norms that regulated and controlled rational and prudent health behaviour'. Doctors gained in prestige and were no longer the subject of ridicule, as they had been, for example, in the cartoons of James Gillray (1757–1815) and Thomas Rowlandson (1756–1827) and in Molière's play *Le Malade Imaginaire* (1673). Later doctors became respected and admired, and their love of science and humanity seemed no longer in doubt. There was ready co-operation in the extension of the idea of 'disease' into new areas of life. Increasingly, medical treatment seemed to be more appropriate and more humane than religious or legal intervention, and this still appears to be a widely held view today.

This attitude has been strongly reinforced by advances in scientific knowledge and medical technology. For the first time in history, doctors have a wide choice of effective treatments for many different conditions. Any extension of medicalisation usually develops in the form of a new fashion and can be analysed as such. It gradually becomes part of mainstream medicine, where it may or may not become a permanent feature.

A spreading influence

The enthusiasm for medicalisation may remain undimmed, but the process has obvious flaws. It encourages the extension of new methods, but often far beyond their true effectiveness. What may seem to be a miracle cure for a few can become a source of danger or anxiety to the many. For instance, modern screening programmes can pick up early cancers and other illnesses, or abnormalities in an unborn child, but the process can create tremendous anxiety in patients, first about the test and then if the result is abnormal. Sometimes the tests themselves are dangerous, or they give false results. These may lead to surgery or other treatment for a nonexistent disease, or to the ignoring of an existing disease. As the result of a misread test, a pregnant woman may be told that her risk of having an abnormal baby is not 1 in 450, as she was told originally, but 1 in 250. Despite the relatively small difference and the continuing strong likelihood that the child will be normal, such a change may induce acute anxiety and panic, with serious contemplation of abortion. There is a tendency for the medicalised feature to dominate the patient's life, even when the risks are small, and even those who have been told that they are healthy are left feeling uncertain.

Another worrying aspect of medicalisation's spreading influence is the takeover by doctors of a wider area than is justified by the situation. For instance, when doctors became skilled at saving mothers and babies in abnormal and dangerous pregnancies, it seemed to many to be appropriate that they should take over 'normal' pregnancies as well, particularly as it can be difficult to detect the abnormal until it happens. This has had some unfortunate results. During the last two centuries many doctors (obstetricians), following the fashions and beliefs of their times, have argued either that all births should take place under the care of a qualified obstetrician, or that pregnancy is a 'disease' in itself, or even that vaginal delivery is becoming a thing of the past and is being, or should be, replaced by universal Caesarean section. Similarly, since doctors can sometimes help those with sexual abnormalities, for example by removing an internal cause of pain or helping in cases of infertility, some have argued and some believe that they are experts in all aspects of sexuality and reproduction. They intrude into areas about which they know little or nothing, rushing into complicated treatments and drugs without considering simple common sense. Herein lies one of the dangers of medical fashion.

Medicalisation is closely allied to the pursuit of power, which is a mainstay and objective of the medical profession, though not necessarily of individual doctors. The medical profession has gained power, and continues to do so, over many aspects of human life where before it played no part. It has done this regardless of whether or not such a step can actually help individuals or society, whether or not it has the technology to improve the situation, and whether nor not it actually intends to try. For instance, during the nineteenth century doctors were powerful in controlling women who did not fit the acceptable domestic mould, perhaps because these women disliked domesticity, sought education or wished to have a role outside the home. The doctors exerted control by performing mutilating operations such as ovariotomy (removal of the ovaries) and clitoridectomy (removal of the clitoris) on those who were psychologically disturbed or distressed. During the twentieth century they took control of contraception and abortion, insisting these were essentially medical matters, though few intended to do much about them and many powerful doctors were determined that as little should be done as possible. Doctors took over 'drug addiction' without admitting that no one knew how to treat it – and they did it in ways that did little to help the majority of patients, but did serve to enhance the prestige of the doctors who purported to treat the problem. Doctors have also become deeply involved in the 'personality disorders' or criminals and of misbehaving children, sometimes without acknowledging that they can do little or nothing to change those personalities. It seems that they, with their auxiliary workers, have in one way or another taken over most groups of people who are problematic to society.

Sometimes, of course, they have had to admit they were wrong and withdraw their influence. One condition which doctors used to 'treat' as a personality disorder and a medical condition was homosexuality, which is now acknowledged to be a normal variation. Another subject that was taken very seriously and regarded as extremely important in the genesis of disease was masturbation. During the late nineteenth century it was regarded as the cause of many illnesses, especially madness. This idea was probably supported by the fact that those suffering from severe chronic mental illness often masturbate openly in public. In a climate of moral condemnation, it was assumed to be the cause rather than a characteristic of the disorder. Nowadays this fashion has ended and masturbation is regarded as mainly normal and of little consequence.

A critical view

In recent years there has been increasing criticism of the behaviour of doctors and doubt about their motives, both individual and corporate. Many people see medicialisation as a system of social control imposed from above – even a step towards totalitarianism. There have been revelations of doctors 'playing God' in deciding whether to treat a patient or to leave him or her to die, and of discrimination against the elderly. Some fear that, if they get the chance, doctors will seize the power to decide, for instance, who is and who is not fit to marry and have children, perhaps through the introduction of a compulsory pre-marital medical visit. The twentieth century, after all, saw doctors who participated willingly in schemes such as the sterilisation of the unfit, doctors who used what they called 'inferior races' for purposes of scientific research, and even doctors who organised and participated in the elimination of the despised and unwanted. The exercise of power and influence over others is a compelling motivation for many.

Some writers have expressed fear about the dangers of allowing medicine to take over matters of everyday life, particularly as ever more powerful drugs are marketed increasingly aggressively and there are ever more sophisticated surgical operations and other 'advanced' forms of treatment. For instance, doctors have extended their control over people's lives through drugs, including manipulating sleep patterns, and even through biochemistry, by suggesting the health benefits of certain diets, exercise, and so on. Ordinary people, impressed by the scientific arguments and the promise of progress for the better, accept all this quite willingly. Apart from an expansionist medical profession, it may be that the worst dangers of medicalisation lie in the fact that it encourages people to submit themselves and their life decisions to 'experts', thus undermining their personal autonomy and development. It is not uncommon for people to consult doctors about whom to marry, whether or not to have children, how to raise them, and questions concerning divorce.

A further danger is the power the medical profession has to impose moralistic views onto society. Drug addiction was mentioned earlier as a subject of medicalisation, and it is a prime example of the moralistic forces at work. Recreational drug-taking has been given the medical diagnosis of 'drug abuse', an expression with clear negative moral overtones which is now widely employed. Moral diagnoses do not – and should not – usually form part of medical diagnosis, however. The doctors are allying their own power of suggestion with attitudes already prevalent in society. It is another case of medical fashion. Society has developed a fashion for the moral condemnation of recreational drug use, a fashion that is both used and abused by politicians and doctors in order to further their own interests. One can see how it came about. Before the current fashion took hold, in the second half of the twentieth century, these doctors were at the bottom of the medical hierarchy, working in the chronic wards of mental asylums with patients regarded as lost, undesirable or of no consequence. When the subject of drugs and their destructive effects became fashionable, or at least fashionable to hate, these doctors gained in status and emerged as chiefs of clinics and consultants in teaching hospitals. Thus can medicalisation and fashion change the status of a group of doctors and work to their advantage. Moreover, politicians tend to support the power of doctors because their power tends to be exercised in authoritarian ways that support the control of the people. Doctors, in turn, tend to support the established order.

Who pulls the strings?

It would be wrong to think that the process of medicalisation was simply instigated by doctors and imposed by them, or that it is necessarily always harmful. It was and still is also demanded by those who will come under its influence. There has been a strong demand for medical services for a long time, and it is impossible to say how far doctors responded to that demand and how far they initiated it. One could argue that what doctors do merely reflects what society asks them to do. Certainly they seldom resist the demands of society, and they have willingly established a whole spectrum of 'disease' in areas previously regarded as none of their concern. Homosexuality, neurosis, child behaviour and even poverty and crime have all been brought at one time or another into the medical empire. The 'disease model' is widely used in analysing and assessing social problems, and this has added status to the medical profession even when they have not brought progress towards greater understanding or power to solve the problems. It has also raised the status of the profession's moral prejudices and enabled doctors to impose these as desirable points of view.

Many doctors have doubted the necessity for such widespread medical intervention and a few have challenged the medical power base, sometimes with disastrous results for themselves. Today an increasing number are thoughtfully critical of the way in which they were trained and the relevance for the present day of the attitudes implicit in that training.

PART II

Medical Fashions

Introduction: Early Fashions

Fashions play an important part in modern medicine. Some fashions may last for only a short period of time, while other last for centuries. Bleeding (blood-letting) and purging were common medical treatments for thousands of years and can therefore hardly be called fashions. They were universal medical treatments that produced visible products and gave the patients bodily sensations that made them feel different. Theories about these practices changed over the years, depending on the current popular theories about the function of the body in health and disease. Blood-letting became unfashionable, or at least less fashionable, during the nineteenth century, when doctors began to realise that it damaged and even killed many patients (the prime minister Robert Peel was a prominent victim of the practice). It was a time when doctors were learning more about the way the body works in health and disease, and were acquiring drugs and other treatments. Many remained ambivalent about the efficacy of bleeding, however. Edward Tilt, a prominent gynaecologist, wrote in 1863 that bleeding had become unfashionable, yet he also asserted that he did not propose to give it up. This was a common attitude. The custom of bleeding lasted well into the twentieth century, when it was still regarded by some as potentially beneficial. By the middle of the century, however, medical students were taught that if an unwell patient could be bled, he did not need it, and if he did need it, his veins would be so collapsed that it would be impossible to bleed him. Since then there has been virtually universal agreement that, except in a few rare conditions, bleeding sick people is harmful.

During the eighteenth century fashion itself became fashionable and affected much of life, including clothes, buildings, possessions and social activities. Medicine followed the new fashion for fashion. In the early part of the century, the most fashionable diagnosis was 'nerves'. As the social classes redefined themselves amid the changes of the Industrial Revolution and the Enlightenment, it became smart to be 'nervous' and many people were now rich enough to pay doctors and spend time and money on their health. It was the age of water treatments and spas, places where prosperous people congregated for social inter-course and medical treatment. Other diagnoses that became fashionable were 'biliousness', 'vapours', 'spleen' and 'hypochondria'. Of the diagnoses still recognisable today, the most obvious is gout, which came to be regarded as a fashionable disease, suffered by people of quality. Late in the nineteenth century the idea of medical psychotherapy developed. The Viennese physician Franz Anton Mesmer (1734–1815) applied the concept of animal magnetism to healing people with psychological problems. Thanks to his efforts, mesmerism became a fashionable form of treatment.

Fashions during the nineteenth century were greatly influenced by changing medical theories as well as by social theories and scientific discoveries. Many diseases were discovered or invented which matched the social theories of the day. Prominent fashions included neurasthenia, ovariomania, hystero-epilepsy and autointoxication.

In the pages that follow we will examine a variety of medical fashions, all once regarded as progress in medicine. I aim to show their ubiquity and the manifold ways in which they can arise and spread. After much consideration of the difficult task of classifying these fashions, I decided that the most satisfactory was to put them into alphabetical order.

Anaesthesia and pain

Anaesthesia differs from most medical fashions in that it came and stayed, then expanded into an important branch of the medical profession that led to many other fashions. Different drugs and techniques in anaesthesia have come and gone, and the subject has become so complex and its practice so skilful that, although medical students are trained to administer anaesthetics, in developed countries doctors now practise anaesthesia only if they have had specialist training. It is generally accepted that doctors who have not had this training should administer anaesthetics only under exceptional circumstances.

It may seem astonishing that after anaesthesia was discovered, it was half a century before it was used. This fifty-year delay is sometimes regarded as one of the mysteries in the history of medicine. One important reason why it did not become fashionable sooner, however, was that it did not accord with contemporary views and attitudes, particularly towards pain. In some ways it actually opposed them.

In 1795 a young chemist called Humphry Davy (1778–1829) made a pure form of nitrous oxide (laughing gas) and discovered that it sent those who took it to sleep. He wrote a treatise about it, describing how it relieved his toothache while he was cutting his wisdom teeth (he was only seventeen at the time). He suggested that it might be used for anaesthesia, both in alleviating the pain of inflamed gums and 'during surgical operations'. In his *Researches, Chemical and Philosophical, Chiefly Concerning Nitrous Oxide, or Dephlogisticated Nitrous Air, and its Respiration* (1800), Davy wrote:

As nitrous oxide in its extensive operations appears capable of destroying physical pain, it may probably be used with advantage

during surgical operations in which no great effusion of blood
takes place.

The turn of the eighteenth and nineteenth centuries was an age of
surgical discovery, expansion and exploration, so one might have
expected such an idea to be taken up immediately, in recognition of its
immense potential for improving and advancing surgery. At the time,
however, few people seemed interested. Those who were aware of the
experiments found other aspects of the drug more attractive. Davy wrote
of 'the pleasurable sensation of warmth' that the drug gave him and of
the inclination to laugh 'at those who were looking at me'. He could not
avoid 'beating the ground with my feet'. After the mouthpiece was
removed, he 'remained in a few seconds in great extacy [sic]'. He tried
it on his friends, including William Allen, a chemistry lecturer at Guy's
Hospital, who in Wilks and Bettany's *A Biographical History of Guy's
Hospital* (1892) remembered:

> We all breathed the gaseous oxide of azote [nitrous oxide]. It took
> a surprising effect on me, abolishing at first all sensations; then I
> had the idea of being carried violently upward in a dark cavern
> with only a few glimmering lights. The company said that my eyes
> were fixed, face purple, veins in the head very large, apoplectic
> stertor. They were all much alarmed, but I suffered no pain and in
> a short time came to myself.

Davy's experimental friends included the poet and critic Samuel Taylor
Coleridge, who wrote:

> I experienced the most voluptuous sensations. The outer world
> grew dim and I had the most entrancing visions. For three and a
> half minutes I lived in a world of new sensations.

For many years the drug was used for amusement, on the stage and at
parties, and there was much analysis of feelings while under its
influence. It was also used occasionally in medical treatment, for
example for 'congestion of the lungs'. Thomas Beddoes (1760–1808),
prominent Bristol physician, set up The Pneumatic Institution for the
treatment of pulmonary tuberculosis by inhalation of gases. There was
little interest in alleviating pain, however, and Davy, who worked with

Beddoes until he left to pursue other interests, intended the inhalation to cure disease rather than pain.

In 1818 Michael Faraday noted that ether had much the same effect as nitrous oxide, but it did not occur to him to use it in surgery or in the alleviation of pain. It was not until 1842 that Crawford W Long (1815–78), a young practitioner in Georgia, accidentally noted the effect of ether in preventing pain. He used it a few times for operations, but did not publish anything about it for fear of being censured in a society that regarded pain as justified by God. Nonetheless, when chloroform was discovered in 1831 and finally became public five years later, the news of it spread and its use rapidly became fashionable.

Why was it that for so long no one followed up Davy's suggestion that anaesthesia might be useful in surgery? Why did it become a fashion when it did, half a century later? Part of the answer is probably that there was considerable religious objection to alleviating pain, which was thought to be part of God's purpose, an idea that changed only gradually with increasing secularisation. It has also been said that there was not enough interest in surgery, for operations were still beset with problems of bleeding and infection. In truth, however, it was a period of considerable surgical activity and innovation. Increasingly, illness or disease was attributed to a single area or organ of the body – a lesion – which, it was thought, might be removed to produce a cure; this immediately suggested that the best treatment was surgery. This was the attitude that promoted the 'advance' of Western medicine, and it has dominated it ever since. In the early nineteenth century, ideas about specific lesions and diseases were replacing more general notions of the sick person. It was also the time when new operations were being developed, including ovariotomy, tenotomy and operations for squinting. In 1841 a London doctor wrote in the *Lancet*:

> The whole history of surgery will scarcely, perhaps, exhibit such an extraordinary number of new operations, and such a number of extraordinary operations within the same given period of time as the last twelve months have produced. A perfect mania for operating has existed ever since the first operation for squinting was declared to be successful.

Yet in 1847 another doctor wrote, 'The whole paying surgical practice of Scotland would scarcely keep one gentleman-like scalpel going.' The two statements are not as incompatible as they may seem. The new operations took place mostly in the great medical centres, and while such major surgery was performed enthusiastically in a few places, it played only a minor role in medicine as a whole, compared with its prominence in later times.

There has been much discussion and many differences about the significance of pain and sensitivity to pain in relation to the development of anaesthesia. Some have tried to argue that the reason why anaesthesia was not used until the middle of the nineteenth century was that people's sensitivity to pain at that time was different from what it became later and did not require it. According to this reasoning, anaesthesia was adopted only after a change in this sensitivity took place. Others have suggested, somewhat implausibly, that the apparent change in sensitivity to pain was a *result* of the use of anaesthetics.

Yet surgeons in the eighteenth and early nineteenth centuries were aware of pain. The Scottish surgeon John Bell (1763–1820) advised on ways to ease it with wine, medicine and comfort. Ephraim McDowell, the Kentucky surgeon who performed the first ovariotomy, gave his patient 'cherry bounce', probably a mixture of alcohol, opium and cherry juice. Before the middle of the nineteenth century, pain control in childbirth – when it was considered at all – had been attempted by the use of opium, and later morphine, often combined with alcohol. This may have been more widespread in Britain and the United States than would seem from the rarity with which it is mentioned in obstetric texts. The concealment happened probably because relieving pain in childbirth was widely regarded as sinful. Moreover, opiates are unsatisfactory under these circumstances because doses big enough to abolish pain tend to weaken the contractions of the uterus, increase the risk of haemorrhage and depress the baby's respiration.

There is plenty of evidence suggesting that people in former centuries were well aware of pain and the suffering it caused. Daniel Defoe in his *Journal of the Plague Year* (1722) said that patients 'unable to contain themselves, vented their pain by incessant roarings, and such loud and lamentable cries were to be heard as we walked along the streets...' (Admittedly, Defoe wrote some years after the plague, but he learned about it from those who had experienced it personally.) Yet pain was not regarded, as it was later, as an evil to be controlled or abolished whenever possible. It was even sometimes regarded as a medical treatment in itself. For example, Benjamin Rush (1745–1813) used a 'tranquillising chair' (said to have been an adaptation of the Inquisition's 'witch chair') which revolved the patient in a forced standing position while he was drenched with more than two hundred pails of water at one sitting.

A modern doctor, Michael Balint (1896–1970), wrote in his work *The Doctor, His Patient and the Illness* (1955):

> Every doctor has a set of fairly firm beliefs as to which illnesses are acceptable and which not; how much pain, suffering, fear and deprivation a patient should tolerate and when he has the right to ask for help or relief... These beliefs are hardly ever stated explicitly but they are nevertheless very strong.

This applies not only to individuals but also to periods of time and their beliefs and fashions. Although there have been attempts to overcome pain as long as there has been civilisation, there seems to have been no *concerted* effort to do so until the mid-nineteenth century – some considerable time after effective means of pain control had been discovered. The attitudes of the early nineteenth century were strongly influenced by Christian funadmentalism and the power of the church to impose attitudes towards pain. There was no Christian tradition that pain should be relieved, despite the biblical assertion that God put Adam to sleep when he created Eve from his rib. The church, particularly the Scottish Calvinist clergy, regarded pain not as a physical malfunction but as part of normal life and perhaps God's punishment. For some believers, such as Descartes, pain was a self-protective mechanism that taught the soul to avoid further damage to the body. Opium and alcohol were known to virtually all civilisations, and many seem to have regarded these as adequate for coping with extreme pain. Paracelsus (1493–1541), the eccentric wandering physician, prepared ether or some such anaesthetic, which he called 'sweet vitriol', saying that 'it quiets all suffering without any harm, and relieves all pain, and quenches all fevers and prevents complications in all illnesses'. Yet he dared not use it on humans, for fear of offending the Church.

There have been enormous changes in public attitudes to pain during the last two hundred years. These changes can be regarded as part of the process of secularisation and the increase in humanitarianism that has gone on during that period. In general, there was decreasing emphasis on a world made bad by sin and increasing emphasis on a world made bad by suffering and pain, combined with an outlook that increasingly peered forward to a freer future rather than backwards to authority. There was an increasingly powerful belief in the progress of civilisation, which came to encompass the reduction of human suffering. Politics became directed more towards diminishing pain than increasing happiness. Humanitarian laws were passed, including the Factory Acts and the laws against slavery. Pain came to be seen more as a passive experience, something that happened to victims, for which they deserved the best treatments and cures that medicine could provide. It no longer seemed rational to face pain as it came and instead seemed sensible – and possible – to escape it. Expectations rose of a pain-free existence, something which would have been impossible before. This could be called a fashion, but it was one that remained and became stronger as the years passed.

It was a remarkable shift in attitude. The belief that pain was something to be conquered and cured created a goal for doctors to achieve. It came, indeed, to be regarded as the main purpose of doctors, their *raison d'être*. As a result, it is difficult for later generations to appreciate the attitudes of a society which possessed the ability to relieve pain yet used it only in frivolous games and theatrical acts. At one time the change in attitude was so striking and apparently inexplicable that the American physician Weir Mitchell (1829–1914) came to the conclusion that the physiology of pain must have changed during the nineteenth century.

Anaesthesia in the form of ether was first used for dental and surgical operations in America in 1846, nearly half a century after it had been discovered and the idea first mooted. On 30 September 1846, the American dentist William Morton used it during a tooth extraction. The next day the *Boston Journal* published an account of the operation.

Last evening, as we were informed by a gentleman who witnessed the operation, an ulcerated tooth was extracted from the mouth of an individual, without giving him the slightest pain. He was put into a kind of sleep, by inhaling a preparation, the effects of which lasted about three-quarters of a minute, just long enough to extract the tooth.

Further operations under ether followed. News of the operation reached England on 17 December. On 19 December a dentist in London used it, and on 21 December the surgeon Robert Liston operated on patients anaesthetised with ether. On 19 January 1847, James Young Simpson (1811–70), Professor of Midwifery at the University of Edinburgh, used it in childbirth and on 10 February he reported its use to the Obstetrical Society of Edinburgh. The news and the custom spread rapidly through France and Germany. In November 1847 Simpson stopped using ether and changed to chloroform, a more dangerous drug but much easier to administer. By 1850 chloroform was used all over Scotland, even in remote villages, while London obstetricians were still reluctant to use it at all. It was said that some women travelled from London to Edinburgh to have their babies delivered under chloroform. Anaesthesia was becoming fashionable.

Despite its increasing popularity on both sides of the Atlantic, however, many operations were still done without it. To begin with, the popularity was confined to the upper classes, and anaesthesia seems to have had little immediate effect on the practice of surgery or on the number of operations performed. One reason for this may have been the continuing dangers of bleeding and infection. Another was the difficulty of administering the anaesthetics, which can produce bizarre, dramatic and frightening reactions, especially when the anaesthetist is inexperienced. There seemed to be no great enthusiasm among the medical fraternity for overcoming these problems in any haste. And despite the embracing of the new fashion for pain control in some sectors of society, many people still clung to the old idea of pain as an unavoidable and even necessary part of life.

This was particularly noticeable in the clash of attitudes towards pain in childbirth. Religious tradition and Victorian attitudes towards women combined to provide powerful resistance to pain relief during labour. The Church taught that it was God's will that women should suffer in childbirth, and God's admonition to Adam and Eve was widely quoted: 'In sorrow thou shalt bring forth children' (Genesis 3:16). This was generally taken to mean that God intended women to suffer pain during labour. James Young Simpson disputed this and insisted that the word 'sorrow' was a poor translation of the original and that 'labour' or 'travail' would be more appropriate. The battle was won in April 1853, when Queen Victoria chose to have her eighth child, Prince Leopold, under the influence of chloroform, administered by Simpson. This remarkably reduced the opposition to anaesthesia, and the fashion gathered momentum. In the same year a medicine labelled as a 'pain-killer' was marketed for the first time in America.

Nonetheless, for a long time the idea of using anaesthesia to control pain aroused anxiety and hostility among both doctors and lay people. There was anxiety that the new procedure might have unfortunate consequences, either from overdosage or from long-term complications. Overdose was particularly likely to occur with chloroform because, unlike ether, there is only a small difference between the dose required to anaesthetise and the dose that causes the heart to stop. There also seemed to be a few people who were particularly sensitive to chloroform and who died after even a small dose. As the century progressed, deaths from chloroform were reported all over the Western world. Various committees were appointed to investigate them, and it is clear from reading contemporary accounts that some of the deaths were due to doctors' inexperience or incompetence in administering the anaesthetic. There was, of course, no formal training in anaesthesiology, and the procedure was distinctly experimental in those early days.

Anxieties were understandable at a time when people knew little about the drugs and nothing about their long-term consequences. Indeed, such anxieties are part of the resistance that always exists towards change and innovation. Until that resistance has lessened with time, usually after the death or retirement of the first resisters, it militates against the development of a fashion into something more permanent. As an illustration of this, an interesting correspondence was exchanged between Simpson and his close friend Francis Henry Ramsbotham, who strongly opposed the use of chloroform. Simpson wrote, 'There is no doubt whatever your grandchildren and mine will… wonder at us dreaming of *not* relieving human agony when we have the power and the means of doing it. As to bad results, I see none.' Ramsbotham, on the other hand, angered Simpson by publishing an account of paralysis that a patient developed many months after child-birth, which he attributed directly to the use of chloroform.

As the nineteenth century progressed, the practice of anaesthetising women in labour grew steadily in popularity, and the religious objections diminished. By the end of the century, science had won and administering anaesthetics to women in labour was both respectable and customary. From then on, discussion became more concerned with methods and choice of drugs, rather than with the rights and wrongs of anaesthesia as a practice. Today it is a highly developed science, increasingly complex, effective and safe. It is hard to imagine life without pain control now.

Appendix

The appendix and operations performed on it led to several medical fashions. Appendicitis is well known in the modern Western world as a painful and potentially dangerous inflammation of the appendix that usually leads to an operation to remove it: appendectomy (or appendicectomy), popularly known as 'having your appendix out'. The danger is that the inflammation may cause the appendix to burst or perforate, spreading infected material through the abdominal cavity, thus causing peritonitis (inflammation of the peritoneum, the membrane that covers the abdominal organs) and the death of the sufferer. Ever since the condition was recognised, it has caused anxiety among both doctors and the public, and it still occasionally kills. As soon as the operation could be done with relative safety, it became one of the most fashionable.

The appendix is a small, worm-shaped organ joined to the small intestine at its junction with the large bowel. In herbivorous animals, such as cattle, it is large and active, but in humans it is small, has no known function, and is regarded as a leftover from an earlier stage of evolution. It has caused much controversy during the last century and a half, during which time reality has mingled with myth, and theory and practice have sometimes been confused by fashion. The fashion for the operation is now largely over, as is the fashion for diagnosing 'chronic appendicitis', but for many years the operation was one of the most fashionable in the history of surgery. An operation that saved the lives of a few acutely ill patients was performed increasingly frequently and became a fashion almost as popular as tonsillectomy. In some communities, children and young people lost their appendices even more frequently than their tonsils. The subsequent decline in popularity does not mean that appendectomy is no longer performed, only that it is no longer done so frequently or for such minor indications.

The success of the original campaign to transform the condition into a surgical disease probably encouraged unrealistic beliefs and the performance of many questionable operations – including fashions in operating for 'chronic appendicitis' and 'grumbling appendix', as a blind guess, or, prophylactically, to prevent a future attack of appendicitis. The development of appendectomy as the commonest abdominal operation created a situation that was likely to produce medical myths and fashions. It is particularly instructive in showing how major surgery was gradually accepted for potentially life-threatening conditions. The operation was relatively safe and its success was impressive. Recovery was usually dramatic. Even King Edward VII had suffered from the condition. His operation, which delayed his coronation in 1902, did not include actual removal of the appendix, but it saved him from death, a fact that greatly increased its popularity. There is probably no quicker way for a medical condition to become fashionable than for it to be diagnosed in a reigning sovereign.

The incidence of appendicitis has varied in different periods and societies. It seems to have been unknown to the ancients and was mentioned only rarely in medical literature before the nineteenth century. Death with abdominal pain was not uncommon, however, usually diagnosed as 'inflammation of the bowels' and later as 'inflammation of the caecum' (the blind end of the large gut), 'typhlitis' or 'perityphlitis'.

Nonetheless, 'appendicitis' had been known to some extent since the sixteenth century. A needle is said to have been found in an appendix in the seventeenth century. Observations on the subject were made in the eighteenth century. The first recorded operation for appendectomy occurred more than a century before anaesthetics, performed in 1736 by Claudius Amynand FRS, surgeon at St George's Hospital, London. In 1759 an appendix abscess was drained. The patient died, but this seems to have been the first time the organ was specifically recognised as the site of disease. It was clearly connected to disease of the caecum, often due to blockage.

The development of pathological anatomy helped locate and understand the problem. In 1812 John Parkinson (son of James Parkinson, who first described Parkinson's disease) was the first to recognise appendicitis as a cause of death when he described a perforated appendix in a boy of five. Thomas Addison (1793–1860) and Richard Bright (1789–1858) both recognised that the appendix could become infected, but inflammation in the region continued to be described as typhlitis or perityphlitis for some time. Typhlitis means inflammation of the caecum; it was generally thought that this was the site of the inflammation. Many patients died of perforation and peritonitis. In 1824 a young French surgeon reported two cases where gangrenous appendicitis was demonstrated at autopsy. In 1834 James Copland, in his *Dictionary of Practical Medicine*, discriminated for the first time between inflammations of the caecum, the vermiform appendix and the pericaecal tissue. In 1836 Thomas Hodgkin recognised the appendix as the commonest source of disease in the right iliac fossa. In 1837 John Burne, physician at the Westminster Hospital, drew further attention to the material difference between inflammation of the appendix and of the caecum. He maintained that it was due to the conformation and situation of the appendix.

Interest in diseases of the appendix was still largely confined to English- and French-speaking countries, but some Germans were also becoming interested. In 1846 A Voltz of Karlsruhe established that perforation was often associated with faecoliths (hardened bits of faeces) and that this was a frequent cause of peritonitis. He demonstrated clearly the role of the appendix in 38 cases followed by autopsy. Others later pointed out that the canal inside the appendix often contained other foreign bodies, such as seeds, hairs, worms or their eggs, shot, pills and gallstones.

By the middle of the nineteenth century it seemed to some surgeons that either appendicitis was becoming more common, or it was being recognised more frequently. Many surgeons were aware that the appendix was a source of disease, but they did not yet think of it being amenable to surgery. In the days before anaesthesia, the treatment for the condition was evacuation, opiates and antiphlogistic remedies. It was not until the 1870s and early 1880s, during the immense growth of surgical practice, that operating for 'perityphlitis' became common.

The surgeons who were most influential in developing and popularising the operation of appendectomy were the Americans R H Fitz (1843–1913) of Boston, Massachusetts, and J B Murphy (1857–1916) of Chicago, and the British surgeons Lawson Tait (1845–99) of Birmingham, and Frederick Treves (1853–1923) of London. Fitz published a seminal paper in 1886 in which he coined the term 'appendicitis' and announced that, in 257 out of 290 cases of perityphlitis, it was the appendix, not the caecum, that was at fault. He gave the first description of what became classical surgical teaching on the diagnosis of appendicitis – abdominal pain starting near the umbilicus and moving towards the groin. He also blamed appendicitis for causing a host of other diseases, mostly infections, including necrosis (gangrene) of the peritoneum, disease of the hip joint and invasion of arteries. Fitz recommended surgical treatment and urged that this be done early. He was, however, referring to the abscess rather than to the appendix itself.

Fitz's article is often regarded as a watershed in the history of the appendix through which appendectomy came to be seen as the flagship operation of the new era. After the paper was published, appendicitis was increasingly regarded as a surgical disease and the important question became *when* rather than *whether* to operate. Acute appendicitis rapidly became by far the commonest of surgical emergencies. John Burke's article 'Early Historical Aspects' in *Surgery* (1951, 30) cited that Fitz 'brought appendicitis from the status of a curiosity to an everyday disease and opened the way for early surgical intervention'. After him, appendicitis became 'almost entirely surgical in character'. During the next seventy years, the operation of appendectomy became increasingly popular until its incidence peaked in the 1950s. Its popularity increased through the powerful influence of Murphy, who insisted strongly that acute appendicitis was a common condition and that immediate operation was necessary if disaster was to be avoided.

In Britain, Lawson Tait, a strong protagonist of the new surgery, was the first surgeon to diagnose acute appendicitis and remove the appendix itself. In 1880 he urged that the abdomen be opened immediately in all acute abdominal conditions, even in the face of peritonitis. This was a revolutionary idea and in keeping with the new enthusiasm for radical surgery. At about the same time, Frederick Treves came to the contrasting conclusion that it was safer to operate *between* rather than *during* attacks. He adopted this practice in about 1888, believing that the risk of perforation, peritonitis and death was justified. The controversy continued for many years. Treves was a distinguished surgeon and his operation on the king greatly increased the popularity of the procedure in Britain.

Paradoxically, or so it seemed at the time, the improved capacity to diagnose acute appendicitis and to operate on it was followed by an increase in its incidence. This was noted all over the Western world and was widely attributed to 'civilisation' or to changes in national diet. In 1910 Owen T Williams, Honorary Assistant Physician to Liverpool Royal Infirmary, suggested that excessive intake of sugar and meat was the cause. In 1920 Rendle Short attributed it to the vast increase in the availability of cheap, processed foods, including white bread, and the decrease of vegetables in the diet. People were eating less coarse bread and fibre. Countries whose diet remained coarse, he said, continued to have low rates of appendicitis. Its apparent increase was also surely connected to the wider acceptance of major surgery, and to the metaphorical halo the condition had acquired after the king's brush with death.

In the 1880s the idea arose that appendicitis could be *chronic* as well as acute. In 1891 a surgeon argued that 'chronic relapsing appendicitis' was actually a mild form of appendicitis which resolved by nature, but in which the inflammation recurred. He advised that the appendix should be removed at the first opportunity. At the time there were also arguments about whether the condition was an entirely surgical one, or whether its management should be a joint decision between surgeon and physician.

Meanwhile, some of the leading surgeons in both Europe and the USA were becoming increasingly radical. Opinion was moving towards early operation, even to the extent that false diagnoses were made in the haste to operate early. Several patients with typhoid were mistakenly given appendectomies. Sir William Osler (1849–1919) warned that movable kidneys sometimes produced the symptoms of appendicitis. Later other disasters came to light. The American Walter C Alvarez investigated the histories of patients with scars in the right iliac fossa. In his article 'Origin of the So-Called Auto-Intoxication Symptoms', in the *Journal of the American Medical Association* (1919, 72), he criticised surgeons who rushed to operate on a small pain and did not bother to take histories, and he warned of the consequences. He found that a little talking or investigation would often have revealed the truth, i.e.:

that the patient was suffering from a stone in the gallbladder or ureter, or with pyelitis, multiple sclerosis, tuberculosis of the cecum or an ordinary irritable colon. The real trouble of two patients was that they had suffered a slight stroke.

A college girl was rushed to the operating table so fast that she had no chance to impress the surgeon with the fact that she had just been on the type of 'walnut fudge bust' which always gave her a violent allergic stomachache. Another woman could not convince the surgeon that she always got an alarming stomachache when she ate onions. One patient had an acute duodenal ulcer, which was not helped by the appendectomy; another had Ménière syndrome, with nausea and vomiting due to active but unrecognised syphilis; another had just had a violent argument with his wife; several schoolteachers were worn out with fatigue at the end of the school term; and one girl had simply vomited her dinner…

> One of the most interesting of the stories…was that of a…woman who always, under any excitement, gets a bad attack of 'mucous colitis'. Naturally, she had one of the most violent spells of her career a few hours before she was to be married, and as a result she was rushed to the operating room and made to spend her wedding night and her honeymoon alone in a hospital cot.

The case that Alvarez found the most remarkable of all, however, was this:

> A woman who gave as the only reason for her appendectomy the fact that on arriving in Los Angeles one day she found a big convention in full swing and all the hotels full. The only place in which she could find a bed was a hospital, so she took it and had her appendix out. She had always wanted to have it done in a routine manner some time, like a tonsillectomy, so why not then?

Increasingly, appendicitis was coming to be regarded as common and the likely cause of any abdominal pain. Thus the operation was becoming idealised as a panacea, and regarded as desirable in itself. As one surgeon put it, appendicitis 'haunts the popular imagination and so perplexes the professional judgment'. As a result, appendectomy was becoming not only life-saving but also a 'frequent source of abdominal catastrophe'. A Bristol surgeon, A R Short, held strong views and stated in 'Clinical Lectures on Appendicitis', *Lancet* (1925):

The most frequent error, in my experience, has been the removal of the appendix when no abnormality whatever could be found in the abdomen and no evidence of disease ever came to light elsewhere... These cases...are most often seen in women over 30.

It is now widely recognised that the diagnosis of chronic appendicitis has been far too frequently made, and that removal of the organ *when the patient has not been seen in an acute attack* has often failed to relieve the symptoms. Some American writers go so far as to say that there is no such thing as chronic appendicitis, but this is an over-statement... The main factor in arriving at a correct diagnosis of chronic appendicitis is to get a reliable history of a definite acute attack.

Short was strongly in favour of early surgery, however, arguing that the mortality in appendicitis was much higher if surgery was delayed.

Sir William Osler was also aware of the prevalence of error – and of the power of fashion. He wrote in *The Principles and Practice of Medicine* (1895):

There is a well-marked appendicular hypochondrosis [*sic*]. Through the pernicious influence of the daily press, appendicitis has become a sort of fad, and the physician has often to deal with patients who have a sort of fixed idea that they have the disease.

Others agreed. For instance, Sir William Priestley commented in 1895: 'Surgery has run wild and there has been a great deal more of operative work than was needed.' Another commentator wrote:

There has arisen a class of surgeons, mostly young, often inexperienced in other safer and more rational methods of treatment, and above all quite callous and indifferent to the true welfare of their patients, whom they look upon merely in the light of subjects to be experimented and operated upon.

Criticism remained relatively rare, however, and the enthusiasm for appendectomy continued to increase. In 1897 the *British Medical Journal* referred to the appendix situation in the USA as a 'boom'. New conditions said to be caused by appendicitis were added continually to the list. For instance, the influential Leeds surgeon Sir Berkeley

Moynihan published, in his book *Essays on Surgical Subjects* (1921), an article on 'appendix dyspepsia' in which he wrote that 'many of the intractable cases of indigestion' were due to diseases of the appendix and could be cured by its removal. He included the 'bilious attacks' of children and the 'sharp abdominal pain, headache and vomiting that can occur after an unwholesome meal'. It gradually became clear that myths were accumulating round the procedure, boosting its popularity beyond what was reasonable. As a result, there were many unnecessary appendectomies, and this led to a rise in the death rate from the condition.

Why did the diagnosis and the operation become so popular? There are many possible reasons. Acute appendicitis which was not operated on was an obvious cause of death, often in otherwise healthy young people. The operation could therefore be perceived to save lives. This was also an age when surgery was becoming safer and was viewed with increasing favour by both doctors and patients. The dominating surgical process of the time was resection, i.e. removing something. The operation, once learned, was small, easy to perform and relatively safe. It became a popular learning operation for young doctors and medical students. It was so simple in relation to other new operations, however, that it was overdone. In 1891 the *Journal of the American Medical Association* complained that from the early 1890s abdominal and pelvic surgery was practised by 'as restless and ambitious a throng as ever fought for fame upon the battle field'. Understandably, these 'cowboy' surgeons would favour a simple operation. Furthermore, this was an age of increasing confidence in doctors and of doctors' increasing surgical enthusiasm and confidence in themselves, which encouraged a policy of intervention. Without anyone saying so, it also provided a method of treating some of the symptoms of neurasthenia, a neurotic condition that so bedevilled the profession when it lacked effective treatment. All this converted appendicitis into a fashionable disease with a fashionable treatment. One surgeon, Robert Weir (1838–1927) of New York, even invented an operation called appendicostomy, which made use of the 'useless appendix' for flushing water through the colon. Thus appendectomy gradually became a powerful medical fashion. Sir William Osler, who had once been opposed to it, gradually changed his views. A new edition of his textbook showed that he had swung towards a belief in early operation.

The argument continued. In America in 1895, Franklin C Wells, a practitioner of some local reputation, developed acute appendicitis and was operated on by his colleague, David Graham. Afterwards Wells, together with George Cleveland, organised a meeting of local practitioners around Chicago to discuss appendicitis. Cleveland started by saying that many cases got better with rest, cathartics, small doses of opium, etc., but he was roundly criticised. During the last years of the nineteenth century there was vigorous campaigning for early operative interference at the hands of a skilled surgeon. The chairman of the Section of Surgery, Massachusetts Medical Society, announced that he was thinking of having a prophylactic appendectomy done on his eight-year-old son. Others echoed this, recommending it particularly for those who rode bicycles, which, it was alleged, were often the cause of appendicitis.

By 1899 there were more than 2,500 books, dissertations and articles available on appendicitis and the overwhelming impression was that the condition was common, which doubtless increased the chance of an abdominal pain, whether acute or chronic, being diagnosed as appendicitis.

Meanwhile, another problem was emerging: the number of deaths from appendectomy. In 1901 in England and Wales appendicitis was made returnable as a cause of death, and the increase was soon shown. The increase in the incidence of acute appendicitis and the development of its surgery was accompanied by an increase in the number of recorded deaths attributed to it. Many sufferers died of perforation and peritonitis. In England and Wales the death rate from appendicitis before 1901 cannot be estimated, but the recorded death rate increased from 38 per million of the population in 1901 to 66 per million in 1910 (or 77 in males and 55 in females). The highest death rate in both sexes appeared to be in later childhood and adolescence. In the United States death rates were even higher, and gradually rose, by 1930, to 150 per million of the population; the mortality from acute appendicitis rose by 22.3 per cent between 1913 and 1923. No one knew how far the deaths were caused by the condition and how far by the treatment, but the increase is likely to have been largely due to growth in awareness of the condition and its burgeoning popularity.

Dr A A Cairns, director of the Department of Public Health in Philadelphia, authorised a survey of the city's hospitals to determine the cause of this increase in mortality and the best ways of reversing it. The clinical records of 5,121 patients in 27 hospitals were studied. The chief cause of death seemed to be delay in dealing with the condition, and also the giving of laxatives, which tended to lead to perforation. A campaign to inform the public was started, including stickers and radio health talks. Both doctors and public were warned of the dangers of delaying action and of giving laxatives to patients with abdominal pain. This strengthened the movement on both sides of the Atlantic for early operation.

In 1903 the mortality from appendicitis at St Mary's Hospital, London, was discovered to be 30 per cent. Questions began to be asked, both about the procedure and the diagnosis, previously so high in favour. It was pointed out, by W McEwan in the *Lancet* in 1904, that 'All this removal of diseased appendices does not bring us one step nearer to the causation of the disease.' In 1904 Bayard Holmes, Professor of Surgery in the University of Illinois, wrote of chronic appendicitis: 'It would almost appear that the appendix is in a state of chronic disease in a large portion of civilized humanity.'

Meanwhile, there was increasing scepticism about chronic appendicitis and a suspicion that, at least in some cases, it might be linked to mental disturbance. A monograph of 1905 by Kelly and Hurdon contained a small section on 'Hysteria and hypochondriasis'.

> These conditions must be eliminated from the diagnosis in some cases of suspected appendicitis, but it is necessary to be always on guard against assuming a nervous manifestation in the presence of a true inflammation of the appendix.

These writers noted the absence of fever and the disappearance of local tenderness when the patient's attention was diverted. They pointed out, as had others, that visceral delusions of the insane are often founded on a pathological condition.

The playwright George Bernard Shaw also involved himself in the argument. In his preface to *The Doctor's Dilemma* in 1906 he called appendectomy a 'fashion for which there is a regrettable demand'. He wrote further:

> **Fashions and Epidemics**. A demand, however, can be inculcated. This is thoroughly understood by fashionable tradesmen, who find no difficulty in persuading their customers to renew articles that are not worn out and to buy things they do not want. By making doctors tradesmen, we compel them to learn the tricks of trade;

consequently we find that the fashions of the year include treatments, operations, and particular drugs, as well as hats, sleeves, ballads and games. Tonsils, vermiform appendices, uvulas, even ovaries are sacrificed because it is the fashion to get them cut out, and because the operations are highly profitable. The physiology of fashion becomes a pathology; for the cases have every air of being genuine: fashions, after all, are only induced epidemics, proving that epidemics can be induced by tradesmen, and therefore by doctors.

In 1914 Edmund Owen, Consulting Surgeon to St Mary's and the Hospital for Sick Children, Great Ormond Street, published *Appendicitis: A Plea For Immediate Operation*, which contained a chapter on 'Imaginary appendicitis'. He wrote:

I do not know if anything has been written about hysterical appendicitis; I do not know, indeed, if the condition has ever been met with. But I am quite prepared to hear of such a case. When disease of the hip joint and of the knee, of the spine, of the breast, and of the elbow are so successfully mimicked, I do not see why one should expect the appendix to go scot free.

Let the case be imagined of a girl of, perhaps, ill-balanced nervous system, who is so circumstanced that she is constantly hearing of appendicitis, and is noticing how much sympathy and attention the subjects of it receive. What more likely than that she should declare herself, or imagine herself, to have a 'touch' of it, or even a serious attack?

While the questioning continued in the background, appendectomy for so-called 'chronic appendicitis' became increasingly routine during the 1920s and '30s and mortality rose proportionately. In 1925 the reports of the US Bureau of Census and of some life insurance companies showed that mortality from appendicitis was still rising. By this time, however, some were beginning to doubt the existence of 'chronic' appendicitis. In 1926 Frank Hathaway, Honorary Surgeon to several hospitals in and near Windsor, stated, 'Experience has convinced me that there is no such thing as a chronic appendix.'

Edmund Owen discussed very frankly the difficulties of convincing patients that this was the case:

The first thing is to convince your patients that they have not got appendicitis, and not allow them to force your hand into operating. So much is known by the general public today about appendicitis, that if they get a pain in the right iliac fossa they are not happy till their appendix is removed. It is often a very difficult thing to make them realize that they are not going about with an appendix which one day may become gangrenous and cause death. Many an hysterical girl with supersensitiveness happens to have her pain more localized in the right iliac fossa and is not happy till her appendix is removed. She is possibly on the safe side, but in six months all her symptoms return… If one surgeon will not operate they will go to someone else who will.

In 1928 a surgeon called C L Gibson recommended exploratory laparotomy (a search through the abdomen) rather than appendectomy in cases of chronic appendicitis. He had found that, whereas the results of appendectomy in acute appendicitis were good, he had a 30 per cent failure rate in 'chronic' cases. He thought this was partly because surgeons were operating as a prophylactic against attacks of acute appendicitis, and partly because they did not first take good histories.

The recognition that appendectomy for chronic appendicitis often failed led to conflict between those who thought it was psychogenic and should not be treated by surgery and those who wished to perform increasingly complicated operations. For example, Dale C Smith, a Californian surgeon, wrote:

> The so-called 'chronic appendix' has forced itself into the picture so often that I am persuaded to present my observations to you in the hope that the 50 per cent unrelieved by appendectomy may be benefited.

He believed that 'the disease known as "chronic appendicitis" may be implicated, but often is a small part of the condition'. But the failure of a cure was so common that:

> there is a growing tendency in the profession to charge the 'chronic appendix' symptom syndrome to neurasthenia and to discourage surgery. We think that is as a great a mistake as the simple appendectomy.

Smith took his arguments from embryology, physiology and pathology. He believed that 'chronic appendicitis…is almost always due to interference with caecal peristalsis, rather than appendicular inflammation'. He thought that a much more extensive operation was indicated.

Those who preached restraint included Sir James Berry, surgeon to the Royal Free Hospital in London. He deplored the current situation regarding appendectomy and wrote in the *Lancet* in 1902:

> An idol that seems to be worshipped today by the majority of our profession, to say nothing of the general public, is the view that acute appendicitis is a terribly fatal disease and that it must be treated by immediate operation whenever possible.

Berry quoted a 'wise old physician' as saying, 'I think the medical profession has gone quite mad about appendicitis.' He described King Edward VII's operation, which avoided removing the appendix, and said that, with the modern fashion in operating, the king would not have lived. He believed that 'the prevalent surgical treatment of appendicitis …is an idol whose pedestal is beginning to totter'.

Berry was out of the mainstream of surgical thought, but he was not alone. Throughout the century, while some surgeons were extremely keen to operate in all suspected cases, others showed concern about the number of normal appendices that were being removed. R W Watkins stated in the *New England Journal of Medicine*:

> There was a time when every patient with a long-continued or periodically recurring discomfort in the right abdomen…must have his appendix out on a diagnosis of chronic appendicitis… In a good many cases that appendix looked quite normal… I still see almost every week a patient carrying one, two or three abdominal scars. The first one is almost sure to be that of a so-called chronic appendix.

As the enthusiasm for appendectomy gradually declined, as it inevitably did, so did the incidence of 'chronic' or 'grumbling' appendix. Doctors grew sceptical about it, at least as a major problem, and lay people followed. In 1976 a review of 403 patients who underwent appendectomy in a community hospital showed that where there was a normal appendix and no other condition requiring operation, there was a higher complication rate and longer hospital stay than in cases of appendectomy for nonperforated diseased appendix. Moreover, a high frequency of removal of normal appendices did not result in a lower incidence of perforation of the appendix. In 1981 F Creed, writing in the *Lancet*, associated non-inflamed 'appendicitis' with depression. In another series of articles, 15 to 20 per cent of patients undergoing emergency appendectomy were found to have normal appendices. This was considered compatible with appropriate aggressiveness in order to avoid perforation and other complications. However, the complications after this exploration could be as high as 15 per cent, with just as many problems as in proven cases of acute appendicitis. The controversy now centred on balancing the complications of appendectomy for a normal appendix with those of a perforated appendix.

The history of appendicitis and its operative treatment is an excellent example of the emergence of a new type of fashion and 'progress' in medicine. It demonstrates very well the problems associated with the accumulation of data and the interpretation of clinical experience. The widespread agreement of the 1920s soon disintegrated, as we have seen.

During the late 1950s and 1960s the incidence of acute appendicitis declined and appendectomy was performed with decreasing frequency. The reasons for this are not altogether clear. It has been attributed by some to improved medical care. Others thought it was due to further change in the popular diet, with greater consumption once again of rough bread and vegetables. Another theory was that there was a connection with sanitation and the acquisition of bathrooms. By 1979 the decline was so marked that the *British Medical Journal* noted that appendectomy was now rare in many surgical units.

In 1994 a young surgeon in Newcastle found that this decrease had continued to such an extent that the frequency of appendicitis in a large district hospital had fallen by 50 per cent during the previous fifteen years. This meant that each junior doctor would perform only one appendectomy for acute disease per month. He pointed out that this dearth was problematic for young surgeons, who had previously acquired skill through the many appendectomies that they used to perform. 'Thus,' he commented, 'the traditional introduction to laparotomy for the surgical trainee is being lost.' The *Lancet* echoed this in an editorial, asking, 'How can today's surgical trainees ever begin to learn their craft?'

Deaths attributed to appendicitis declined correspondingly. In 1930 there were 2,941 deaths in England and Wales from appendicitis. In the USA in 1935 there were 16,142 such deaths. In 1973, despite an increase in population, there were only 1,066 deaths from appendicitis in the UK.

Autointoxication

An important source of medical fashions in the early twentieth century was the theory of autointoxication, itself once a popular fashion. Autointoxication is the theory that the body is poisoned by the contents of its own large intestine.

The theory is ancient. The word 'autointoxication' was coined in 1887 by Charles-Jacques Bouchard (1837–1915), a French pathologist who was later awarded the Légion d'Honneur for his work. During a famous debate on 'alimentary toxaemia' (one of a number of synonyms and near-synonyms for autointoxication) at the Royal Society of Medicine in 1913, it was said that the condition had been discovered in 1880 and an account published in the *Lancet*. In fact, the theory goes back at least to the ancient Egyptians. It simply reappeared and was seized upon at a time when many Victorian doctors and others believed that the bowels, especially when constipated, were a source of poisoning. Fluid absorbed from the colon was said to damage red blood cells and to produce a form of blood poisoning. Like many fashions, the basis of this idea was flimsy or nonexistent, but it fitted the fantasies of the time.

The theory of internal poisoning has waxed and waned for many centuries. Its history shows how fashions can fluctuate, how physicians must, to some extent, go along with their patients' ideas about the nature of disease, and how the enthusiasm of one tends to influence the other. At times autointoxication was believed to be the cause of most disease. At other times and among other people the theory has been regarded as rubbish. It became prominent in conventional medicine in the late nineteenth century, and is still strong in popular medicine today. Many systems of complementary medicine insist on the presence of toxins and poisons that need to be detoxified or purified. Modern advertisements warn of the dangers of self-poisoning and extol the virtues of, for example, colonic irrigation, perhaps by a registered colonic therapist, or 'spring-cleaning the body'. A typical advertisement might run: 'Colon Cleanse – the natural vegetarian food supplement to form a friendlier health technology... A well-balanced diet may not be enough... Get one month's supply FREE!' Widespread advertisements based on the theory suggest that it appeals to many people.

The theory of autointoxication has long been discredited in orthodox medicine, and many eminent medical libraries now scarcely mention it in their subject indices. Yet it still sometimes resurfaces, even in orthodox medical thought. During the 1980s, for example, there was a return of the fashion for colectomy (removing the colon or large bowel) to treat intractable constipation. The operation was performed in respectable and skilled hospitals, but it was a strictly localised fashion and soon passed.

There are many possible reasons why the theory of autointoxication has been so popular and so persistent in widely differing times and conditions. People in all human societies find faeces distasteful. At the same time, small children show an interest which their parents discourage. Toilet training is a variable but important part of child-rearing and small children are often rewarded for 'performing' in the right place. Some remain fascinated by faeces and, when this links with sexual development, they occasionally develop the perversion of coprophilia (sexual attraction to faeces), or have fantasies about it. Some have ambivalent feelings, perhaps being revolted by faeces but at the same time feeling satisfaction at 'relieving' themselves. This is sometimes combined with the parsimony and desire to control (or the fear of loss of control) of the 'anal' character. In a *Lancet* article in 1880, one doctor, R Bell, referred to 'Constipation Viewed as a Disease "per se" and as an Exciting Cause of Disease'. The double entendre may not have been unintentional.

It is widely known that faeces can spread disease. This reinforces the distaste, the desire to 'train' small children and the provision of rewards for 'good' behaviour in the matter. Before the days of scientific medicine, purging was one of the few procedures that a physician could perform with visible, often impressive, results and without immediate or obvious dangers. It is especially impressive to those who retain their childhood fascination with the subject of bowel evacuation.

During the late nineteenth century the theory of autointoxication was reinforced by the demonstration of the existence of germs and how they can lead to disease. These discoveries led to the adoption of antisepsis and, later, asepsis, which in turn made surgery safer and so encouraged its development and practice. Initially it was difficult to decide which germs were harmful, so there was a tendency to regard *all* germs as harmful and even to attempt to sterilise the gut and keep it sterile. There was little knowledge of or interest in the bacteria that take part in normal digestion.

Autointoxication is also a theory of anxiety. It articulates fears of attack (from both inside and outside) and also fears of disorder, which were particularly powerful in the late nineteenth century. It provides a theory of disorder that avoids and denies the idea, long resisted by the medical profession, that physical symptoms sometimes begin in the mind and can only be cured through the mind. Thus the theory of autointoxication supports the basis of modern medicine, the body as a machine with working parts, quite separate from the mind (see Chapter 1). It is also a theory of power, particularly the power of doctors who have purged people for centuries when they could do little else to help or impress them. Many doctors have built large practices and fortunes in this way.

Over the years the theory of autointoxication has adapted to current beliefs and at times has seemed eminently logical. Most commonly in the late nineteenth and twentieth centuries it was associated with the idea that the intestinal contents putrefy through the action of bacteria, forming toxins that lead to chronic poisoning of the body. Various factors have been blamed, especially stasis, meaning slow (or delayed) passage of food through the gut. Another factor thought to be involved was mechanical obstruction, such as 'dropped' organs.

At times the theory has had a powerful influence on the practice of medicine, generating many fashions. It provides a system that enables doctors to do something for their patients, and it helps those who feel uncomfortable or anxious about themselves, or who like to devote time to their bodily functions. During the seventeenth century the idea of autointoxication became popular among the upper classes, especially in France, where the fashion for 'visceral clysterisation' (often in the form of up to three large medicated enemas every day) became widespread even before fashion had become a driving force in medicine. It is recorded that Louis XIII of France (1601–43) had 212 enemas, 215 purgations and 47 bleedings in one year. He died at the age of 42. His successor, Louis XIV, received several thousand intestinal douches in the course of his life. A celebrated legal case of the time concerned payment for 2,190 enemas all given to a canon of Troyes within two years, an average of three per day over the whole period. The idea went on to become fashionable in both England and America.

In the eighteenth century the theory of autointoxication was encouraged by the theories of Johann Kämpf (d. 1753), who advocated the doctrine of infarctus which asserted that impacted faeces originating in the liver vessels and intestine were the cause of virtually all disease. Kämpf distinguished two kinds of infarctus, the black bilious and the mucous. To eliminate the dangerous product, he recommended frequent 'visceral cylsters' (enemas). The theory waxed and waned thereafter, but gained new power and popularity during the late years of the nineteenth century.

Other physicians presented autointoxication in less humoralistic terms. In 1765, for example, Albrecht von Haller (1708–77) held that in constipation foul water was absorbed from the faeces, filling the blood with rancid parts which produced fever, haemorrhage, consumption and insanity.

It came to be believed that the absorption of noxious materials from the colon was the principal cause of death in cases of bowel obstruction, an idea that was initiated by the Frenchman Jean Amussat (1796–1856). According to his Parisian friends, he formed the theory after the death in 1838 of his friend Broussais, who died a horrible death from intestinal obstruction due to cancer. This affected Amussat deeply and he vowed not to allow such a thing to happen again. O H Wangensteen (1898–1981), a modern surgeon and medical historian, commented in his book *The Rise of Surgery* (1978) that it was 'a theory since invoked as a solace by many a surgeon disappointed over his poor accomplishment in the management of bowel obstruction'. The modern idea of autointoxication based on chemistry was first expressed in 1868 in an article written by the Frenchman Charles Bouchard (1837–1915). The idea was that the putrefactive decomposition of proteins produced toxins harmful to the host. An increasing number of people devised chemical experiments and tests involving this theory.

The popularity of autointoxication reached its zenith after the discovery of micro-organisms and the general acceptance of the germ theory. Bouchard's article gives a picture of how the subject was understood at the time. He proposed that the degree of toxaemia could be estimated from the amount of ethereal sulphates excreted in the urine. He believed that colonic stasis in itself was not injurious, and even that it was beneficial ('constipation ought to be regarded as a protection against autointoxication'), as bacteria tended to die out in dry, hard faeces. Paradoxically, he encouraged later believers in colonic toxins by stating that the intestines eliminated most of the poisons formed there by putrefaction, but not all, because the slow movement of the bowel's contents allowed some toxic absorption to take place. He believed that poisons were constantly produced in the body but were mostly neutralised by the liver. 'The healthy man is both a receptacle and laboratory of poisons.' He also believed that autointoxication resulted where there was excessive production of normal toxins so that the liver and kidneys could not deal with them, or where abnormal chemicals were produced. 'Man is in this way constantly living under the chance of being poisoned; he is always working towards his own destruction; he makes continual attempts at suicide by intoxication.'

The article demonstrates the intellectual chaos that existed when chemists, with insufficient knowledge and technology, began to analyse bodily fluids and identify the chemical substances produced from the breakdown of foodstuffs and by bacteria. Bouchard also started the fashion of giving antiseptics to disinfect the intestine. A later critic wrote of him, 'Whenever he could get splash sounds in a woman's stomach he ascribed all the symptoms or pathologic findings she had to "autointoxication".' This became a common attitude of medical men.

Belief in autointoxication and its evils was continually reinforced by the revelations of scientists, and the theory became scientifically more respectable through developments in bacteriology and biochemistry. The accumulated literature on the subject is enormous, though little regarded today, and much of it is tedious to read and difficult to understand. A lengthy text designed to sum up the evidence is virtually incomprehensible to the modern reader, but purports to give biological evidence for the disorder.

The theory was further reinforced by the discovery that the intestines of newborn babies are sterile but collect microbes during the first few days. These beliefs led to the conclusion that the large number of microbes that are always present in the adult human bowel must be a cause of disease and should be destroyed or avoided. By the beginning of the twentieth century microbes were thought to be useful in digestion, but important questions remained. Were these microbes pathological even if they did aid digestion? Were they indispensable? Could they become dangerous under certain circumstances? It was difficult to decide, and no one knew for sure.

Support for the theory of autointoxication also came from the discovery of bacteria related to specific diseases such as tuberculosis, gonorrhoea and diphtheria. These included gonococcus, 1879; salmonella typhi (typhoid), 1880; streptococcus, 1881; tubercle bacillus, 1882; cholera vibrio cholera, 1883/84; corynebacterium diphtheriae, 1883–4; clostridium tetani, 1884; meningococcus, 1887; salmonella enteritidis (food poisoning), 1888; haemophilus influenzae, clostridium welchii (gas gangrene) and pasteurella pestis (plague), all during 1892; clostridium botulinum (botulism), 1896; shigella shigae (bacillary dysentery), 1898; salmonella paratyphi, 1900; treponema pallidum (syphilis), 1905; haemophilus pertussis (whooping cough), 1906.

With all these diseases shown to be associated with specific bacilli, it is not surprising that some doctors behaved in ways that might seem paranoid today, pursuing micro-organisms through experiments that had little or no relation to circumstances that might be encountered in real life. For example, filtered cultures of cholera vibrio could produce severe gastrointestinal symptoms if injected into the cavity of the abdomen, but had no effect when injected into the lumen of the bowel – yet neither of these situations could occur in normal life.

The word 'ptomaine' became popular at this time. It referred to putrefying animal or vegetable matter, but it also meant 'a misfortune, calamity or disaster'. It was increasingly applied to various causes of gastrointestinal upsets and systemic diseases and was much used to suggest poisoning from the products of putrefaction, particularly from sausages and shellfish. It also included chlorosis. Sir Andrew Clark (1826–93), a popular society doctor who was prominent in the Royal College of Physicians, believed that constipation was caused by tight corset lacing, insufficient diet and irregular bowel habit, leading to excessive formation of ptomaines, which destroyed the red blood cells in circulation. It seems likely that he explained this theory to his rich and fashionable patients, who spread it among their friends and acquaintances. This is another way in which medical fashions are formed and propagated.

Some doctors seemed keen, even desperate, to find the evil effects of autointoxication in every situation. For example, someone calling himself 'M.A., M.B.' wrote to the *Lancet* asking for more information about autointoxication in pregnancy. No reply was published, but the subject was discussed a few years later at the International Congress of Medicine and the idea that pregnancy was pathological was implicit. No one disputed the statement that 'every pregnant women is in a condition of autointoxication', which was discussed approvingly.

The theory of autointoxication and the fashion for diagnosing it spread everywhere and many doctors, as well as patients, came to believe that it was the cause of most disease. As with visceroptosis (the theory of 'dropped' organs, or 'ptosis' – see page 165) there was disagreement about how to treat the condition, but few if any doctors questioned its existence or its dangers. One observer suggested later that the readiness with which these ideas were accepted must have been partly because 'they fit into this great background of inherited belief'.

In 1897 the list of articles on autointoxication occupied five columns in the Surgeon-General's Catalogue and the subject had a substantial entry in many respected catalogues, textbooks, encyclopaedias and indices of medicine. Some of the most prominent doctors largely ignored the subject, however. In the first edition of his successful text-book *The Operations of Surgery* (1889), the surgeon W H A Jacobson clearly did not regard autointoxication as a fit subject for a surgeon to discuss. He was concerned only with serious conditions such as tumours, strictures and fistula. Nonetheless, many others believed that autointoxication was the cause of dysentery, typhoid, fever, enteritis and peritonitis, among other afflictions, which shows how confusing it must have been for those trying first to understand the new evidence supporting the theory of germs and then to decide which germs were and were not harmful.

In the early twentieth century, new fashions developed in ideas about stasis and autointoxication, as well as an increased interest in evolutionary ideas and comparative anatomy. Popular ideas, still prevalent today, concerned the disadvantage of human beings' upright posture and the unsuitability of 'civilisation' for our current stage of evolutionary development. Such arguments were used as a rationale for fashions in radical treatment. E Barclay-Smith, in *Proceedings of Cambridge Philosophical Society* (1903), wrote:

From his herbivorous ancestors [man] has inherited not only a bacteria infested colon but a tendency to a caecal diverticulum. Further, one great penalty he has had to pay for assuming the erect posture is to add yet another factor, viz. gravity, to favour the stay of the intestinal contents at the proximal end of the large gut. He has done his best, as it were, to adapt himself to these untoward circumstances.

W K Sibley, writing in the *Lancet* in 1906, offered the following explanation:

Man has adopted a vertical attitude, while his internal viscera are still arranged for a horizontal one. He is thus at a great disadvantage for the regular performance of some of the animal functions.

Modern civilisation has also so altered the character and methods of preparation of his food, that he now finds himself with an internal mechanism which has to perform duties for which he is not yet properly adapted.

Man is burdened with some feet of large intestine, a remnant which is probably not only more or less useless, but to which the origin of many of the ills to which flesh is subject can be traced. In this large bowel the excreta from the foodstuffs are apt to collect or to remain much longer than is desirable; this is designated constipation.

Some doctors were also developing the idea that micro-organisms might play an important part in the digestive process, at least in animals. This went with strong and overtly aggressive ideas of control and fears of loss of control. E Barclay-Smith wrote:

Obviously it is a physiological necessity, in the first place, that bacterial activity should be limited, and in the second place that it should be localised.

If...there was indefinite bacterial invasion of the small intestine, they would seize upon and convert to their own use the material which was the result of normal digestive secretions. Being thus robbed...the animal might starve to death.

Barclay-Smith reached the climax of his paper with what he called 'an important practical application as regards the large intestine as found in man'. Still in fighting mode, he described the 'adenoidal tissue in the intestinal wall' as containing 'defensive energy': 'Strained to the breaking point either from an irresistible onslaught or from the weakening of its vital resistance, these accumulations prove weak spots in the armour of the first line of the body defence ...' There was, he said, 'a constant war to the death between them and the bacteria infesting the caecum'. He added, 'I am convinced that the large intestine is practically a useless encumbrance.' This idea spread and affected theories of medical and surgical practice.

Recognition of the existence of bacteria in the large gut (and their absence in the newborn) also led to the idea that the colon should be sterilised. Understandably, there was confusion about which micro-organisms were dangerous and which were not. Diseases such as typhoid were prominent in doctors' minds, mingled with ideas about costiveness and constipation.

> SIR, – For about a quarter of a century autointoxication has been on my mind... [I]n all cases of obstinate bowels [I] have always aimed at trying to render the intestines septic.

Here Thomas Dutton, a London physician who specialised in diet, indigestion and health, in his letter, above, to the *British Medical Journal* in 1908, uses the word 'septic' to mean 'germ-free', an occasional use of the word as in 'the septic value of salt', perhaps associated at the time with 'septic tank', a receptacle for purifying sewage that was, and still is, a method used where there are no main drains. Such ambiguity may reflect the conflict that existed in many doctors' minds at that time.

There was also much confusion as to the causes of the mysterious disease of autointoxication. In one sentence the *British Medical Journal* in 1908 gave seven different causes or predisposing factors, some of them overlapping and none of them a convincing explanation: 'food used up beyond normal limits', insufficient emptying of the intestine, disturbance of digestion, deficient intestinal motility, want of exercise, unsuitable diet and 'habitual suppression of the normal action'.

Meanwhile, there was increasing interest in regulating the bowels, with a growth of emphasis on the dangers of constipation and efforts to define it or at least to confirm bowel function as being within the medical sphere. One doctor, Grant, in the *British Medical Journal* in 1904 defined constipation as follows:

> The mutational motion ought to be the debris of the food con-sumed during the previous day, and if it is so, constipation does not

exist. While if it is the debris of the food consumed some days previously, constipation does exist.

This doctor devised 'A Test for Constipation' which involved eating charcoal. It caught out 'a patient who was under the impression that because she went to stool every morning, she could not be constipated'. Here we have a good example of the gradual medicalisation of body functions and their regulation by the doctor seeking control (see Chapters 2 and 5). Constipation was an increasingly fashionable diagnosis. The charcoal test was to become popular as more doctors concerned themselves with regulating the bowels of their patients.

Increasingly, autointoxication became the object of scientific study and measurement. In 1906 the three Goulstonian Lectures of the Royal College of Physicians were given by H Batty Shaw MD, FRCP, Lecturer in Therapeutics at University College, London and Assistant Physician to University College Hospital. Introducing the first lecture, he said, 'It is the object of these lectures to consider the possible effects due to autointoxication when from any cause the organs and tissues of the body are made to disintegrate; to study the effects of the dissolution of cells of various organs and tissues as shown by the toxic effects of their products.' There follow many graphs of blood pressure and other clinical measurements which are difficult to understand, at least in their relation to autointoxication. There is, for example, discussion of 'intracellular ferments' and a histological picture called 'Section of the aorta in the neighbourhood of a rupture which occurred in a child aged nine years: showing cloudy degenerated areas in the media', and the statement, 'Seeing that raised blood pressure occurs so often in uraemia, it is reasonable to think that the latter also may be due, in part at least, to the entrance into the system of toxic material...'

In the same year another old theory was incorporated into the developing idea of autointoxication – the theory that pregnancy can be classified as a disease. At the Fifteenth International Congress of Medicine in 1906 it was asserted that 'every pregnant woman is in a condition of autointoxication.' The fact that some women felt unusually well during pregnancy was explicable by the fact that a small quantity of toxin had a stimulating effect. Professor Charrin said he had proved the importance of intestinal toxins in pregnancy and believed that toxins also originated from the *foetus* and the *placenta*.

The fashionable theory of autointoxication continued to dominate the thinking of many doctors during the first third of the twentieth century. One can see this, for instance, in the meeting on the subject at the Royal Society of Medicine in 1913, attended by large numbers of doctors. During the five-week debate, no one actually challenged the *concept* of autointoxication. The influence of the theory eventually declined more because influential doctors such as Sir James Goodhart, Sir Arthur Hurst and Sir Clifford Allbutt questioned its prominence rather than its existence.

By the middle of the twentieth century autointoxication was an outmoded concept, but it lived on to a certain extent. It was taught in British medical schools until after World War II, but was then finally dropped, remaining popular only among self-medicators, supporters of popular medicine and those seeking physical explanations for inner anxieties. It is still promoted by practitioners of some forms of complementary medicine and by purveyors of patent medicines. It is no longer a respectable diagnosis, though it sometimes infiltrates conventional medicine in a different guise and with a different vocabulary. Before it waned, however, the concept was extended into other theories and had considerable influence in ways quite different from what had gone before. Toxins and 'detoxification' are prominent subjects in numerous features and advertisements for alternative medicine.

Few modern writers have been interested in the subject of autointoxication. Although it was one of the most powerful fashions in medical theory and one of the most common diagnoses in the late nineteenth and early twentieth centuries (demonstrated, for instance, in the frequency with which it appears in contemporary medical literature and lay memoirs), it is now largely ignored by practising doctors, scientists and medical historians. 'Autointoxication' is often omitted from modern medical indexes and catalogues. It is absent from Charles Singer's authoritative history and from Garrison and Morton's list of important diseases in medicine. Wangensteen mentions it only to dismiss it and it is scarcely mentioned in the subject catalogue of the Wellcome History of Medicine Library in London. Its disappearance seems to follow the general principle of all but the most perceptive medical history that, however influential it was in its time, anything that has been disproved or discredited must be forgotten and ignored. The theory of autointoxication always had its critics, of course, and it may be significant that even in its heyday it was never mentioned by name in any question in the examination for the Membership of the Royal College of Physicians. It seems that, whereas virtually all doctors believed it to some extent, the concept became more popular among the lay public and the lower echelons of medical practice than it did among the medical élite. There are 'diseases' in a similar situation today, such as ME, fibrositis, fibromyalgia and rheumatism.

There have been a few attempts to set autointoxication and allied subjects into their historical background. In 1928 H Bedingfield, who investigated the subject, said that Bouchard beguiled thought by 'false imposture and force of words' with the term autointoxication. Quoting Allbutt, he said that the word had survived 'to oppress and mislead us, as other ghosts do, when the underlying thing has dissolved'. Norman O Brown, in his *Life Against Death* (1959), discussed the development of Freud's concept of anality and gave an account, now dated but still useful, of its connection with giving and taking, money, retention and excrement. There are several published accounts of ancient theories and lucid histories of the idea that putrefaction of the stools causes disease, dating from ancient Egypt. It is easier to find accounts of such theories and customs in ancient than in modern literature. Clysters and enemas have attracted a certain amount of historical interest, not all of it verifiable, but in the main there is silence about the profession's enthusiasm for autointoxication and the reliance that doctors placed on it even within living memory. Its very closeness to our own time may be a source of anxiety and thus a reason for ignoring it.

This raises the question of how doctors, scientists and medical historians deal with fashions that have been rejected, particularly those that might make recent or fairly recent activities of the profession look foolish. Some may look at rejected knowledge dispassionately and historically, but some judge it to be inherently inferior to current and accepted knowledge. They may treat it peremptorily and indifferently, or may ignore it, dismiss it or explain it away, justifying the original rejection of the idea. Not so long ago autointoxication was regarded as extremely important, but few in the mainstream of medicine are willing to discuss it with any respect today.

One theory related to autointoxication that supported a powerful fashion in early twentieth-century medicine was 'focal sepsis' or 'focal infection', the idea that a pocket of hidden infection was causing the symptoms of which the patient was complaining. It gradually spread, reinforcing and to some extent replacing concepts of visceroptosis, stasis and autointoxication. Focal sepsis was the theory that many diseases were produced by a focus of infection, often round the teeth, from which toxic products spread to different parts of the body. Like autointoxication and intestinal stasis, it had no experimental foundation but seemed logical and in accord with the scientific thinking of the time. It was widely accepted and formed part of the general background of medical theory and belief in the first half of the twentieth century. All three theories were stimulated by the new knowledge of germs and all led to surgery that would now be regarded as invasive and unjustified. These theories also demonstrate how ideas believed to be 'scientific' may have little or no background in science but are essentially and even totally formed by social and economic factors, based on beliefs held by both professional and lay people.

Other related theories and fashions can be understood only against the background and beliefs of the time. They included the theory that 'atypical' complaints were caused by overlooked infection in one of the mucous surfaces of the body, and there was a theory that 'the pennies of ill health' (the typhoids and tuberculoses being 'the pounds') were mostly caused by 'diseased orifices'. Another theory of 'intestinal kinks' was devised by the surgeon Sir William Arbuthnot Lane, who developed the operation of colectomy, or removal of the large gut, for severe constipation.

By the early years of the twentieth century the 'disease' of auto-intoxication had appeared in many guises and fashions and was linked to other 'diseases' which we now know to have been fanciful. A casual count of these disorders yields 66 names, many of which overlap. There was a cluster of labels that suited different symptoms and the fantasies of those who tried to understand and treat them. They include alimentary toxaemia, chronic abdomen, chronic infection, chronic constipation, adhesions (without previous surgery), chronic appendicitis, coprostasis, colonic infection, dropped organs such as stomach, kidney or liver – known as ptosis – focal sepsis, gastric fermentation (flatulent dyspepsia), inner cleanliness – or its opposite, intestinal stasis or intoxication – nervous dyspepsia, neurasthenia, ptomaine poisoning, putrefaction, septicaemia and subinfection. Few of these diagnostic fashions are recognised today. Those that are, such as flatulent dyspepsia, constipation and ileo-caecal obstruction, have different meanings from those of a century ago, but the symptoms that caused them all are still found and new diseases and fashions have taken the place of the diagnoses which have fallen out of use.

Childbirth

There have been more fashions in the management of pregnancy and childbirth than can be described in the space available here. Avoid black cats. Be an invalid. Rest as much as possible. Exercise as much as possible. Eat for two. Don't eat for two. Gain very little weight. Put on weight. Turn the baby if it is a breech. On no account turn it. Pull the baby out with forceps as soon as possible. Leave the baby alone in all circumstances.

Many fashions have been forms of interference, sometimes not so much for the sake of the patient as for the convenience of the doctor, saving him time or increasing his control. These fashions include obstetric procedures such as induction of labour (by breaking the waters), episiotomy (cutting skin and muscle to enlarge the birth passage), and using forceps as a routine rather than waiting for the baby to arrive in its own time. Others include routine pubic shaving and enema at the start of labour, fixing the mother's feet in stirrups or turning her onto her left side, administering twilight sleep and – a more modern fashion – the use of a birthing pool in which the baby may be born under water. Some of these fashions have been perpetuated largely by the mothers, for example the birthing pool, some by midwives, such as preparation for labour, and some, particularly those that save time or require special medical training, by the doctor.

There have always been fashions in managing the 'lying-in' period. Older readers will remember that in the early years of the NHS, women were expected to stay completely in bed for at least eight days after the birth and to remain in hospital for twelve days. At an earlier period this lying-in was even longer, a month or more. At a time when there was no blood transfusion (patients were even liable to be bled) and many women were exhausted and anaemic from frequent childbirth, caring for a number of small children and often also eating a poor diet, this was probably sensible, but it became a fashion that was strictly imposed on everyone.

In eighteenth-century England, the following was the fashion:

> She is covered up close in bed with additional cloaths, the curtains are drawn round the bed, and pinned together, every crevice in the windows and door is stopped close, not excepting even the key hole, the windows are guarded not only with shutters and curtains, but even with blankets, the more effectually to exclude the fresh air, and the good woman is not suffered to put her arm or even her nose, out of bed, for fear of catching cold. She is constantly supplied out of the spout of a teapot with large quantities of warm liquors…

Charles White, the Manchester surgeon who wrote this piece, disapproved of the practices it described and he tried to change the fashion. He kept the windows of the lying-in room open and allowed no fires, kept his patients cool, and banished everyone from the room except those who were essential for the care of the patient. He insisted on scrupulously clean bedlinen and the absence of all smells and vapours that he believed created 'the putrid miasmas that caused puerperal fever'. The theory that disease was carried by bad air or miasma was common and powerful in the days before it was established that infectious disease was associated with micro-organisms.

Childbirth was the sole domain of midwives until the obstetric forceps began to be used in the eighteenth century. Then it was gradually taken over by male accoucheurs, who became, and have remained, fashionable for the upper social classes. The old customs and fashions of the midwives declined while the changing fashions of the obstetricians reigned, greatly influenced by scientific discoveries and constantly shifting social fashions.

Delivering a baby by forceps is one fashion that has waxed and waned depending on circumstances and individual doctors, and with its own outspoken protagonists and antagonists. In Georgian England the forceps became widely used and sometimes caused terrible injuries from unskilled and often unnecessary use. In 1737 a Mrs Sarah Stone of Piccadilly wrote *A Complete Practice of Midwifery* and declared, 'I am certain that when twenty women are delivered with instruments (which has now become a common practice) nineteen of them might be delivered without, if not the twentieth.' In Mrs Stone's own practice of three hundred cases a year, instruments were needed only four times. Yet one obstetrician used forceps in 29 out of 60 births, and another began to 'cut and slash as soon as everything was not precisely normal', leading to the death of the mother in 20 per cent of cases. Dr Nicholls, a friend of William Smellie, the inventor of the forceps, attacked unnecessary instrumental deliveries in his 'Petition of the Unborn Babies'. Mrs Kennon, one of the royal midwives, was so delighted that she gave him £500.

By the end of the eighteenth century, the pendulum had swung right back the other way. In 1788 Thomas Denman, London's most prominent obstetrician, decreed that forceps were to be used only 'to supply the total want or deficiency of the natural powers of labour'. In his view, instruments were never to be used while progress, however slow, was being made. This policy was continued by Denman's son-in-law Richard Croft, the royal obstetrician, and was responsible in 1817 for the death in childbirth of Princess Charlotte, the only child of the Prince Regent and heir after him to the throne. Keeping strictly to the Denman tradition, she was left in the second stage of labour for many hours, even though the baby's head was visible. Eventually the baby was stillborn before the mother collapsed and died, leaving no obvious heir to the throne. The sons of George III had many bastards, but no legitimate children, and were told to produce some. The result was the birth in 1819 of Princess Victoria of Kent, who became Queen Victoria. Thus did the fashion for leaving childbirth to nature lead to momentous changes within the royal family and the royal succession.

Since that time, the fashion for forceps has had a mixed existence. The practice has varied from hospital to hospital and from doctor to doctor. The most extreme accoucheurs have even tried to deliver with forceps all but the most precipitous babies. The best known of these was Dr J B DeLee (1869–1942) of Boston, founder of the Chicago Lying-In Dispensary (1895), which became the Chicago Lying-In Hospital. DeLee believed that the pressure on the baby's head in unaided birth led to brain damage and mental handicap and he advocated intervention, in the form of chloroform and forceps, in all possible cases.

During the late nineteenth century it became possible to deliver women by Caesarian section. This, too, has had its fashions and its problems. Recently other childbirth fashions have been changing once again towards increasing interference. Not only has the incidence of Caesarian section increased enormously, but also the practices of inducing labour and delivery with the aid of instruments. The motives behind these changes include financial considerations (of both doctors and hospitals), shortage of hospital beds, a strong belief in scientific progress and the scorned situation of women said to be 'too posh to push'! There has been much criticism of these fashions, and there is pressure to change them back to more 'natural' customs.

Children and doctors

Before the mid-nineteenth century doctors took little interest in children. William Buchan's *Domestic Medicine* (a book of popular medicine published from 1769 onwards) reveals the traditional prejudice against calling in doctors for small children:

> The management of children...has been generally considered as the sole province of old women while men of the first character in physic have refused to visit infants even when sick.

There had been little study of child development and little interest in it. The considerable anatomical and physiological differences between children and adults were not yet appreciated, and in the climate of increasing intervention and greater surgical power, a child who differed from a normal adult (as all children do) was liable to be regarded as abnormal and treated as such, often drastically. Such ideas complicated debate about whether children's diseases were different from those of adults, or whether they merely needed different treatment. Doctors were also worried by the need for extreme care with dosages and the fact that certain drugs and applications were known to be unsuitable for children.

Children, in fact, did not become popular as patients until late in the nineteenth century. Charles West, founder in 1852 of the Hospital for Sick Children, Great Ormond Street, recorded the new attitude when he lectured solely on the diseases of childhood and warned his audience, 'You will feel...as if entering a country whose inhabitants you expected to find speaking the same language... [and] ...you observe manners and customs such as you had never seen before.'

This, then, is the background to the various medical fashions that have been applied to children over the years, including circumcision, tonsillectomy, lancing gums and pink diseases (see pages 123, 212, 140 and 152 respectively).

Circumcision

The operation of circumcision was, and to some extent still is, a strange and dramatic medical fashion for children. It has a long history as an important ritual in many countries and for many religions, of course, but during the nineteenth century in the Western world it became a social fashion without religious significance. It was thought to prevent venereal disease, cancer of the penis and, most importantly in people's minds at the time, masturbation. It was also said to be a treatment for alcoholism, epilepsy, asthma, hernia, gout, rheumatism, curvature of the spine, headaches and many other conditions. At a time of increasing emphasis on cleanliness, it was held to be an aid to hygiene, and was also believed to improve sexual performance and to be a punishment for wicked practices. Many doctors believed that all boys should be circumcised. An article in the *Lancet* advised that the operation should be performed without anaesthetic 'so that the pain experienced may be associated with the habit we wish to eradicate'. This opinion was echoed in 1888 by J H Kellogg, the pioneering vegetarian who founded the Kellogg food company. By this time 15 per cent of the American male population was circumcised. Kellogg had strong views on masturbation, and in *Plain Facts for Old and Young* (1888) wrote:

A remedy [for masturbation] which is almost always successful in small boys is circumcision… The operation should be performed by a surgeon without administering an anaesthetic, as the pain attending the operation will have a salutary effect upon the mind, especially if it be connected with the idea of punishment.

The fashion for circumcising newborn boys without religious reasons for doing so grew exponentially. In 1860 only 0.001 per cent of the male population in the United States was circumcised. By 1871 it had increased a thousand times. By 1887 the figure was 10 per cent, and there were ever more rationalisations for performing the operation, some of them ridiculous. L L Sayer claimed in the *Journal of the American Medical Association* in 1887:

> Hip trouble is from falling down, an accident that children with tight foreskins are especially liable owing to the weakening of the muscles produced by the condition of the genitals.

In the same year, in his book *Treatment of Disease in Children*, Angel Money wrote:

> There can be no doubt of [masturbation's] injurious effect, and of the proneness to practise it on the part of children with defective brains. Circumcision should always be practised. It may be necessary to make the genitals so sore by blistering fluids that pain results from attempts to rub the parts.

The sadism behind many of these recommendations is obvious. Not only was the foreskin seen as detrimental to health, but some doctors wished the treatment to go further. One, J Hutchinson, writing in the *British Medical Journal* in 1890, recommended:

> Measures more radical than circumcision would, if public opinion permitted their adoption, be a true kindness to many patients of both sexes.

In his *Handbook on the Diseases of Children* (1895), C E Fisher asserted:

> In all cases in which male children are suffering nerve tension, confirmed derangement of the digestive organs, restlessness, irritability, and other disturbances of the nervous system, even to chorea, convulsions, and paralysis, or where through nerve waste the nutritive facilities of the general system are below par and structural diseases are occurring, circumcision should be considered as among the lines of treatment to be pursued.

The anti-masturbatory fashion was common not only in private practice but also among the working class, and circumcision was even the subject of advertisements. For example, a circular was sent to those mentioned in the birth columns of newspapers. It recommended the operation not only for the newborn babies, but also for their fathers, and warned of the evils of neglecting it.

Circumcision, or clitoridectomy, was also performed on girls. This fashion was short-lived in Britain, where in 1867 a surgeon called Isaac Baker-Brown was expelled from the London Obstetric Society for performing the operation. It continued to be done in America, however, where it was often combined with cautery of the spine and genitals and where surgery for masturbation was recommended even after 1925.

By 1900 25 per cent of the American male population had been circumcised, and by 1920 the figure was 50 per cent. In 1928 the editor of the *Journal of the American Medical Association* recommended 'routine circumcision at birth'. Soon after this, however, a movement against routine circumcision began to develop. It was led by the psychologists. In 1942 Helen Deutsch, a famous disciple of Freud, wrote:

If surgeons only knew how much damage is done, for example, by a circumcision performed as a hygienic measure during the early years of childhood, they would feel like so many Herods.

In 1949 a British paediatrician, Douglas Gairdner, led the medical movement against circumcision in an article that was influential everywhere except America. He pointed out that the foreskin at birth is nonretractable in nearly all cases and that there had been little critical assessment of the situation. For instance, whereas enthusiastic circumcisors were claiming that most newborn boys suffered from phimosis (narrowing of the aperture, making urination a strain), Gairdner said that he had never seen such a case.

The argument continues to this day. Circumcision is still held to be of some social status and medical benefit, although the so-called 'benefits' have all been shown to be illusory. In that respect the operation has proved to be one of the toughest and most persistent fashions of the English-speaking world.

Constipation

Constipation is a grand old condition in medical fashion. The Latin word *constipare* means 'to press together', and since the sixteenth century it has usually referred to the bowels. Since then there has been much interest and many fashions in the subject.

In the eighteenth century it was regarded as important that body waste should be efficiently expelled, and bowels that worked well were held to be vital to a healthy life. 'Constipation' was seldom more clearly defined than in vague terms such as 'costiveness', as Roy and Dorothy Porter remarked in their book *In Sickness and In Health* (1988), but 'Diarists constantly bewail their constipation, and dwell on their bowel motions, and the number, size, shape, hue, odour, and texture of the stools they produce.' Such preoccupation with the matter was often accompanied by anxiety about poisoning.

Doctors thrived on these preoccupations. It was, after all, one of the few aspects of body function that they were in a position to regulate. The diet of well-off people in those days consisted largely of meat and pastry with little fruit, vegetables or fibre, and during the nineteenth century influential doctors promoted a fashion of producing a large stool after every meal. Failure to do so led to purging with ever stronger laxatives, emetics (drugs that induce vomiting), sudorifics (drugs that induce sweating), enemas, and even, when surgery became sufficiently advanced and safe, total removal of the colon or large gut – all of which kept the fashionable doctors satisfactorily busy.

The great surgeon and teacher John Abernethy (1764–1831), like many others, insisted that regularity was essential to health. William Buchan's *Domestic Medicine* (first published in 1769 and popular for a century) stated:

Few things conduce more to health than keeping the body regular. When the *faeces* lie too long in the bowels they vitiate the humours; and when they are too soon discharged, the body is not sufficiently nourished. A medium is therefore desired, which can only be obtained by regularity in diet, sleep and exercise. Whenever the body is not regular, there is reason to suspect a fault in one or the other of these.

Until well into the twentieth century constipation, which came to be known as 'the British disease', was thought to be extremely serious in that lack of regularity led to serious disease. In the later part of the century, this view became less fashionable. It was realised that there are wide variations in habits and that people are not poisoned by their own products. In recent years much less attention has been paid to it and the fashion for regular 'dosing' of both adults and children has declined.

Fletcherism

Some fashions are initiated or maintained by one individual, usually a person of powerful personality, often with a limited but vociferous following. Such a person was Horace Fletcher (1849–1919), a well-known and influential food and health faddist in early twentieth-century America who was nicknamed 'The Great Masticator'.

Fletcher was immensely energetic, a world traveller, millionaire businessman, amateur painter, speaker, author and self-taught nutritionist who perfected and fanatically distributed his doctrine of 'Fletcherism' for 24 years from 1895 to 1919. His idea was that all food must be deliberately masticated and not swallowed until it had turned to liquid. He believed that this prevented overeating, led to better systemic and dental health, helped to reduce food intake, and consequently conserved money. He warned people not to eat except when they were 'good and hungry', and to avoid dining when they were angry or worried. He also said they could eat any food they fancied as long as they chewed it until 'the food swallowed itself'. The fashion was endorsed by the *Lancet*, but it was never universally accepted or adopted.

Gynaecology

Women's reproductive organs have probably inspired more medical fashions that any other human part. Specialisation in gynaecology as well as abdominal surgery developed from these fashions. Women were regarded as suitable subjects for experiment, and sometimes they still are. The experiments have sometimes been official or semi-official in the form of research, and sometimes personal, pursued by individual doctors.

Women have been the subject of medical trials, experiments and fashions ever since medicine began to 'progress'. They have probably always tended to be more compliant than men, more available as patients, more prone to physical symptoms and more likely to complain about them. Their reproductive systems have been regarded as suitable for extensive examination and intervention. When anaesthesia and antisepsis became part of medical practice, it was possible for the speciality of gynaecology to develop – and this coincided with a period when middle-class women, many with money and servants, were unable to work, attend university or receive serious education and were largely confined to their homes, children and 'feminine' occupations such as embroidery and socialising. Unsurprisingly, it was also a period when 'hysteria' and 'neurasthenia' were common diagnoses, along with a concentration on the body and its functions.

OVARIOTOMY

Many women developed cysts on their ovaries, as they still do. These sometimes grew large, weighing as much as 100lb or more (the record was 149lb), and were resistant to all forms of drug treatment. The only

129

way to remove them was by surgery, which became feasible during the nineteenth century through the operation incorrectly known as ovario- tomy – oophorectomy, or ovariectomy, is the correct name for the surgical removal of an ovary or ovarian tumour, whereas ovariotomy is in fact the surgical incision into an ovary. Surgeons practised on corpses and on hospital patients (i.e., on poor women). When they had lowered the death rate to no more than about 20 to 30 per cent, the operation was regarded as relatively safe and the fashion for it grew.

These pioneer surgeons did not match their skill in performing the operation with knowledge of female physiology, however. Little was known of the ovary's function, but this did not deter them. From the middle of the nineteenth century it became known that menstruation depended on the ovaries rather than on the uterus, as had been believed earlier. The ovaries became 'the grand organs of sexual activity', but throughout the century there were instances of leading surgeons revealing profound ignorance. As late as 1891 the president of the American Gynecological Society observed with surprise that in his experience of 144 cases of removal of both ovaries, menstruation had ceased in every case.

The death rate from ovariotomy was still so high that the gynae- cological surgeons of the day were careful to operate largely only on serious cases. This practice, of course, simply increased the death rate. The minimum size for an ovarian cyst to be operated on seems to have been about 'twice the size of a baby's head'. There was criticism of those who did the operation and some overt hostility, especially in France, where it was rejected by the French Academy and regarded as 'une audace humaine'. Nonetheless, it slowly became fashionable as surgery grew safer and easier.

The fashion for the operation was boosted when it began to be per- formed for psychological and ideological reasons, in cases of hysteria, neurasthenia, and various spurious conditions such as 'ovariomania', 'nymphomania' or 'ovarian epilepsy'. These were all fashionable contemporary explanations of women's behaviour when this did not conform to conventional expectations. It was simply assumed that this kind of ovariotomy, done when there were no signs of a diseased ovary, was a cure for female ills. Such practice began with a skilled and highly moral American surgeon, Robert Battey (1828–95) of Augusta, Georgia. In 1872 he published a paper with the unfortunate title of 'Normal Ovariotomy', and he was criticised for operating on 'normal' ovaries. He justified his actions by arguing that any woman with symptoms whose cause was not obvious *must* have something wrong with her ovaries, which were better removed. For him, the prime indication for doing the operation was 'any grave disease which is either dangerous to life or destructive to health and happiness, which is incurable by other and less radical means'. At the American Gynecological Society meeting in 1877, he gave four indications:

1. When life is endangered in the absence of a uterus.
2. With obliteration of the uterine cavity or vaginal canal that cannot be surgically restored.
3. In cases of insanity or epilepsy caused by uterine or ovarian disease.
4. In cases of protracted physical or mental suffering associated with monthly nervous and vascular perturbations. Later he refined the indications to 'oophoromania', 'oophoro-epilepsy' and 'oophoroalgia'.

This was Battey's first report on his operation for removal of normal ovaries. Later he published other reports under the titles 'Is there a proper field for Battey's operation?' and 'Extirpation of the functionally active ovaries for the remedy of otherwise incurable diseases'. Meanwhile, the diagnosis of 'ovariomania' found increasing favour. It suited the entrepreneurial spirit demanded of the recently organised medical profession and provided a huge supply of middle-class patients, which was what doctors needed for building up their practices. It is important to realise that most doctors at the time genuinely believed that the ovaries were the source of virtually all female sickness, and many believed that women were inherently sick simply because they were women. The operation of ovariotomy was further popularised in America by W L Atlee (1808–78), one of two brilliant brothers who were both surgeons. English and German surgeons also took it up enthusiastically, especially Lawson Tait in Birmingham. The French were not so keen.

Later Battey maintained that he operated not on 'normal' ovaries but only on those he believed were causing gynaecological disease such as menstrual disorders, including severe menstrual pain. However, others were not so careful and operated for a wild variety of reasons. Essentially, 'Battey's operation' was the removal of healthy ovaries with the aim of relieving other symptoms by producing an artificial menopause.

Battey may not have been too careful about describing the indications for the operation, but he liked to promote himself. He described many cases of success, for example, 'entire cessation of the epileptiform and at times cataleptic, convulsions', 'gratifying improvement in general health', 'good and satisfactory cure'. One patient who had been bedridden and 'requiring the constant use of opiates to allay her pain... bounced like an India rubber ball at once into a state of perfect health and comfort'. He had followed her up for twelve years after the operation. Case V, a housemaid, was 'wholly unable to earn her support' through 'oophoro-epilepsy'. The operation resulted in 'complete cure'. Case XVI, bedridden for four years, 'made gratifying improvement'. Case XXIX 'was a great sufferer'. She still had 'slight nervous disturbances', but 'the contrast in her condition is so great that the case may well be classed as a complete cure'. He noted, however, that the operation did not cure drug addiction.

Battey was at least honest and moral, if misguided. He firmly maintained that the ovaries were always diseased in the cases he chose. He also tried to analyse his own motives. He referred to his 'feeling of dissatisfaction and unrest when foiled in my attempts to relieve suffering women through the orthodox means', and said he was 'an earnest seeker after truth and wisdom'. He added as motivation his belief that 'insanity is not very unfrequently caused by uterine and ovarian disease'.

The removal of normal ovaries has, in fact, a long and ancient history. Women were castrated in ancient Lydia, and women with male singing voices were entertainers in India as late as 1841. John Hunter (1728–93) wrote that he could see no reason why a woman should not suffer spaying safely, as did other animals. Most of the women who had the operation were young; the average age was thirty. Following Battey, the idea was taken up with varying degrees of enthusiasm by most of the leading gynaecologists of the day, who combined with the psychiatrists in what became a profitable practice. In 1889 the gynaecologist Skene remarked how 'the boundary lines which divide the gynaecologist and the psychologist often touch and cross each other'. Thus the stage was set for the widespread practice of operations for 'ovariomania'.

There were critics of the operation, and some ignored it altogether. Lawson Tait, the innovative Birmingham surgeon who was later to become such a strong protagonist of the operation, did not mention it in his 1877 book, *Diseases of Women*. In 1879 the eminent New York gynaecologist Emmet criticised the operation in his textbook. Spencer Wells (1818–97), who had done the operation himself many times before deciding that it was unethical, warned about its use in the context of psychiatric conditions. In 1886 he explicitly declared that it should not be done for nymphomania, insanity or any other form of mental disease.

The use of ovariotomy in psychiatry was probably the practice that did the most to discredit it. Yet it continued to be done, often for persistent masturbation. William S Stewart of Philadelphia described 'a remarkable case of nymphomania and its cure'. In his 1886 *Textbook of Surgery*, the London surgeon Frederick Treves included a section on 'Oopherectomy; Battey's operation; spaying; castration of women', which he described as 'the removal of ovaries that are either apparently normal, or that present other structural changes than those of a new growth'. He wrote reassuringly, 'It may at once be said that in the great majority of the operations already performed, the ovaries have presented some evidence of structural disease.' He said that the indications for doing the operation 'have not yet been very distinctly formulated, and considerable difference of opinion exists as to the propriety of performing oopherectomy for certain of the conditions for which it has already been adopted'. He describes indications for doing the operation, 'keeping as far as possible to structural changes'. These were Treves' indications:

1. Persisting hyperaemia of the ovary, i.e. profuse menstruation with intense pain, often with a displaced uterus.
2. Ovaritis, acute or chronic – due to injury or cold, sepsis after labour, extension of inflammation from uterus or vagina. He thought that gonorrhoea was probably the most common cause.
3. Amenorrhoea with hystero-epilepsy, which he said could result from advanced chronic ovaritis with enlarged, nodular ovary.
4. Occlusion or absence of the uterus or vagina.
5. Fibroids – to lessen their growth and encourage their atrophy.
6. 'Neuralgia of the ovary, and in some cases of mania, epilepsy and hysteria.'

He commented that it was under this last heading that 'the application of the operation is exceedingly questionable':

Indeed, so far as practice has at present proceeded in this direction, it would appear to be unjustifiable to remove the ovaries in these causes unless there is evidence that they are diseased, are beyond the reach of other treatment, and are the principal cause of the nervous or mental disorder.

Others were not so cautious. In 1887 Harvey Cushing (1869–1939), a distinguished early endocrinologist, in his 'Report of a Case of Melancholia; Masturbation; Cured by removal of Both Ovaries', hailed it as 'one of the unequalled triumphs of surgery'. William Goodell, Professor of Obstetrics and Gynecology at the University of Pennsylvania, advocated Battey's operation for all cases of insanity, and others soon followed. Enthusiasts accused others of inhumanity, cruelty and criminal neglect if they *failed* to perform it. Others condemned it as 'spaying' and 'castration'. In 1886 Lawson Tait wrote to the *Lancet*, criticising the journal for confusing 'spaying' (done before puberty to improve the food supply) and 'removal of the human uterine appendages' (done after puberty with 'no other purpose than the saving of life and the relief of suffering'). The two operations, he said, 'have therefore no conceivable resemblance', and to talk of 'spaying women' was to display ignorance and 'indulge in wilful misrepresentation for purposes of giving offence'.

At this time fantasies about the operation were also developing in connection with current ideas of racial purity and the sterilisation of the unfit. This was the era in which the treatment of the insane was moving more and more towards sterilisation, isolation and dehumanisation. Powerful people, such as P Munde, writing in the *American Gynecological and Obstetrical Journal* in 1898, saw 'America as a beleaguered island of WASP righteousness, surrounded by an encroaching flood of dirty, prolific immigrants, and sapped from within by the subversive practices of women'. Yet, ironically, most of the patients who were sterilised were WASP women. They were also nearly all middle class, as were those diagnosed as suffering from hystero-epilepsy. In 1895 the gynaecological cases seen at Mount Sinai Hospital, New York, were analysed. They were mainly poor women, and among more than 3,000 cases treated, there was no case of hystero-epilepsy.

Gradually Battey's operation was discredited on both sides of the Atlantic and its popularity decreased, but it has been calculated that before this happened, and including relatives as well as patients, about half a million people must have given active consent for the procedure. By the last years of the nineteenth century, there was marked hostility to the operation. Although it was still being performed quite extensively, the gynaecological authority H A Kelly did not mention the operation in his textbook of 1896, and that set the tone for subsequent attitudes.

The history of this operation demonstrates clearly how the medical profession can espouse untested procedures and unproved theories because they happen to fit in with current beliefs and prejudices. Battey's operation was important in the development of abdominal surgery, but it is also a good example of the way in which a medical fashion develops and is sustained.

DILATATION AND CURETTAGE

One of the many gynaecological fashions of the nineteenth century was for a minor operation on the womb known as 'dilatation and curettage', or D&C, which entailed dilating the opening of the womb (the cervix) with a series of rods, each larger than the one before, then introducing a curette (a metal instrument with a curved, sharp end) and scraping the lining of the womb. The operation is relatively easy and safe to perform, though it can lead to perforation of the uterus and peritonitis. Joseph Recamier (1774–1852), the French surgeon who invented the operation in the 1840s, noted three deaths from this cause. It normally involved an anaesthetic and a short stay in hospital, but it could also, with greater risk, be performed in an office rather than a clinic and without an anaesthetic.

The operation, like many others, was never properly evaluated. During the height of the fashion, which began to decline only in about 1960, the operation was performed on huge numbers of women. It was the commonest gynaecological operation and the commonest of all elective surgical procedures in the West. It was used for many gynaecological conditions and as a preliminary to further diagnostic procedures and treatment. From scraping the inside of the womb with the curette, its lining could be examined, which was, and still is, of considerable use in diagnosing cancer. It was also thought to be a treatment for heavy periods or irregular or unexpected bleeding, and the fashion for this idea continued long after it was shown that the procedure was no use as a cure for these conditions.

The operation is also a method of inducing abortion in the early stages of pregnancy.

Until about 1960, a full gynaecological examination included a 'scrape' as routine. Then doubts arose, especially in America. It was noticed that dilatation and curettage seemed to miss many pathological conditions and was not as effective in treatment as other methods. Also, more rigorous methods of testing were being introduced and it was realised that the effectiveness of the operation had never been properly evaluated.

The fashion lasted longer in Britain than in America, perhaps because more sophisticated alternative techniques were developed earlier and more quickly in the USA. Between 1977 and 1990 the number of D&Cs performed in England and Wales was stable at nearly seven times the US rate. Then the rate declined rapidly. In 1994–5 the number of D&Cs performed in England was only 87,210, compared with 169,230 in 1989–90. Nowadays the Royal College of Obstetricians and Gynae-cologists no longer recommends it for women under forty years old.

The growth of the fashion for D&C was part of the general development of popular gynaecological operations in the nineteenth century. Without strict evaluation, it seemed to be an impressive procedure and its importance seemed sensible and self-evident. For decades, gynaecological operating lists began or ended with a few D&Cs. They could mostly be left to the junior staff, even the most junior. The operation was visibly effective, in that there were 'products', however scanty, and these could be sent to the laboratory, which would produce an impressive report. When it was done in order to procure an abortion, which became extremely common after the passing of the Abortion Act of 1967, the operation was virtually always successful. Huge numbers of women aged over fifty in the Western world have undergone the procedure.

We can only guess why the fashion lasted so long when there was in fact little or no evidence that it was effective in most conditions, least of all in heavy bleeding, the condition for which it was most commonly performed. (Its use in abortion is a separate issue.) The absence of complications or the gratitude of the patient often seemed to be a justification for a specific medical procedure. D&C was a minor operation and caused little pain, discomfort or inconvenience, but it was dramatic in that it took place in an operating theatre and involved an anaesthetic and a few days in hospital. The operation entered the popular imagination in that most women knew about it and many talked about it and expected to have it if they had menstrual complaints. It became part of the conventional wisdom of both doctors and laity. As with tonsillectomy (see page 212), this is a powerful combination in the promotion of a fashion.

HYSTERECTOMY

Hysterectomy, the operation for removing the whole womb, would have pleased Victorian surgeons as a treatment for female problems, including hysteria, but they almost never performed it. At that time it was dangerous and liable to kill the patient. This partly explains the popularity of ovariotomy.

The operation of hysterectomy developed as a treatment for cancer of the womb. There was little understanding of the condition before the late eighteenth century, and any growth in the uterus was called a 'mole', described in the following manner by a French surgeon in 1817:

> The housewives believe that moles not only take the form of certain animals, but that they even walk, run, fly, try to hide themselves, even to re-enter the womb from which they came; indeed, if no obstacle be offered they will kill the woman just delivered of them.

Several surgeons suggested that the womb might be removed for cancer, but they did not attempt it. In 1825 the distinguished Scottish surgeon John Lizars described a case and his editor, the controversial James Johnson, referred to the operation as follows:

> We consider extirpation of the uterus, not previously protruded or inverted, one of the most cruel and unfeasible operations that ever was projected or executed by the head or hand of man. We are very far from discouraging bold or untried operations, but there is a limit beyond which it may not be prudent to go, even should a solitary instance or two of success rise up as precedents to bear out the operation.

In the middle of the century there was still opposition to the operation, especially from those with conservative tendencies, typified by

Charles D Meigs (1792–1869), Professor of Obstetrics at Jefferson Medical College, who was a writer and teacher of great power. In 1848 he wrote, 'I detest all abdominal surgery, save that which is clearly warranted by the otherwise imminent death of the patient.' Instead he emphasised, 'Much may be done in a way of wise counsel and prudent prescription.' One is not surprised to learn that it was said that Meigs, powerful as he was, and an eminent professor of women's diseases, had 'never held a knife in his hand'. Meigs was as hostile to anaesthesia as he was to abdominal surgery. (He also opposed Oliver Wendell Holmes when he asserted that puerperal fever was contagious.) He was not alone. Fifteen years later, in 1863, James Simpson wrote of hysterectomy:

> Judging of it a priori, we should regard the operation as unjustifiable, and experience serves only to confirm this judgment... I have no hesitation in saying that it should even then be rejected, as an utterly unjustifiable operation in surgery.

Early attempts to perform hysterectomies were indeed failures, and many of the patients died. The commonest cause of death in ovariotomy was peritonitis, but in hysterectomy there were the added dangers of haemorrhage and shock. There was much professional opposition to the operation, but gradually it became safer, more popular and an increasingly fashionable substitute for ovariotomy. The fashion has persisted to the present day, and the operation still attracts both criticism and praise. It is now a safe routine, but many people, including many experts, believe that it is done too often. At present there is a campaign against the frequency with which it is performed.

Joints

The replacement of arthritic and damaged joints by artificial prostheses has saved much pain and discomfort and can be regarded as one of the great medical advances of the second half of the twentieth century. It began with replacing the hip and does not seem to be what one would now regard as a 'fashion' because it has been so successful. However, there are fashions in how it is done and in the materials used. In 1993 an editorial in the *British Medical Journal* referred to the 'hip industry' as a 'fashion trade' and warned that it was costing the health service many millions of pounds each year and, more importantly, was causing patients unnecessary pain and distress through 'early failure of unproved implants'. In 1995 the high failure rate led to a call for improvements, which has had good results. Meanwhile, the operation of knee replacements has made steady progress and is much more successful today than it was even a few years ago.

Lancing gums

For many centuries, the surgical knife known as the lancet has been a symbol of medical practice and medical competence. Since ancient times it has been used for blood-letting, opening abscesses, circumcision and other minor operations. One of these operations was slitting the gums of babies because it was believed that this helped them to cut their teeth. The fact that we still use the phrase 'cutting teeth' shows how old concepts persist. A more modern view is that a child's teeth push up rather as plants push their way up through the earth.

Until the twentieth century the death rate among infants and small children was high, as it still is in many developing countries. In some places and eras, four out of five babies have died each year. Most of these deaths occurred between the ages of six months and two years, the age of cutting the first teeth. It is not surprising that teething was widely believed to be a common cause. In 1839, 5,016 deaths in England and Wales were attributed to teething. In 1910, the figure was 1,600.

Some older remedies for teething were violent and included blistering, bleeding, placing leeches on the gums and applying the cautery to the back of the skull. The French surgeon Ambroise Paré (1510–90) introduced a more professional and (for the times) more logical treatment: lancing babies' gums. He described how he got the idea from a postmortem on a baby:

When we…diligently sought for the cause of his death, we could impute it to nothing else than to the *contumacious hardness of the gums*… When we cut his gums with a knife we found all his teeth appearing…if it had been done when he lived, doubtless he might have been preserved.

The idea grew that failing to lance gums contributed to infant death. This idea recurred frequently in the literature of the next four centuries while the fashion lasted. It was also fashionable in the eighteenth century for a successful doctor to carry in his waistcoat a small lancet, often with an elaborate handle of ivory or mother-of-pearl. These lancets were symbols of the profession as much as practical accessories. New varieties served different purposes: the gum-lancet – priced at 2/6d (12½p) in tortoiseshell and 8/6d (42½p) with a tenaculum or hook with a French catch – was one of the most popular. With few exceptions, both physicians and surgeons advised gum-lancing as a remedy for every disease or ailment, whether the tooth was evident or not.

Lancing the gums became common practice. The British surgeon John Hunter (1728–93) would lance a baby's gums up to ten times. The American J Marion Sims (1813–83) described his treatment of an eighteen-month-old baby: 'As soon as I saw some swelling of the gums, I at once took out my lancet and cut the gums down to the teeth.' The physician Marshall Hall (1790–1857) wrote that he would rather lance a child's gums 199 times unnecessarily than omit it once if necessary, and he instructed his students to do it before, during and after the teeth appeared, sometimes twice a day.

By the mid-nineteenth century it was becoming clear to some that teething did not cause serious diseases in infants. Opinions were increasingly divided and ambivalent, as is often the case when a fashion or a long tradition is losing popularity. Charles West (1860–98) of Great Ormond Street wrote that teething was 'a perfectly natural process', yet he continued to advocate gum-lancing, advising that 'it may be necessary to repeat your scarification several times with the same object'. By 1867 the American physician Samuel Gross was complaining that young doctors were not using their lancets; yet in 1883 distinguished physicians were still insisting that dentition was 'a powerful predisposing cause of diarrhoea and enteritis'. By this time there was wrath and rivalry between the two camps. The Liverpool physician Boyd Joll taught that teething was 'normal' and that lancing the gums exacerbated diarrhoea. He evoked anger in some quarters by advising students to leave the 'lancet in their waist-coat pocket'.

The conflict centred on the changing meanings and uses of ideas about teething in medicine and surgery. Increasingly humanitarian attitudes and new thoughts about the nature of childhood were associated with dissatisfaction with violent treatments and greater belief in the reparative powers of nature in acute diseases. As doctors became more confident and powerful, they tended to interfere more, yet lancing the gums declined at a time when other forms of surgical interference (e.g. tonsillectomy, tenotomy for clubfoot and surgery for cleft palate) were becoming popular. It is possible that the adoption of the germ theory and the development of antisepsis and asepsis in surgery militated against 'pocket-knife surgery', because elaborate knives and showy lancet cases were revealed as sources of germs and therefore as potentially dangerous.

In 1884 the prestigious Medical Society of London held a meeting on the subject. Edmund Owen FRCS, Surgeon to the Hospital for Sick Children, Great Ormond Street, announced that the lancet and the leech now 'lie together in the same dark tomb'. Most participants disagreed, both with Owen and with each other. Some were convinced that diarrhoea and convulsions were caused by teething, or had seen many cases relieved by lancing the gums. Others dismissed this as 'mere hypothesis'. One thought that children, by sucking the blood from lanced gums, were in danger from loss of blood. At the end Owen commented that the great diversity of opinion justified him in bringing the subject before the society. Even this statement elicited hostile criticism from subsequent correspondents: to one, lancing gums was such a self-evident benefit that he was surprised that anyone thought otherwise, another found it 'incredible' if doctors did not 'accord their chief and most obvious triumphs to the lancet and the gum-lancet', while others evoked John Hunter or repeated the old idea that failing to lance contributed to the high rate of infant mortality.

While the debate among 'experts' raged on, the fashion for lancing gums continued to decline. By 1896 some observers were even going so far as to say that the growth of teeth causes no more symptoms that the growth of hair. In New York the pioneer paediatrician Abraham Jacobi (1830–1919) was drawing attention to the social factors that underlay paediatric problems. In 1898 he announced, 'Lancing the gums has lost most of its charms.'

Child health was improving and infant mortality was falling, but some, especially dentists and pathologists, still regarded teething as potentially pathological and continued to advocate lancing to lessen the danger. There seem to be no records of complications. Most doctors, even when they opposed the operation, seem to have agreed with John Hunter that lancing was never attended by dangerous consequences. In

1918, in the *British Journal of Children's Diseases*, there were still paediatricians who asserted that 'teething can give rise to serious symptoms', including 'diarrhoea, vomiting, eczema, bronchial catarrh, and convulsions, as well as screaming fits and strabismus.' Medical texts, especially those of dentistry, also still advocated gum-lancing. As late as 1938 one of these advised consulting the dental surgeon 'with a view to lancing the gums' and gave instructions about performing the operation. This persistent view among dentists and pathologists may have been related to their striving for professional advancement and recognition.

Belief that teething is a problem remains common, especially among mothers – and attributing high fever to teething rather than more serious illness continues to delay calls to the doctor. Commercial interests still try to foster anxiety in doctors as well as in mothers, yet no one in the West now lances gums. In the developing world, however, there are still myths about teething that lead to lancing. Perceptions of teething are more likely to invoke interference where infant mortality is high, but they are also related to the prevailing structure of medicine, to the state of 'folk' medicine and self-medication, and to changing ideas about the causes of disease in general.

Mastoid

The mastoid process is a hollow, bony prominence in the skull behind the ear. During the eighteenth century a fashion developed in which deafness was treated by opening it, though the mastoid has nothing to do with hearing. In the days before antibiotics, the mastoid process frequently became infected in children in a condition known as mastoiditis. For many years it was fashionable to treat this by puncturing the eardrum.

The development of treatment of the ear, nose and throat was handicapped because it was a regarded as a speciality, which meant that it lacked respectability among the élite of the medical profession, who initially tended to despise specialised medicine as a form of quackery. The problem as it existed in the 1880s was described by one aspirant, Greville MacDonald (1856–1944) in his *Reminiscences of a Specialist* (1932):

> Even a consulting-room in Wimpole Street could not give me a place among the really elect. The Throat Hospital, in spite of its new and irreproachable staff, was still looked upon by a carefully censorious profession as simply *not respectable*. The distrust of this newest specialty in medicine was chiefly due to the prevalent disapproval of specializing in general; for it was considered that all qualified practitioners were competent for everything.

Some advances were made despite the obstacles, however. In 1853 Sir William Wilde of Dublin, a famous Ear, Nose and Throat surgeon and father of Oscar Wilde, recommended incision of the mastoid through the skin to remove pus in serious cases. A few years later it became technically possible to look deep into the ear with the otoscope, and the speciality of otology developed from this. Mastoiditis was common, and the operation of mastoidectomy (removal of the mastoid process) became fashionable and remained so until the arrival of antibiotics – after which mastoiditis became rare. This is an example of a successful and effective medical fashion that became outmoded and unnecessary due to other medical advances.

Masturbation

Many medical fashions have been directed *against* something and none of these has been more popular, more powerful or more vigorously pursued than the fashion for preventing, punishing and 'curing' masturbation. For many years this was a dominant theme in medicine and the campaign against masturbation created one of the most powerful and prevalent medical fashions of the nineteenth and early twentieth centuries. An almost universal belief that masturbation was the cause of much ill health increased in ferocity during the nineteenth century, and amounted among some people almost to frenzy. It became the basis of much Western medicine. Its power was linked to a number of other beliefs and motives, political, ideological, economic and religious. For instance, it linked with religious notions of 'uncleanliness' and bourgeois traditions of self-control set against a background of population growth and the interests of the London venereal trade. Physical and mental symptoms attributed to masturbation were connected with some of people's deepest anxieties concerning virility, gender, identity and personal confidence.

The ancient doctrine of semen conservation has a long philosophical history in Europe and Asia. In Sanskrit semen is equated with *sukra*, the life force. During the eighteenth century the theory of semen conservation re-entered Western medicine. In about 1716 an anonymous tract called *Onania* was published in London. It cited masturbation as a cause of epilepsy, as well as of 'cessation of growth, phimosis, paraphimosis, strangury, priapism, fainting fits, epilepsy, impotence, and in women, fluor albus, hysteric fits, consumption and barrenness'. By 1760 this tract had gone into nineteen English editions and was also published in German and French. What made the anti-masturbation movement really popular in England, however, was the series of famous treatises popularised by a prominent French physician, Simon André Tissot (1728–97). His medical connections increased the influence he had on the profession. Ideas about masturbation became the basis of theories of degeneracy which came to play an important part in medical theory, profoundly affecting ideas about disease in general and about mental disease and hysteria in particular.

The anti-masturbation idea was strongly supported by religious beliefs, despite the fact that the Bible has no definite condemnation of masturbation but only the brief and enigmatic reference to Onan's sin (see Genesis 38). During the eighteenth century, the term 'masturbation' came into use as a condemnation. A moral offence gradually became a 'disease' which was believed to cause a host of other diseases, many of them psychological. In medicine, and particularly in psychiatry, 'causes' are difficult to ascertain and we tend to see them in any activity which is itself thought to be harmful.

The idea that overindulgence in sex is harmful to health is ancient, but none of the classical writers seems to have made specific reference to masturbation. The Church had always preached against it as a 'sin against nature', but without being specific about *why*. Medieval theologians classified it as a mortal sin, but it seems that local confessors treated it as venial. Ignatius Loyola's *Spiritual Exercises* (1548) did not even mention it. Most people considered it a less serious offence than fornication, adultery or sodomy. It became a cause for concern in its own right only from the late sixteenth century. In the 1630s the Puritan divine Richard Capel, in his *Tentations*, declared 'self-pollution' to be the worst and most polluting of all sins of 'uncleanness' and said that it caused bodies to 'rot and weaken'. In 1716 Richard Baxter, a nonconformist divine and author, wrote:

> Those that were never guilty of Fornication, are oft cast into long and lamentable Troubles, by letting Satan once into their phantasies …especially when they are guilty of voluntary active Self-pollution.

Increasingly, discussions of masturbation were accompanied by dramatic descriptions of its harmful physical effects. In 1760 Tissot wrote that it caused cramps, convulsions, epileptic fits, 'vapours', hypochondria, hysteria and melancholy. Later, in the nineteenth century, came the introduction of the idea of 'masturbatory insanity'.

Why did the subject of masturbation become so prominent? There have been various theories. One is that the preoccupation had a social cause, in the light of early puberty and later marriage, but others suggest quite different influences, including a medical profession eager to medicalise the subject and bring it under their expertise. Moreover, it was a subject which easily became connected with some of the most powerful contemporary concerns, moral, religious, social and political. It was even regarded as an epidemic. It linked to new ideas about the body, along with notions of physical integrity, masculine selfhood and control over the body's orifices. During the eighteenth century many Georgian writers wrote of masturbation as a sin, a vice, and a character weakness, and as ruinous to health because it supposedly induced wasting conditions. Reproductive biology increasingly promoted the idea of semen as a vital fluid, and it was believed that wasting it led to adolescent consumptions.

Probably the first doctor to suggest that masturbation was *not* a harmful practice was the British surgeon John Hunter. His views went against what most of his eighteenth-century contemporaries believed. He realised that if there was any harm in masturbation, it came from 'the idea' rather than from the practice, meaning that it was psychological and stemmed from guilt feelings. He denied that the practice led to impotence: 'It appears to me to be far too rare to originate from a practice so general.' After Hunter's death in 1793, a third edition of his *Treatise on the Venereal Disease* was published, edited by his brother-in-law Sir Everard Home. In it Home brought the writing more into line with current thought. He omitted some of the text and suggested that 'onanism' was more harmful than Hunter had suggested.

By the nineteenth century the idea that masturbation caused insanity was firmly fixed in both lay and medical minds. It came to be seen as a social evil, a threat to society, requiring harsh measures to eradicate it. It was a time of increasing prudery and emphasis on respectability. Medicine was increasingly mixed with morality. Lewdness and immorality were seen as threats to middle-class life. The campaign against masturbation became a 'crusade', with pressure on parents to guard their children. In 1816 the distinguished French physician J E D Esquirol (1772–1840) gave his authority to the belief that masturbation led to insanity. 'Masturbation is recognized in all countries as a common cause of insanity,' he wrote. He followed this in more detail in 1822:

Onanism is a grave symptom in mania; unless it stops at once it is an insurmountable obstacle to cure. By lowering the powers of resistance it reduces the patients to a state of stupidity, to phthisis, marasmus and death.

The apparent link between masturbation and insanity was strengthened by the observation (easily made even today) that mental patients, confined and lacking in both inhibitions and occupation, tend to sit and masturbate.

A few professionals doubted the conventional wisdom. One of them was John Gideon Millingen, resident physician to the County of Middlesex Pauper Lunatic Asylum at Hanwell, who wrote:

Masturbation has been considered a very frequent cause of insanity. I doubt it. That this vice is often attendant on the malady, is a well-established fact; that the moral and physical exhaustion that must arise from its indulgence aggravates the disease, is also certain; but I apprehend that it is frequently an effect rather than a cause.

The doubters were lone voices, however. In 1843 the *Lancet* published the case of a testicle that atrophied as a result of excessive masturbation. No one seems to have expressed doubt about the cause. The following year the entry under 'Insanity' in Copeland's *Dictionary of Practical Medicine* referred to exhausting factors that led to insanity, of which masturbation was the greatest.

In 1849 Samuel Grindley Howe (1801–76), an MD of Harvard, a social reformer and founder of the Massachusetts School for Idiotic and Feeble-minded Youth, discussed 'self-abuse' in flowery terms as a cause of idiocy:

One would fain be spared the sickening task of dealing with this disgusting subject; but as he who would exterminate the wild beasts that ravage his fields must not fear to enter their dark and noisome dens, and drag them out of their lair; so he who would rid humanity of a pest must not shrink from dragging it out from its hiding-places, to perish in the light of day.

The attitude of medical leaders reveals much about their individual temperaments. In 1868 the misogynistic Henry Maudsley, founder of the Maudsley Hospital, discussed masturbation in terms of self-indulgence and self-abuse. He wrote of 'that kind of insanity which is brought about by self-abuse', saying, 'Once the habit is formed and the mind has positively suffered from it...the sooner he sinks to his degraded rest the better for himself and the better for the world which is well rid of him.' He went on:

> Nothing is more certain than that either of these causes will produce an enervation of nervous element which, if the exhausting vice be continued, passes by a further declension into degeneration and actual destruction thereof. The habit of self-abuse notably gives rise to a particular and disagreeable form of insanity, characterized by intense self-feeling and conceit, extreme per-version of feeling and corresponding derangement of thought, in the earlier stages, and later by failure of intelligence, nocturnal hallucinations, and suicidal or homicidal propensities.

James Paget (1814–90), one of the most distinguished and original doctors of his day, was also appalled at the idea of masturbation, but his observations were more charitable. He wished he 'could say something worse of so nasty a practice; an uncleanliness, a filthiness forbidden by God, an unmanliness despised by men', but said it did no more harm than any other indulgence in excess and certainly did not lead inevitably to the lunatic asylum. The pioneer surgeon Lawson Tait expressed similar views:

> [The] evil effects of masturbation have been greatly overrated, thanks to a reticence on the part of those who know all about it, and this has permitted a disagreeable subject to fall into the hands of those who live on the ignorance and misfortunes of their fellow beings.

Many other influential figures, however, including Lord Baden-Powell, founder of the scouting movement, held definite and negative views on the subject. Referring to 'self-abuse' in his *Scouting for Boys* (1908), Baden-Powell wrote that it 'brings with it weakness of the head and heart, and if persisted in, idiocy and lunacy'. Sigmund

Freud was another one of those who believed that masturbation could cause illness.

The 'treatment' of masturbation also had its fashions. In the first half of the nineteenth century, it was treated mostly with hydrotherapy, diet and other gentle methods. Then surgery became fashionable, and for a while it was believed that castration helped make the patient more amenable to other forms of treatment. In time the fashion for gentler treatments returned. In 1899, for example, the German physician Hermann Rohleder urged that children who masturbated should be whipped, but 26 years later he had changed his views and advised patience and understanding.

Nowadays masturbation in moderation is seen as normal in both sexes. In excess it is regarded as the result of mental and other disturbances.

Pink disease

Many diseases and medical problems, whether fashionable or not, arise from nonmedical fashions or are made worse by them. An obvious example is smoking, now a well-known cause of cancer and disease of the lungs, heart and circulation. Unsuitable fashionable shoes can lead to foot problems such as corns and bunions, and whenever the fashion for platform shoes recurs, there is an 'epidemic' of broken and sprained ankles. The custom in Japan of eating certain fish has led to outbreaks of poisoning, and eating polished rather than whole rice has led to severe vitamin deficiency (beri-beri) in some countries, even in children of wealthy people. The fashion for junk food has damaged many hearts, and the custom of providing alcohol at every kind of hospitality event doubtless encourages alcoholism.

Pink disease was a curiosity in the history of medicine. It was an unpleasant disease that affected babies between the ages of six months and two years. Doctors in Western countries first noticed it at the end of the nineteenth century and it was common, at least in children's clinics, for the next fifty years. Today, older doctors can remember miserable babies and toddlers, bright pink or red in colour and photophobic, with 'raw beef' hands and feet, loss of appetite and peeling skin. Reports abound of children too miserable to acknowledge their mothers, such as the child who kept repeating, 'I am so sad.' One unhappy mother was quoted as saying, 'My child behaves like a mad dog.' In most cases the condition improved spontaneously, but sometimes it left the child with permanently damaged lungs or kidneys. The death rate from pink disease varied from 5.5 per cent to 33.3 per cent, but was usually about 7 per cent. Although there have now been almost no cases for forty years, there still exists a society for long-term sufferers, many of whom feel angry that their health was destroyed in early childhood.

For half a century paediatricians puzzled over the cause of the disease. Then, in the middle of the twentieth century, it was discovered to be a form of mercury poisoning due in most cases to the fashion for mothers to give teething powders to their babies. This fashion was not new, but during the nineteenth century it increased greatly. The increase coincided with the development of sophisticated methods of advertising by the manufacturers of the teething powders, and increased literacy among mothers meant that many more could read the advertisements.

Why did manufacturers put mercury into babies' teething powders? At first glance it seems an odd and dangerous thing to do. Mercury was known by then to be poisonous. The symptoms and signs of its poisoning were well known to nineteenth-century doctors, though people do not seem to have related these signs to the children suffering from pink disease. (The signs of mercury poisoning included tender teeth and inflamed gums – just the symptoms for which mothers gave their children teething powders in the first place.) Mercury had been known to ancient Arabian physicians and was recognised as a powerful drug in the sixteenth century, most notably by Paracelsus, who popularised calomel, a common form of the drug. Before the days of antibiotics, mercury salts were used as a powerful antibacterial substance, probably the most powerful known. The *British Pharmacopaeia* for 1910 listed 25 mercurial preparations and stated that one part in 2,000, the strength commonly employed in surgery, 'kills all known bacteria'. It warned of its danger to the kidney and in scarlet fever and eclampsia, and also of chronic poisoning 'in certain trades'. The tradesmen most commonly affected by mercury poisoning were the hatters, and the disease was known as 'hatters' shakes'. In eighteenth-century America, Benjamin Rush even induced mercury poisoning as part of the treatment for many diseases.

Why did it take so long to discover the cause of pink disease? The answer tells us much about medical thinking and medical fashion.

Describing and recognising the disease was indeed a slow process, and in the course of it one can trace trends in medical thought as they grew and changed. Pink disease was first described fully in 1903 by P Selter, a German, though it had been recognised in Australia several decades earlier. There seems to have been little interest in trying to understand the disease, however. Nonetheless, a fact that was obvious to anyone who studied it was that, although in English-speaking countries patients were usually aged between six months and two years, in German-speaking countries they were usually older, perhaps five or six years old. This important observation seems to have made little impression at the time. Later it turned out that in countries where children with pink disease were older, the cause was usually not teething powders but similarly marketed worming medicines (*Wurmschokolade* in German).

In 1914 an Australian doctor called A J Wood came to England to discuss the subject with the English paediatricians George Frederick Still and Archibald Garrod. They both agreed that they recognised the symptoms, but had no idea of its cause or pathology and knew of no literature on the subject. Wood began to search for more cases in his native Australia. By 1920 he had collected 88 cases, of whom the oldest was three years and six months old and the youngest four months. Most were between six and eighteen months old. By 1935 he had found at least 140 cases and discovered that 'it was not a new disease in Australia for during the last fifty years it has been recognized by medical men specializing in diseases of children in Melbourne and Sydney'. Following current thinking, he believed that the disease was probably 'either a passing bacterial invasion leaving a trail of disordered body function, or else a prolonged mild infection which has evoked but little reaction'.

This was before the days of antibiotics, and infection was still a serious problem. Wood thought that the infecting organism might be a virus 'which is widely spread throughout the community in a non-pathogenic state', through carriers who might 'react slightly from time to time' and thus produce immune bodies. Occasionally the organism would assume a pathogenic role 'in a highly susceptible individual, usually a child aged between eight and eighteen months'. This was a time when the fashion for diagnosing virus infection for unknown causes – still widespread today – was just developing.

In 1920 the disease was discovered independently in three separate areas in the United States, where it was described as 'a polyneuritic syndrome resembling pellagra-acrodynia' that had occurred in seventeen patients. In 1921 a Dr Brown of Toronto considered the disease as more or less like pellagra. Agreeing with this, a Canadian paediatrician wrote some years later from Niagara Falls to say, 'We see a great deal of this disease owing to our long winter.' He added, 'It is undoubtedly a primary infection.' What made it 'undoubtedly' infectious was the current fashion for attributing the unknown to viruses.

Pink disease was first reported as a distinct, recognised disease in England in 1922. In 1923 it was described as a 'peculiar neurosis of the vegetative nervous system in young children'. In 1930 the Australian H Swift advocated artificial sunlight and wrote later that this treatment 'was as nearly as specific as it is possible at present to obtain'.

Pink disease was becoming important. In 1931 the sixth edition of *The Nomenclature of Disease* (drawn up by a Joint Committee appointed by the Royal College of Physicians of London) included it for the first time, listing it under 'Disease due to disorders of Nutrition or of Metabolism'. In 1933 C Rocaz of Bordeaux thought it was 'probably of infectious origin...one of that group of diseases which appear intermittently in this world...apt to be signalled as new diseases...' He wondered whether it was the same as an epidemic in Paris in 1828, but decided that it was more like pellagra. He noted (as did many after him) that it often appeared in healthy breast-fed babies, and suggested that it was due to 'an unknown neurotropic virus which produces diffuse lesions in the central nervous system and the vegetative nervous system.' He added that this view 'now seems to be definitely established.' There was no firm evidence to justify this conclusion. He probably came to it because it was a currently fashionable theory to explain mysterious diseases. He did not try to explain why the disease was more or less confined to babies and toddlers. The story emphasises that fashions in diagnosis are usually related to other currently fashionable ideas. Thus does fashion lead to fashion and influence other fashions!

Pink disease entered the medical literature during a period when the idealisation of childhood, so prominent in the second half of the nineteenth century, was giving way to political concern for the health of children in the face of national decline and depopulation. As the twentieth century got under way, the belief was growing that the influences of childhood to a large extent determine the events of adult life. The new century was to be 'the century of the child' as depicted in Ellen Key's influential book of that title. The same year, 1900, Margaret McMillan's *Early Childhood* was published. During the nineteenth century the first European hospitals for children had been founded, including the Hôpital des Enfants Malades in Paris in 1802 and the Hospital for Sick Children, Great Ormond Street in London in 1852.

Children were becoming popular patients. It may seem odd that pink disease had not been publicised earlier, but it may be that no doctor had seen enough cases to describe it. Until the acceptance of the germ theory most of the young patients admitted to these hospitals suffered from longer-term or chronic, rather than acute, illnesses.

Once it had been described, pink disease was soon reported in nearly every developed country in the world, with a preponderance of cases in certain areas, particularly Australia, North America and Central Europe. Pink disease baffled the doctors. Its origin was unknown, but its similarities with pellagra (a nutritional disease identified in 1914 as being due to lack of vitamin B) led some people to maintain that faulty nutrition might be a cause – despite the fact that most of the patients with pink disease seemed to be perfectly well nourished. The fashionable pathology of the time was infection, and most people continued to hold to this as a cause.

Little thought was given at the time to the influence of social (as opposed to occupational) influences, so it is not surprising that no one seems to have considered the current social customs that affected children, and speculated publicly on why a 'virus' should be confined to so narrow an age group. Furthermore, little was written in the medical literature about maternal customs and folk remedies in child-rearing, and it seems likely that the doctors concerned did not think of them. It was noted that the disease occurred where there were water courses, that sometimes several children in a family were affected (leading to the idea that it was 'hereditary'), and that it often developed after infectious illness. Rocaz concluded that diet was 'probably of no essential significance'. No one seems to have suggested that it might be due to poisoning, and at least one consultant at Great Ormond Street, Sir James Goodhart, actually advised his students to treat cases of difficult teething with the mercury powders that were eventually to be revealed as the cause of the disease.

In 1922 the American John Zahorsky did comment on the similarity of pink disease with mercury poisoning, saying that several of his patients 'had been given large doses of calomel at the outset of the disease, and the swollen gums, loosened teeth, with salivation, gave support to this.' He dismissed the theory, however, because 'cases were encountered in which no history of calomel administration could be elicited.' He decided instead that 'some powerful protein poison must be present.'

It is interesting to see that, having devised an unfashionable theory to explain the disease, Zahorsky was so easily deflected from it. Why was he deterred from pursuing the idea? It is hard to maintain a theory which is alien to contemporary thinking, and a tentative originator of such a theory may be put off more easily than might be the case with a theory that matches current beliefs more closely. At that time, theories of nutritional deficiency or virus infection were more likely to be accepted than any new theory. Similarly, although the idea of poisoning was suggested from time to time, the idea that the disease might be due to something that mothers gave their children was not part of medical or lay thinking at the time. There was still much idealisation of mothers and their role, and the suggestion that they might – even unwittingly – be harming their children would have been difficult to accept. Furthermore, doctors did not usually occupy themselves with the small details of their patients' daily lives. They were more attuned to 'scientific' causes, particularly those that might be adduced from tests in the increasingly important laboratories, rather than inferred from conversations with their patients.

At the time when all these discussions about pink disease were taking place, the sales of patent medicines were increasing rapidly and the British Medical Association was concerned about the inherent dangers. Despite its vigorous campaign, however, achieving the regulation of patent medicines was a long, slow process. In the last third of the nineteenth century, patent medicines in Britain were relatively free from control, and the campaign against them was aimed largely at preparations that contained opium. These preparations became increasingly difficult to obtain as the concentrated campaign slowly took effect, while those containing active constituents such as mercury benefited from the relative lack of regulatory attention. Among those advertised were teething powders, some of which 'sold in very large numbers'. The BMA simply hoped that 'the spread of instruction as to the common-sense management of infants' would 'gradually lead to a great diminution in the custom so prevalent among the poorer classes of dosing infants.'

In 1904 the *British Medical Journal* began a specific and energetic campaign against what it called 'secret remedies'. This culminated in the publication in 1909 of its successful book *Secret Remedies*, which sold over 62,000 copies in less than a year. Among the preparations it criticised were teething powders, supposed to soothe babies' pain but which actually poisoned.

The advertisements and accompanying circulars for mercurial teething powders emphasised the dangers of teething and the teething period. The leaflet that accompanied packets of Stedman's teething powders, for example, suggested subtly that babies were liable to die unless they were given the powders. It informed its customers:

> The returns of the Registrar-General tell us that the period of Dentition is one of more than ordinary peril to the child... [W]e may fairly congratulate ourselves when this time of Teething is past. To pass this time safely, and with the least risk to the child, one of 'Stedman's Teething Powders' should be given about twice a week, during the whole time of Dentition.

Another type of teething powder emphasised the good effects of 'Fifty Years' Experience' of this 'Much-Valued Medicine', while yet another boasted:

> The constantly increasing sale of these justly esteemed Powders proves them to be the most effectual Medicine that can be given to young children during the troublesome and anxious period of teething.

These advertisements were taking advantage of the ancient belief – among both medical and lay people – that teething was a dangerous process requiring medication.

By 1935 there was still no convincing evidence about the cause of pink disease. In that year the Annual Meeting of the British Medical Association was held in Melbourne, and much time was given to the condition. A J Wood began by discussing the possible causes of the disease as first, vitamin deficiency, second, light hypersensitivity, and third, infection – 'maybe a virus which is widely spread throughout the community in a non-pathogenic state'. Dr S F McDonald of Brisbane supported the idea of a neurotropic virus. He said that several cases sometimes occurred in the same family, and that one attack seemed to bring on a lifelong immunity. He had treated sixteen cases with liver, with very good results. Dr Robert Southby of Melbourne also supported the idea of the neurotropic virus by mentioning its apparent close analogy with poliomyelitis and the predisposition in certain families to this type of infection. He had treated some patients with pooled normal human serum. Dame Jean Connor, a physician from Melbourne, suggested that it 'might be due to contact with some substance which was innocuous until the patient was exposed to light', and she drew an analogy with the effect on lambs of the active principle of St John's Wort, which led to erythema (redness) and urticaria (hives). Dr Robert Hutchinson, assistant physician to the London Hospital and to the Hospital for Sick Children, Great Ormond Street, had difficulty in accepting either the infective theory or the deficiency theory, but had no positive alternative suggestion. Dr Ian Wood, also of Melbourne, said that the search for a virus had been unsuccessful. The Australian physician Sweet referred to 'this fascinating but elusive complaint'. No one was any the wiser.

In 1938 the English paediatrician J C Spence (1892–1954) of Newcastle put forward a new idea. He wrote:

> Many observers have remarked that it is more likely to occur in the children of well-cared-for families than in those of poverty-stricken families; further, in so many instances the infant's diet has been reinforced by orange juice, cod-liver oil, Marmite, and other foods rich in vitamins that the possibility that it is a disease of over-nutrition must be considered.

This emphasises a situation in which it seems that no one yet had a mental image of poisoning as a possible cause of disease in children. It required radical thinking to extend ideas about what had hitherto been regarded as an occupational disease.

The mystery began to be solved in 1945 by Josef Warkany (1902–92) of the Cincinnati Children's Hospital. He and his assistant, Donald Hubbard, found large amounts of mercury in the urine of a child with pink disease. They did not publish their findings until 1948, however, and it is noteworthy that the news seems not to have spread through the small and tightly knit paediatric world, where everyone knew everyone else. Ideas contrary to those prevailing tend *not* to spread.

In 1947 Guido Fanconi (another paediatrician famous for original thought) and others reported pink disease in 39 children who were known to have received calomel as a treatment for worms. Pink disease usually developed on the eighth day after administration and led to varied eruptions and other typical signs. The connection was not pursued.

In the same year the World Health Organisation's *International Classification of Disease* classified pink disease under 'Diseases of Nerves and Peripheral Ganglia'. In 1949 the fourth edition of Paterson and Moncrieff's textbook classified it under 'Organic Diseases of the Nervous System' as 'an encephalo-myelitis'. The section called 'Aetiology' included the 'social' factors of age, seasonal incidence, sexual equality and grouping. The only comment regarding the possible cause was, 'There is no evidence that diet or lack of vitamins plays any part in the causation of pink disease.' It also commented on its 'similarity to other forms of encephalomyelitis of virus origin that opinion in this country, America and France is in favour of an infective agent, probably a neurotropic virus'.

By 1950, much evidence had been published incriminating mercury as the cause of pink disease, but Alan Moncrieff, Professor of Child health at the Hospital for Sick Children, Great Ormond Street, and medical correspondent of *The Times*, was not convinced. In an article on the subject in the eighth edition of Price's *Textbook of the Practice of Medicine* (1950), he mentioned the opposing theories of exposure to and protection from sunlight, but he did not mention mercury. He wrote that pink disease was 'generally ascribed to the effects of a widely diffused toxin which shows a predilection for the autonomic nervous system' and concluded, 'The balance of present evidence favours a virus.' He only mentioned mercury in passing in the next edition of Price's textbook, in 1956: 'Mercury poisoning has been blamed, especially in the USA, following the use of teething powders containing calomel, but very many babies are given such powders and do not develop pink disease.'

In the United States, by contrast, the idea was gaining ground. Emmett Holt's textbook *The Diseases of Infancy and Childhood* (1940) was among the first to acknowledge the work of Warkany. In 1951 Warkany and Hubbard strengthened their theory when they reported on 41 children with pink disease from all over the United States. There was mercury in the urine of 38 of them (92 per cent) compared with 15 per cent of the controls. The source of the mercury was teething powders or diaper rinse. In the same year, an important British textbook on paediatrics presented the Warkany and Hubbard work as a new theory which it was 'too early to assess'. A new British textbook published the following year made no mention of pink disease at all.

In 1953 Dr Murray H Bass, consulting paediatrician to the Mount Sinai Hospital, New York, writing in Holt's textbook, wondered whether mercury was 'the only etiological factor' and remarked, 'No satisfactory explanation has been advanced for the failure of acrodynia [pink disease] to be recognized during the many decades of the nineteenth century when calomel was administered almost routinely to any infant or child with fever.' Still no one seemed to have considered social conditions such as the huge increase in advertising and in sales of patent medicines during the last decades of the nineteenth century, and the increased literacy of mothers after the introduction of compulsory education in 1870. Such thoughts were not part of the medical thinking of the time.

   The theory that mercury poisoning caused pink disease was gradually accepted, but against much resistance, as are most new ideas. The story raises an interesting point about traditional attitudes of the medical profession towards defined diseases and new knowledge. Reading the textbooks and professional journals of the day, it is striking how much interest was shown in diagnosis and the delineation of new or rare diseases and how little in their causes. The tradition was not to separate cause from effect, and many doctors were content to describe diseases without speculating on their origins. In textbooks of the time, many sections entitled 'Aetiology' were no more than descriptions of age group, sex and social class and did not even speculate on origins or causation, let alone provide any firm facts. Any speculations that were included were frequently confined to the main interests of the moment without involving wider considerations. In the early twentieth century, when pink disease first generated interest, the general focus was on infection, viruses had recently been discovered and speculation about nutrition was just beginning. A diagnostic scheme taught to generations of medical students and probably dating from this time ran: 'Congenital; traumatic; infective – acute; infective – chronic; neo-plastic; degenerative.' There was no mention of nutrition, poisoning or psychogenic influences. This scheme was still used in the 1950s and reflected the profession's relative lack of interest in causes. Obscure and speculative 'viruses' were often considered adequate explanation, just as they are with many lay people today. The word 'idiopathic', used in the sense of 'origin unknown', was freely used, as though that was sufficient and satisfactory explanation.

   It is also interesting to note that doctors showed little or no interest in the medicines that their patients were receiving outside their own professional fields. They did not, for example, consider what the children might have been given by their mothers in their 'search' for causes. Although pink disease came to the fore at precisely the time when the British Medical Association was campaigning to control patent medicines on the grounds that they were dangerous, and although the symptoms and signs of pink disease were the same as those of mercury poisoning, it was nearly half a century before anyone made the connection. The resistance to the evidence that the disease was caused by mercury poisoning declined only when the opponents and sceptics grew old and disappeared from the scene. The tendency of people and professions to create such static situations is well documented.

Eventually there was change, albeit slow. In 1957, for instance, the *WHO International Classification of Disease* still listed pink disease under 'Diseases of the nervous system and sense organs', with the subheading 'Erythroedema polyneuritica: Acrodynia, Pink disease, erythroedema polyneuritica, Swift's disease'. In 1958, for the first time, *British Pharmacopeia* omitted calomel, the main source of mercury poisoning in children. In 1960 the Royal College of Physicians listed pink disease as both 'Disease of skin' and 'Disease of undetermined cause'. It mentioned mercury poisoning and gingivitis as caused by mercury, but did not mention a link with pink disease. Perhaps significantly, in contrast to the section on dermatology, it mentioned no author as having written the section on poisoning, perhaps another indication of the lack of interest in poisons as causes of illness. In 1967 the *WHO International Classification of Disease* listed pink disease in the index (though not in the text) in the section for 'Injury and Poisoning' under 'Toxic effects of substances chiefly non-medical as to source', and 'Mercury compounds'. This was repeated over some years.

The message was getting through, and at last it seemed that pink disease might become a thing of the past. Mercury was withdrawn from most teething powders after 1954, initially through voluntary action by the manufacturers after adverse publicity. Later in the decade the theory had become widely accepted, and soon babies with pink disease were rarely seen.

It did not disappear altogether, however. Cases are still reported from time to time. Calomel continued to be used and to cause poisoning. The last mercurial compounds were removed from the *British Pharmacopeia* only in 1958. Anxiety about the toxicity of mercury reappeared in the context of dental amalgam fillings and contact with mercury vapour. There have also been instances of chemists selling old teething powders. Incidents of mercury poisoning have been caused by absorption of mercury in dusting powders through broken skin and from house paint. Other forms of chronic mercury poisoning have been reported from time to time, for example primary renal tubular acidosis and Minemata disease. A description of a child poisoned by mercury spilled by his father reminded the medical profession of the continued presence of mercury in children's environments. But at least the connection of the disease with the fashion for teething powders was broken.

For many years that seemed to be the end of the story. Then, in 1993, an article appeared in the *British Medical Journal* that brought it to life again. It was a report on Young's syndrome, a condition of infertility due to lack of sperm in men with chronic chest disease, first described in 1970. These men formed a large proportion (45 per cent) of 274 azoospermic men who attended a single urologist and had genital operations at a London hospital. W F Hendry, the surgeon, noticed that many of them mentioned that as children they had suffered from pink disease. It was also known that mercury poisoning damages the cilia, the tiny, waving structures that move small objects through the nose, bronchi, fallopian tubes and male epididymis. Hendry postulated that, if the damaged cilia were the result of pink disease, there would be a higher proportion of men born before 1955 with the condition than there would be of those born later. This proved to be the case. Moreover, the sale of calomel had been discouraged by the Food and Drug Administration in the United States from 1933, and few examples of Young's syndrome have been reported there.

Pink disease can, like some other diseases, be viewed as a social disease exacerbated by a fashion, exploited by manufacturers. It shows the importance of social factors, and offers an insight into the medical profession and its way of thinking during the early twentieth century. First, there was the centuries-old tradition of using mercury to treat many disorders, including those in small children. Second, there was the traditional fear of teething and its 'dangers', which was widespread in the community and from which even progressive medical men were unable to free themselves. These fears were increased and perpetuated by the high death rate in children aged from six months to two years which, inevitably, was associated in people's minds with teething. The social circumstances that perpetuated this mortality rate have been widely discussed. They include urbanisation and its problems, particularly with drainage and sewage, poor living conditions and sanitation, poor diet and dietary ignorance, general poverty and ubiquitous, uncontrolled infection. Third, exploitation by manufacturers of patent medicines also played a part. This was increased by new and sophisticated techniques of advertising and the failure of the medical profession to persuade the government of the day to control the patent medicine trade and make it safer. The effect of this may have been increased by a fourth factor, education. Between 1840 and 1900 levels of illiteracy in adult women fell from 50 per cent to 10 per cent. This meant that more mothers could now read the advertisements for mercury powders.

Increasing specialisation in medicine and the development of outpatient clinics led to numbers of similar cases being seen by the same doctors, so that less common but nevertheless specific conditions were more likely to be recognised. Yet the attitudes and customs of the medical profession and their sometimes rigid modes of thought inhibited a realisation of the true cause of the disease. The problem awaited someone like Josef Warkany, knowledgeable in the field yet capable of stepping outside the conventional wisdom of the day. It is perhaps depressing that everyone else seems to have been content with speculating on the relative merits of well-worn paths of thought.

The disease is also remarkable because evidence suggests that in some cases it has caused adults to suffer from chronic chest disease and infertility. Other childhood diseases have long-term consequences (e.g. polio, rickets, rubella), but who would have thought that the actions of mothers following fashionable patterns of behaviour in trying to help their teething infants could have had such devastating and long-term effects on their children?

There seems to be no publication as yet concerning the possible long-term effects of pink disease on women. Yet cilia, the structures damaged by mercury, are also found in the female genital tract, where they waft the ova gently down the fallopian tubes. Tubal failure is often attributed to other causes, including infections such as gonorrhoea. Some women feel ashamed and believe that the problem is their 'fault'. It may be, however, that pink disease in childhood will turn out to be the cause of their infertility, just as it may be the cause of some cases of kidney failure in adults.

Ptosis

Ptosis was a strange fashion in medicine which developed as a result of a misleading interpretation. In the second half of the nineteenth century the idea grew that each organ of the abdomen had a fixed place in the body and caused symptoms if it moved, so that it then needed to be treated. The Frenchman Frantz Glénard (1848–1920) described the condition in detail.

It is not difficult to see how this idea became popular. The Victorians liked things to be neat and tidy. A favourite motto was, 'A place for everything and everything in its place.' It was a period when surgery was developing rapidly and practical anatomy, in the form of dissecting dead bodies, was becoming common. Without an understanding of the principles of sepsis, however, it was generally still too dangerous to operate on the living abdomen, so its interior was rarely seen. Thus surgeons had plenty of experience of dead abdomens and little or none of living ones. Bodies immersed in preservative are stiff, and the position of organs relative to other organs is therefore constant. In the living body, most parts are also generally in a fixed relationship with each other, but in the abdomen the gut moves constantly and it is misleading to give precise details of how the positions of the different organs relate to each other. Even the 'fixed' organs, such as the kidney, are slightly movable. The stomach and intestine move extensively during digestion. Modern medical students are taught to examine the kidney by moving it, but at one time it was believed that mobility was abnormal.

Nineteenth-century doctors believed that if the position of an organ differed from what was regarded as standard in a corpse, this was abnormal and the cause of adverse symptoms. *Gray's Anatomy*, first published in 1858 and regarded as an anatomical bible ever since, gave precise relationships for all the organs of the abdomen – and it still does.

It was believed that when an organ became displaced, because of the influence of gravity it 'slipped' downwards. Hence the process came to be known as 'ptosis', from the Greek word for 'slipping'. The idea grew just as the practice of surgery was becoming safer and developing rapidly. Surgeons were seeking new operations, many of which concerned the abdomen. At that time women had few opportunities in education or work and many developed a preoccupation with ill health and multiple symptoms. The idea of ptosis became fashionable and led to the invention of many new operations which were, like so many before them, mostly performed on women, in a proportion of seven or eight to one man.

In the late nineteenth century the belief that the condition of abdominal ptosis both existed and was abnormal gradually merged with other endemic ideas such as 'putrefaction', 'infection' and 'poisoning'. These ideas helped to form new syndromes, 'diseases' and 'disorders', such as 'intestinal poisoning', 'focal sepsis' and 'chronic appendicitis', and such lines of thought mixed with ideas of stasis, chronic obstruction, autointoxication and the belief that retarded gut movement had bad consequences. The changes were influenced by increasing knowledge (not all of it accurate) and awareness of germs and the revelation that at least some of them could kill or damage the human body. Nevertheless, the 'pure' (if one can call it that) idea of ptosis persisted. The concept of the abdominal organs 'slipping' or 'dropping' can be seen down the years, and traces of it can still be found today.

In 1914 the subject clearly took someone's fancy at the *Lancet*, which published a curious little editorial on the subject. Called 'Floating Kidney', it pointed out that 'this affection' occasionally 'gives rise to such unusual symptoms that even a clever diagnostician may be deceived and his mind led to think of diseases entirely different'. It mentioned 'biliary colic and jaundice' (from 'decompression of the duodenum'), 'congested states of the appendix and pelvic organs', ptyalism (excessive salivation, thought to be due to 'irritation of the salivary glands through the sympathetic'), 'sciatica and pain when lying on the sound side', also 'polyuria, mucous colitis, and paralysis of the lower limbs'. It then described a 'further unusual and, it appears, hitherto unrecorded symptom', which had recently been published in Italy:

A young woman who presented all the usual symptoms and physical signs of floating kidney on the right side complained also of continuous pain in the spine. Further investigations disclosed the fact that when asked to pick up an object from the ground she was unable to do so without bending the leg on the thigh and the thigh on the abdomen of the left side and keeping the right leg extended. An operation...discovered the right kidney not much enlarged but surrounded by many adhesions. The author's explanation of the phenomenon is that the right kidney had, owing to its mobility, developed a condition of irritation which resulted in a slight paranephritis, as shown by the adhesions found at operation. As the psoas muscle is inserted into the lateral aspect of the bodies of the twelfth dorsal and first four lumbar vertebrae, the displaced kidney came to occupy a position on that muscle, which contracted when the patient flexed the thigh on the abdomen and caused pain. The existence of any spinal lesion was disproved by the fact that this unusual symptom disappeared after the operation.

Here the article ends abruptly, a neat piece of gobbledegook and spurious and mechanistic rationalisation without comment or discussion.

Those who continued to concern themselves with ptosis were not only surgeons who could not keep up with the times. Some were innovative and anxious to improve techniques and results. Some even continued to invent new operations for the condition, such as one designed in 1914 to 'guarantee against recurrence of undue mobility' and 'an assurance that the fixation shall be satisfactory, by restoring and maintaining the normal position of the organ'. The operation consisted of sewing the 'offending' kidney to the wall of the abdomen. It was called nephropexy.

There are many other examples demonstrating that the study of ptosis continued to flourish. At a meeting of the Urological Section of the Royal Society of Medicine in London on 28 October 1920, the surgeon Victor Bonney described a new operation for fixation of the kidney. In 1927 a new book on clinical diagnosis contained a section on 'enteroptosis', a word that covered all forms of ptosis of the gut. At least until 1928 it was a common operation in many hospitals, especially the Glasgow Royal Infirmary.

The first edition of Price's *Textbook of the Practice of Medicine* (1922) devoted four pages to movable kidney and also contained a six-page article on the subject of dropped visceral organs by the British expert Sir Arthur Hurst (1879–1944), who had done original research into the subject. He was a strong critic of 'unnecessary' abdominal surgery, but at first he did not doubt the existence or importance of ptosis (though he later revised this idea), which, he wrote, 'is most frequently due to a fall in intra-abdominal pressure caused by weakness of the abdominal and pelvic muscles, the normal tone of which maintains the viscera in position.' He went on:

> The degree of ptosis of the different organs depends upon their weight and upon the length and elasticity of their peritoneal attachments, which in the absence of their natural support, act as true ligaments... It is possible...that the general effects are commonly of more importance than those due to ptosis of individual organs.

He devoted several pages to diagnosis and treatment and was in favour of 'exercise and Swedish gymnastics' as well as 'abdominal support' and 'small meals'. Hurst was, however, adamant about surgery: 'In no circumstances should any operation be performed for fixing dropped viscera.' He did modify this statement:

> ...except incidentally in the case of the caecum and ascending colon when an appendicectomy or appendicostomy is performed and a pelvic caecum has given rise to unpleasant symptoms, and in certain cases of nephroptosis.

But then he becomes firm again:

> ...the effect of such operations is rarely permanent, and the neurasthenic condition of many of the patients makes surgical interference of any kind most undesirable.

Nonetheless, he feared there were exceptions to this rule. It is difficult to write a textbook so that everyone will be satisfied – Hurst was more forthright when lecturing at his own hospital. Meanwhile, he continued:

> Short-circuiting operations are very rarely required for the purpose of overcoming kinks in the alimentary canal. [Here he seems to

have changed the subject.] Gastro-enterostomy is never followed by any improvements in cases of gastroptosis; in rare cases of severe kinking at the splenic flexure a short-circuiting operation, such as an anastomosis between its limbs, may be required, and the results obtained are generally satisfactory.

Price's *Textbook* has long been one of the most popular for both medical students and graduate doctors working for higher examinations. Yet this confusing entry remained much the same for a large part of the twentieth century – while 'ptosis' was increasingly regarded as a normal anatomical variation rather than as an abnormal condition or 'disease'. By the sixth edition, in 1937, Hurst, now with long experience behind him, showed his increasing scepticism.

In no circumstances should any operation be performed for raising dropped viscera. I have never seen the slightest benefit follow, and the anxious mental condition of many of the patients makes surgical interference of any kind most undesirable.

There are now no ifs or buts. He knows what he thinks and he says so, confident that medical public opinion is behind him. Commenting on this in his autobiography, he wrote:

In the first editions a good deal of what I wrote was founded on tradition which had been handed on from one text book to another. In the later editions there is scarcely a single statement for which I cannot vouch from my own knowledge.

Hurst died in 1944 and his section of Price's *Textbook* was taken over by others. In the ninth edition (1956), his article was slightly shortened and the phrase 'Kidney belts and special pads to support the movable kidney are no good' was inserted. By 1973 all mention of visceroptosis had disappeared.

In the specialised literature, the most important comprehensive contribution to the subject of visceroptosis was probably a book by R C Coffey, published in 1923. Coffey was surgeon in chief at Portland Surgical Hospital, Oregon, and 'clinician in surgery' to the University of Oregon Medical Department. He was asked by the Editorial Committee on Surgical Monographs of Appleton and Company to write a monograph on gastro-enteroptosis. Before signing the contract he consulted friends. 'Almost with one accord, the advice was against it, some thinking the subject was too trivial, others that it was too dangerous.' He went ahead anyway. *Gastro-Enteroptosis* begins with an 'Appreciatory Note' by the British surgeon Berkeley Moynihan (1865–1936), who, Coffey says, 'probably has as large a perspective on the surgical problems of the abdomen as any one in the world.' The book seems to have been the product of mutual admiration. Moynihan urged Coffey to write it by mentioning 'a number of London surgeons who were working along this line', and suggested that he ignore the critics:

> 'For,' said he, 'they know that in the mountain of rubbish there is a gem of purest truth. There are so many men about these days who seem to consider this a proper subject to drivel over, it is high time that some one, who above all must be a sane man, should burn the rubbish and cherish and preserve the truth.' After this encouraging and highly complimentary statement, the contract for the production of the monograph was signed.

In his contribution to the book, Berkeley Moynihan pointed out that operations formerly of 'great difficulty' were now 'standardised' and 'a fairly simple matter'.

> The surgeons [*sic*] greatest task now is to decide in what circumstances an operation should be performed or avoided... This facility in the conduct of operations has led sometimes to their performance by surgeons of little skill and of less wisdom, with the result that an operation has perhaps suffered eclipse and become discredited, not for any defects in it as a technical procedure, but in consequence of its improper application to the individual case.

Moynihan then turned to 'the whole subject of visceral prolapse', which he said was:

> ...as difficult a surgical subject from which to unravel the truth as any with which I am familiar... Here is material in abundance for the surgical adventurer. Regardless of all else, the stomach may be lifted up and fixed by suture, the kidney anchored to the last rib,

and constipation for the moment relieved by a short-circuiting or abstracting operation.

He continued this tale of disaster:

> The lot of the patients is hard. Constipation will soon return, the other kidney will fall down or the anchored one break loose, and the distress of the fixed stomach greatly exceed that felt in its vagrant days...

Coffey tried to give a history of gastro-enteroptosis, its surgery and his own experience with it. He first operated for gastroptosis in 1901 and for ten years, he said, 'my surgical efforts were limited to bedridden patients who were approaching the terminal stages of this condition and were suffering from the end results.' Since the condition is now believed not to exist or at least not to be harmful, let alone 'terminal', one can only speculate about the conditions from which these patients suffered.

Coffey made several trips to Europe. He wrote of his visits in 1912 and 1913, 'I observed that my medical colleagues were producing very remarkable results by forced feeding, fattening, and by certain exercises and orthopedic measures,' and he realised that x-ray studies were showing the importance of fat in the aetiology of ptosis. In December 1913 he delivered the Muetter Lecture in Philadelphia, in which he gave his 'conception of the ptosis question', his intention being 'to present the fundamental underlying truths for the consideration of a group of highly trained specialists, both medical and surgical'. However:

> Owing to the hostile criticism of anything pertaining to this question, by many of the leading men of the country, I decided not to publish the lecture until sentiment had somewhat softened.

He believed that the time to publish had now come 'in view of the fact that the most hostile critics must now concede that there is something very important in the subject.' Nonetheless, he admitted that 'no new fundamental principles have developed since the delivery of the lecture', and that significant clinical work had been done in the intervening nine years by only 'a few individuals in this country and in England', all of whose reports were 'favourable'. He cited, among others, George Waugh's article in the *British Journal of Surgery* reporting nearly three hundred cases of colopexy (fixation of the colon), as 'Right-Sided Ptosis', and Rovsing's 'many hundreds of cases of what may be termed "Mid-line Ptosis" '. He said, 'Men of ability and vision have been earnestly working on this question for a generation.' Like Moynihan, he warned against unscrupulous surgeons:

> I concede that in bringing forward this subject of ptosis and stasis, we are opening one of the most dangerous fields for surgical abuses that has ever been opened to the surgical 'confidence man', who needs no other excuse for performing a surgical operation than the consent of the patient.

He believed that the use of x-rays could increase these dangers:

> X-ray observation is of inestimable value in the study of these cases, but is, I concede, the most dangerous agent yet placed at the disposal of the unscrupulous surgeon, because it is so convincing to the laity, and at the same time so meaningless when considered independently of the history of the case, and not properly interpreted.

He adds, in perhaps the sternest warning of all:

> This warning is necessary because of the fact that there are probably more people afflicted with this abnormality than with any other disease known to human-kind, there being probably fully twenty per cent of individuals who are potentially ptotic.

This was a dire warning about a disease that did not exist – but ptosis was very much a disease to Coffey, and one of the most common and important. He gives the impression of being a thoughtful and vigilant, if overenthusiastic, surgeon. His book contained more than three hundred pages, discussed every aspect and surveyed all the literature. The 'disease' of ptosis is not even mentioned in the textbooks today, yet in the early twentieth century no one seems to have doubted its reality. Disagreements were about the treatment, not the existence, of the condition.

Coffey ranged over almost every possible aspect of the subject according to scientific and mechanical knowledge at the time. He gives detailed descriptions of the anatomy and physiology of the abdomen, its shape, structure, suspensory supports, intra-abdominal and intravisceral pressures, motility, function, development and pathology, including bacteriology, toxicology and mechanics. He describes 'abdominal ptosis', 'general ptosis', 'right-sided ptosis', 'mid-line ptosis' and even 'Virginal Gastrocoloptosis' as well as 'Maternal Gastrocoloptosis'. Most of these conditions are illustrated with elegant drawings, many of them of abdominal dissections and most of them, to the modern mind, incomprehensible or at least unconvincing as demonstrations of disease. Of special interest to us here are two chapters towards the end of the book, 'Intestinal Stasis and Radical Surgery' and 'General Indications for Surgical Treatment'. He aligned the subject of ptosis with that of stasis and the current beliefs that serious disease was caused by the absorption of bacteria from the gut. He was, however, 'unable to see any convincing proof that such diseases as cancer of the breast, tuberculosis, ulcer and cancer of the stomach are directly caused by bacterial absorption from the alimentary canal'. Coffey believed that 'the harmful effects of stasis are chemical more than bacterial'.

We do not know how many people had major surgery for ptosis or what they suffered as a result. Coffey confidently went on to describe various other surgical operations and techniques, ending with the view that:

> ...if any radical operation is absolutely required for intestinal stasis...the removal of the ascending and first half of the transverse colon should be the operation of choice.

He attached a diagram and added:

> The operation is easy, the ileocaecal valve is preserved, and in two cases of mine, at least, the operation has been a complete success.

Thus, towards the end of this long and impressive book, he based this important conclusion on his experience of just two cases. He also wrote that he believed that 75 per cent of cases of ptosis could be satisfactorily treated by medical means, and a further 15 per cent could probably 'be made very comfortable by a skilled internist'. This left a final 10 per cent who would require 'a surgical procedure in addition to these [medical] measures in order to give the patient the greatest degree of comfort'.

In his final chapter Coffey gave his views on the indications for surgery in ptosis (which seems, in the course of the book, to have embraced or become stasis or constipation).

> If it were possible by magic to eliminate operative mortality, postoperative morbidity and other inconveniences, I would unhesitatingly say the great majority of cases should be operated upon.

He then analysed the results of various surgeons and concluded:

> Gasto-enteroptosis is a subject which deserves much more thoughtful consideration from the thinking members of the profession than it has received... Being a mechanical and physical condition, largely, mechanical and physical measures are essential to its proper treatment... There is a certain proportion of the cases in which it is necessary to use surgical measures in order to get results. It is probable that my estimates are ultraconservative... I unhesitatingly state that there is no part of my surgical work which has been more satisfactory than that pertaining to the ptosis question.

Coffey attempted to examine every possible aspect of the subject, yet he omitted the psychological aspects of the condition. This is typical of medical thinkers and practitioners of the time, and is not uncommon today. He defined 'neurasthenia' rather casually as 'extreme cases [of] that low state of health ordinarily referred to as "asthenic"'. He discussed it towards the end of his book, though without mentioning it in his full table of contents. His description is worth quoting because it expresses vividly an attitude – mocking and dismissive while at the same time recommending surgery – that has become part of Western medical tradition, in which fashion succeeds fashion.

> The most important manifestation indicating surgical treatment for right-sided ptosis is right-sided pain or distress. [He does not define 'right-sided distress' and it is not clear what he means by this.] Right-sided pain or distress was formerly considered as positive evidence of organic disease. In the early nineties, the ovary was supposed to be the cause of much right-sided pain. Therefore, the right ovary or both ovaries were removed and the

patient made a nervous invalid thereby, while she remained unrelieved. A few years later, chronic appendicitis became the vogue and many of these patients whose ovaries had been removed now had the appendix removed – without relief. Many of these patients had stomach troubles for which gastro-enterostomy was sometimes performed – again without relief. The gall-bladder was drained in many cases without relief, until removal of the gall-bladder came to the front – this also without relief. The enthusiastic and optimistic surgeon who had removed the patient's ovaries, later her appendix, done a gastro-enterostomy, fixed her right kidney, drained her gall-bladder and finally removed her gall-bladder, each time felt sure he was going to solve the problem even in the absence of demonstrable organic pathology, but the patient went on with pain and distress. Finally, after having failed to relieve her, he gravely pronounced her a 'neuroasthenic'.

He went on to say that most cases of abdominal pain could now be accurately diagnosed:

With our modern clinics and means of investigation, the differentiation of organic and inorganic disease can usually be made. Most organic conditions can be diagnosed or eliminated. All the acute conditions, such as perforating ulcer, pancreatitis, gall-stones, appendicitis, etc., are easily diagnosed. There is no excuse for a careful surgeon failing to determine an obstruction of the ureter, a stone in the kidney, a cystic ovary, etc.

He suggested, without actually saying so, that other conditions were likely to be due to ptosis and should be operated on.

In short, I believe that surgery is justifiable and advisable in all chronic pains in the right side of the abdomen which are of sufficient severity to warrant a diagnosis of an organic lesion...

So much for 'neurasthenia' and psychological insight. Psychological concepts impinged on surgeons in 1923 even less than they do on many today.

In the same year as Coffey's magnum opus, Robert Orton Moody, Associate Professor of Anatomy at the University of California and later Honorary Demonstrator in Anatomy at University College, London, published with his associates, Roscoe G Van Nuys and W E Chamberlain, the results of x-ray and fluoroscopic examinations of six hundred healthy adults. They concluded that the stomachs of 80 per cent of their subjects were in positions that would be diagnosed as ptosis, yet almost none had symptoms and the state of the abdominal wall was not related to the position of the stomach. Thus began a new era in which ptosis was viewed differently, although the change was slow. Others, including radiologists, also concluded that the position of the stomach had nothing to do with its function. In 1927 Moody published a study of 1,150 students, 'not one of whom had a history of chronic gastric or intestinal trouble'. His conclusions included the statement that 'transverse colons dipping far into the true pelvis are normal'. His comments were thoughtful: 'These facts justify the conclusion that enteroptosis, gastroptosis and coloptosis seldom or never exist as pathological conditions.'

In 1930, in the Clinical Lecture delivered at Guy's Hospital, Sir Arthur Hurst included movable kidney, gastroptosis, pelvic caecum and dropped colon in his list of 'mythical maladies':

As the normal kidney is movable, a 'movable kidney' cannot be regarded as a disease, and simple mobility never gives rise to symptoms, in spite of the fact that a single Birmingham surgeon has fixed 1,500 movable kidneys in the last thirty years...

Many thousands of kidney belts have been supplied to the unfortunate owners of kidneys which were sufficiently palpable to be easily discovered on abdominal examination.

The x-rays have not proved an unmixed blessing for medicine. It takes a good deal to compensate for a diagnosis of gastroptosis, a pelvic caecum or a dropped colon – three 'diseases' which we owe to the radiologist. It would not matter so much had not each of these so-called diseases led to the invention of an operation for its cure.

Just as some people have long noses and others have short noses, so some have long stomachs and others have short stomachs, which are nothing more than normal variations from the average.

Hurst made friends with the radiologist A E Barclay, 'the first and only British radiologist to investigate the normal physiology and anatomy of the oesphagus, stomach and intestines'.

[Barclay] described mass peristalsis of the colon about the same time as Newton and I published our description of it, and he was the first to discover the great variations in the position of the stomach and colon of normal people with changes of posture. For twenty-five years he has fought with me against the popular radiological diagnosis of dropped stomach and dropped colon, which encouraged surgeons to perform quite useless operations and made the fortunes of many of the makers of abdominal supports, which we both showed have the effect of pushing the organs still further down instead of holding them in their supposed normal position. We have always taught that the so-called dropped organs are not in any way abnormal, there is no evidence that they ever occupied a higher position, and they never give rise to symptoms until their owners are told about them, when they soon become a constant source of anxiety.

One might think that the ghost of ptosis was laid to rest, yet even in the twenty-first century one still comes across an occasional person who has had or has been recommended surgery for 'dropped' internal organs.

Race

The relationship between medical fashions and contemporary beliefs, prejudices and interests is shown very clearly in the relationship between medicine and race, particularly in the United States. In times past, a black skin has been regarded as a disease in itself. In 1792 Benjamin Rush, the doctor who signed the Declaration of Independence, saw a negro with vitiligo, a condition in which there is loss of pigment in the skin. He supposed that all negroes suffered from a mild form of congenital leprosy whose only symptom was blackness.

In the Deep South, many medical conditions were thought to be related to race. These included pneumonia and pulmonary congestion, 'bilious and adynamic fevers', scrofula, yaws, consumption and a host of psychological conditions, including drapetomania, which was 'the desire of a slave to be free', and 'rascality' or 'hebetude of mind and obtuse sensibility of body', which caused the slave to be 'like a person half asleep'.

Nowadays it is fashionable to compare the incidence of various diseases in different ethnic groups. It is acceptable to say that skin pigment protects against the sun's rays, and can encourage the development of rickets. Some diseases, such as sickle cell disease and thalassaemia, are known to occur in people of particular ethnic backgrounds, but it no longer fashionable or permissible to attribute medical conditions, especially psychological conditions, to skin colour *per se*.

Railway spine

Social and industrial change as well as scientific inventions have a strong influence on medical fashion. A nineteenth-century fashion with both these origins was a 'disease' called 'railway spine'. It developed from theories that arose in two quite different fields: the coming of the railways and coincidental ideas about the nervous system.

A new invention that affects human function in ways previously unknown is liable to create anxiety. The building of railways created concern about the possible ill effects of travelling on them, rather as people in our time have been worried about such things as space travel, genetically modified food and cloning. Before the railways were built, no one had travelled faster than the speed of a horse. There were rumours that travelling at more than fifteen miles per hour was dangerous and would cause blood to pour out of the ears. Even after this was shown not to be case, anxieties persisted about the effect of rail travel on the spine.

At the same time the nervous system was the centre of much scientific study and was widely believed to be the centre or co-ordinating structure and force of the body.

The development of the railways led to anxieties which revealed themselves in medical speculation and theory. In 1842 the first railway accident in France left a powerful impression, followed by America's first serious accident in 1853, in which a train fell into a river, killing 46 people. In 1861 one of the first enquiries into the dangers of rail traffic was held under the auspices of the *Lancet*, and in 1866 John Erichsen (1818–96), Professor of Surgery at University College, London, developed the idea that relatively small injuries could lead to major physical damage. He wrote a book about it, which was influential.

People came to believe that travelling by train was dangerous to health and could lead to a number of symptoms, directly traceable to the effect of train travel on the spine. As a result, many millions of pounds and dollars were paid out by railway companies to individuals claiming compensation for their illnesses, and the whole business became part of the development of the insurance industry and the idea of 'compensationitis'.

Small babies

Medical fashions mostly concern doing things to patients, which is part of traditional medical practice. Some fashions, however, have been for *not* doing things. This can be seen in the history of premature and dangerously small babies, whose treatment has been greatly influenced by their country's attitude to matters of population. For example, at the turn of the twentieth century, France, in need of an increase in population, cherished its weak babies, was a pioneer in their treatment and developed various methods and fashions for coping with the premature. The American attitude was more eugenic and opposed to 'weaklings', both deformed and premature.

In the late nineteenth century babies began to be weighed at birth and it was recognised that those below 2,500g (5½lb) were especially vulnerable. It was realised that one of the problems was loss of heat, and this led to a fashion for incubators – initially inspired by poultry-keeping methods. The development of incubators also became closely connected to show business, and some doctor-showmen travelled with underweight babies in incubators, advertising 'The Smallest Baby on Earth', and so on. In the USA, a *St Louis Post-Dispatch* contained a drawing of a 1lb 12oz baby being placed in a man's shoe.

The French physician Stéphane Tarnier was the pioneer in incubator use. In 1879 he saw a chicken-hatching exhibit at the Paris Zoo and commissioned the zoo's instrument-maker to build one to hold two human infants. In 1883 an incubator was in use in London's Lying-In Hospital, and in 1898 incubators were in use at the Hospital for Sick Children, Great Ormond Street. There was some criticism of this practice, and the *Lancet* warned of the dangers of 'baby-farming'. An increase in interest in babies coincided with this concern. There were certainly some dubious things going on. Advertisements for 'Bargains in Unwanted Babies' were not uncommon. In 1898 a *Lancet* writer warned that at fairs an incubator was 'a side-show, nestling between the five-legged mule, wild animals, and the bearded woman'.

The design of most early incubators was unsatisfactory. In 1900 Dwight Chapman, an eminent New York paediatrician, used incubators on hospital wards to care for premature babies from tenements. In one type, only 2 out of 73 babies survived and in another, all 40 infants died. The death rate was so high that some doctors did not record those who died in the first few days. Others did not admit babies who weighed less than 1,200g (2lb 10oz). Body temperature was one of the problems. While it was recognised that a premature baby could not maintain a normal body temperature, no one knew what the correct temperature should be. Estimates varied from 70 to 100°F.

Feeding and breathing were also big problems for premature babies. In the early twentieth century it was thought that feeding should begin as early as possible after birth to prevent death from starvation. Yet many premature babies could not cope with milk delivered through a glass tube, and they either asphyxiated or developed pneumonia from inhaling the milk. By contrast, some believed that the babies retained an excessive amount of fluid so that early feeding was unnecessary and even harmful to the kidneys. Thus the idea developed that the babies should be starved for a while after birth, and this notion became a fashion. For the next fifty years many paediatricians followed it. The recommended period of starvation varied from twelve hours to three or even four days. The practice of delayed feeding first became popular in the United States, but was soon followed in Britain. By the 1940s it had become almost universal practice, despite evidence accumulating against it – an example of the strength of a fashion at its height. A clinical trial by a German paediatrician, published in 1955, showed that there was an increased death rate of 28 per cent in these infants, but no one seems to have taken any notice of this. The fashionable treatment fitted the ideology of the age, and these ideologies are the hardest to shift.

In 1962 a brave and innovative paediatrician, Dr Victoria Smallpiece, went against the fashion and fed the babies with undiluted milk from birth. These babies did better than those who had been starved. The belief grew that nutrition in premature babies should be interrupted as briefly as possible, but it encountered opposition. By the mid-1960s the fashion for early feeding was spreading, but the *Lancet*, which tended to employ older doctors and members of the medical establishment to write their leading articles on clinical subjects, said that the advantages of early feeding were outweighed by the risks, arguing that early feeding went against 'Nature'. It said that normal babies chose to fast:

If the healthy mature baby chooses to fast for several hours after birth, we should bow to his superior knowledge, and profit from his example in our care of the premature, less able to fend for themselves. We may not always understand the ways of Nature, but if she has created the human infant to observe temperance and moderation over his first drink, then presumably she knows best.

Dr Smallpiece and her colleague Davies replied that normal babies do not fast:

Finally, just where does your study of Nature lead us? We have watched many healthy mature babies who were seemingly unaware that Nature intended them to observe 'temperance' and 'moderation' over the first feed. We are surprised that you should quote her as our model for the care of the premature baby. Are we not correct in thinking that her neonatal mortality in this group in the animal kingdom is nearly 100%?

Smallpiece and Davies pointed out that the foetus is fed continuously in utero, so it seems irrational to interrupt the process just when a baby is exposed to greater risks. Smallpiece and Davies also showed that many of the infants who did survive this regime suffered brain damage as a result. Without a controlled trial, they won the day, the practice of delayed feeding eventually ceased – and the mortality figures fell.

Until about 1953 the death rate in very small babies had declined slowly. Then the improvement ceased and the death rate actually increased for more than a decade. By that time innumerable fashions had developed in the care of newborn and premature babies. As the *Lancet* described it in 1974:

Modern neonatal iatrogenesis reached a peak when almost every major error in newborn care was widely practised, at least for a time by overextended paediatricians using inadequate equipment.

Often in incubators that became chilled, resuscitated at birth with large doses of nikethamide or by intragastric oxygen, they showed an increased risk of kernicterus [severe jaundice of the newborn] from excessive Vitamin K and sulphonamides.

By the 1970s the wheel had turned full circle, at least as far as feeding went. It became fashionable to give the babies milk, preferably mother's milk, from birth, and theories about the benefits of starvation gradually died. From 1965 the death rate in the newborn began to fall again, a trend that has continued ever since.

Breathing was another problem in the newborn, particularly in very small babies, and this led to other fashions. Immature lungs often could not sustain the child, and it became fashionable to give them oxygen, often in high concentrations and somewhat indiscriminately. This turned out to be one of the most unfortunate medical fashions of all. As the fashion gained popularity, many premature babies became blind with a serious condition known as retrolental hyperplasia, caused by immature eyes being exposed to high tensions of oxygen. Many of these babies also had other signs of brain damage.

Sudden death in childhood

Sudden death may seem a curious topic to relate to fashion, but a medical fashion can arise from the need to treat or explain a problematic situation. Sudden death in childhood, now known variously as 'cot death' or 'sudden infant death syndrome' (SIDS), has exercised many able minds in our time and before. The history of the medical approach to infant and childhood death leads back to 'status lymphaticus', a fashionable diagnosis among doctors at the end of the nineteenth century. It persisted for half a century, apparently killed all its victims and was listed as an official cause of death. Then it was realised that the disease did not even exist.

Doctors thought that status lymphaticus was caused by an enlarged thymus gland, a small structure of lymphatic tissue that straddles the windpipe in the neck. A large thymus had long been regarded as a dangerous condition and the new 'disease', causing death in 100 per cent of cases, was clearly dangerous. The *Lancet* even announced, in 1908, that 'the status lymphaticus problem is a much more serious one than the majority suppose', and it added, 'there is no disease of greater medico-legal importance than the status lymphaticus.' Later, although no 'cure' had been found, status lymphaticus dropped from the textbooks so completely that today many younger doctors and medical historians have never heard of it. It was a fashion that filled a need at the time and prevented awkward questions.

During the nineteenth century there was increasing pressure on doctors to register deaths and to record the 'cause' of death, even if they had no idea what this was. In 1837 came the Births and Deaths Registration Act which required the registration of all deaths. Soon afterwards certification of cause of death was also demanded. For the

185

first time doctors were required to distinguish between 'natural' and 'unnatural' deaths, which required a whole new way of thinking about death and its causes. This created difficulty in the courts, where medical witnesses were increasingly required to give evidence in both criminal cases and in the adversarial common law courts of England and the United States. There was growing pressure for more accurate diagnosis. Older diagnoses, such as 'act of God' (a favourite in former times) were no longer acceptable. In his first report in 1839, the medical statistician Dr William Farr deplored the varied diagnoses that he received for the same condition and called for uniform naming. In 1853 the First Statistical Congress was held in Brussels, at which Farr was invited to draw up a classification of diseases for international use. In 1869 a committee appointed by the Royal College of Physicians drew up the first edition of *The Nomenclature of Disease*, which was then revised frequently. When a medical practitioner gave a cause of death that was not recognised, the Registrar-General communicated with him in an attempt to arrive at an acceptable diagnosis. In 1874 another Births and Deaths Registration Act made it compulsory to register every death and give the cause. Doctors had to get used to registering their patients' deaths and deciding on a cause of death that was 'scientific' and acceptable to the authorities. The making of myths and fashions was almost inevitable as they attempted to fill the many awkward gaps.

A particular difficulty for doctors was to give the cause when death occurred suddenly and for no apparent reason. These deaths were sometimes in children and young people and included cases of what today we would call 'cot death'. There had been a worrying increase in sudden deaths during surgery, a practice that was expanding but still rather experimental; inevitably it led to more deaths. Many of these were attributed to chloroform, and many were in children – these attracted particular attention, and were an embarrassment for the medical profession.

Individual chloroform deaths were chronicled in the medical journals. Week after week, case histories were published under the headlines 'Another death from chloroform', 'Yet another death from chloroform', 'Two more deaths from chloroform'. There were deaths at St Mary's, at Guy's, in Edinburgh, Boston, Paris, Berlin, and it was suggested that many more such deaths occurred in private practice and were being covered up. Clearly, medical establishments throughout the

Western world were seriously worried about these deaths. Typically, the *Lancet* pronounced:

> The profession and the public at large are...becoming alarmed at the repeated instances of death brought on by the inhalation of chloroform, and it is for ourselves a melancholy duty to record these unfortunate instances.

That was in 1853. It was to get much worse. In 1869 the *British Medical Journal* published a long editorial called 'Chloroform accidents', which began:

> Recent facts have been by no means encouraging as to any diminution in the dangers of anaesthetics and comparing the situation to 'a plank bridge across the Thames – safe for some but hardly to be recommended for general use'.

Some doctors believed that the deaths were due to lack of skill on the part of anaesthetists and the reports suggest that this was so, but, understandably, many anaesthetists disagreed, especially when they witnessed one of these mysterious deaths themselves. Then they were more inclined to think that there must be a specific pathological cause, something wrong with the patient that had not been detected. There is a long medical tradition of blaming the patient when unfortunate events occur that are not fully understood.

Reading through these cases, it seems certain that some of the deaths *were* due to careless or inexperienced anaesthetists, but many of them happened at the hands of experienced and careful practitioners. The *Lancet* bewailed the fact that 'fatal cases have occurred with the most practised and scientific chloroformists'. It added, darkly, 'chloroform takes away *pain* but it also takes away *life*'.

There were enquiries and committees and chloroform commissions, but people still wanted to know why these deaths occurred. The basis already existed of a possible explanation that was in accord with current thinking. There was, handily, a condition that had been mooted for some time which could be brought out, adapted to the current need and turned into a medical fashion.

There was a long history of sudden death in infancy and early childhood related to noisy breathing and laryngeal obstruction; the 'crowing' symptom was known as laryngismus stridulus. It was uncommon, but here is a typical case in a one-year-old child with a history of 'crowing fits', described in 1844:

> The child was sitting on the floor amusing itself with some playthings... They saw the little thing stoop forward suddenly, as though in play... As it remained in that position, however, they went to it, took it up, and found it dead. It had perished suddenly, no doubt in one of the paroxysms of laryngismus.

Laryngismus stridulus was listed in the 1837 paper of the Royal Colleges on death certification, a decade before the introduction of chloroform. It was thought to be due to strangulation from pressure on the windpipe of an enlarged thymus gland, so this could not directly explain the mysterious deaths under anaesthesia.

Like other lymphatic tissue, the thymus is relatively large in small children and gradually diminishes in size as the child grows. We now know that the thymus is important in the developing immune system, but, although its existence was possibly known as long ago as the time of the ancient Egyptians, its function was unknown until late in the twentieth century. In the nineteenth century there was a trend in surgery to remove structures that the body could apparently do without, and thymectomy became an authentic surgical operation.

Our distant forebears gave the thymus quasi-magical qualities. The new scientific doctors were unable to ascertain its function and tended to assume that it had none. They sometimes removed it to prevent its strangling the child, although it later became obvious that it could not do this. Before the twentieth century there was little effort to discover the average size of the thymus or how much it varied between individuals. The variation turned out to be considerable. Some people realised that the thymus is large in infants and gradually declines in size, but many doctors diagnosed as 'large' any thymus that was not obviously small. This was usually done, not by weighing but from judgments with the naked eye at postmortem. It was the exception to try to establish norms of weight, even from postmortem material.

Most children who died had suffered from severe or debilitating illness, during which the size of the thymus had diminished as the child wasted. This was not recognised, so it was not understood that healthy children who die suddenly tend to have bigger thymuses than those who die slowly. It was unusual, therefore, to see a large thymus in a dead child and so it was assumed that this was the cause of the death. Thus the death of any child who died suddenly without apparent cause could be attributed to status lymphaticus, or sudden death.

The idea that a large thymus was a sign of health rather than disease developed only gradually. In the 1860s the physician Samuel Wilks (1824–1911) taught that the 'plump and rounded bodies' of children with large lymph tissue were a sign of health, but he was unusual in his belief. Later, in 1886, the shrewd Guy's physician Charles Fagge wrote in his textbook, 'As a matter of fact, it is now certain that there is no relation whatever between laryngismus and the state of the thymus.' The clearest statement came much later, from the physician Humphry Rolleston in 1936. He commented on the thymus: 'Its real size is seen only in cases of sudden death in health, and these are the cases in which it is commonly regarded as enlarged.'

Even when more was known about the thymus, however, the myth persisted that a large size was dangerous. The false belief about the thymus was the basis of the fashion for diagnosing status lymphaticus to explain sudden death. Quite apart from the belief that a large thymus could lead to sudden death in children, there was another theory also gaining credence. In 1830 the German J H Kopp had drawn attention to what he called 'thymic asthma'. These were attacks of breathlessness on inspiration which sometimes led to death and were believed to be due to mechanical pressure from an enlarged thymus. Sudden inexplicable deaths without previous breathlessness but with a 'large thymus' were also often equated with the previously mentioned laryngismus stridulus (the crowing noise) or laryngismus (contraction of the throat), sometimes being regarded as variations of the same.

[It is] characterized by crowing inspirations, or by momentary suspension of the act of respiration; these attacks occur suddenly, and at irregular intervals, are of short duration, cease suddenly, and are unaccompanied by cough, or other signs of irritation of the larynx. If the disease progresses, it becomes associated with other convulsive symptoms, as strabismus, distortion of the face, carpopedal spasms, or general convulsions.

The condition described here in 1883 by Meigs and Pepper was sometimes classified with the neuroses and was genuinely thought to be due to strangulation by a large thymus gland. In one reported series of 30 cases, 24 of them were children aged under one year old, and all were under four.

Nonetheless, strangulation by the thymus gland was difficult to justify as the cause of sudden unexpected death without previous symptoms, for example under chloroform. Some people postulated spasm in the throat, but this was unsatisfactory. In 1858 a German physician, A Friedleben, announced, *'Es gibt kein thymic Asthma'* (There is no thymic asthma). Yet the popular view in the profession continued to be that pressure from an enlarged thymus could cause sudden death, and cases continued to be reported into the twentieth century.

In 1889 and 1890, in two parts of the same investigation, the Austrian Professor Richard Paltauf finally came up with an explanation that fitted the need. He doubted that mechanical pressure from the thymus could kill. He had examined many corpses after unexplained sudden death and described widespread hyperplasia of the lymphoid tissues. He suggested that there was a peculiar 'lymphatico-chlorotic' constitution in which there was enlargement of all lymphoid tissues and which caused a predisposition to sudden death. He linked it to the 'hypoplasia of the heart and aorta similar to that described by Virchow in chlorotic subjects'. This came to be called 'status lymphaticus' or 'status thymicolymphaticus'. Like the other pathologists, Paltauf gave no measurements and no standards of normality or abnormality.

This idea fitted comfortably into current theory with its ideas about diathesis – a constitutional tendency towards disease or a particular disease. This was related to the old idea of disease as an imbalance of humours, a condition thought to be related to decline and degeneration. Thus, in a convenient combination of old and new theories, 'thymic' death came to be regarded as the result of a condition inherent in the patient, who was predisposed to sudden death from trivial causes. Such explanations freed the increasingly anxious anaesthetists from blame and also created a new medical fashion.

The idea caught on, largely because the conclusion that constitutional (or 'diathetic') imbalance was the underlying explanation satisfied all sides. It provided an explanation for the awkward fact that the actual cause of death could not be attributed to any single postmortem finding. It exonerated clinicians, surgeons, anaesthetists and pathologists. It was such a satisfying explanation, in fact, that the diagnosis was accepted by most people involved for the next sixty years. A subsequent researcher counted more than 820 papers on the subject published in the following 32 years. In Britain it created much interest. It was widely taught that a typical status lymphaticus death was a child who saw his friend nearly run over and immediately dropped dead himself.

Almost everyone seems to have believed in the fashionable theory of a lymphatic diathesis predisposing to sudden death. The race was now on to diagnose status lymphaticus before sudden death occurred, and to apply treatment that would prevent it. In 1898 Sir William Osler discussed the 'lymphatic constitution' whose subjects 'have a diminished vital resistance, and are especially prone to fatal collapse under ordinarily very inadequate exciting causes'. Others linked the condition with exophthalmic goitre (enlarged, toxic thyroid) and large adenoids. The idea developed that children with status lymphaticus were well fed, pale, pasty, flabby and rather inert and effeminate, with large thymus and tonsils. This verbal picture was repeated many times, at least until the mid-twentieth century. Clifford Allbutt and Humphry Rolleston, distinguished authors of standard textbooks (and John Thomson, who wrote the relevant section in 1908), were more sceptical, but accepted the theory in the absence of better and wrote that there was no treatment.

It is not surprising to find that anaesthetists were especially keen on the theory. As one of them wrote, 'The most important thing to us as anaesthetists is the diagnosis of this condition.' Once the diagnosis was established and accepted, it conveniently exonerated many doctors. In 1909, for instance, following the case of a sudden death attributed to a persistent thymus, the *Lancet* commented that 'the circumstances of death might have sustained a charge of manslaughter in the absence of a necropsy'. Clearly trying to protect the profession, the *Lancet* also emphasised the importance of diagnosing the condition lest death be attributed to 'anaesthetic, poisoning or overdosage' or 'wrongly attributed to drug toxaemia'.

Some said there was no treatment possible, but others said there was, and this led to another, albeit smaller, fashion. This was thymectomy, the surgical removal of the whole thymus. Since it had no known function and its absence was compatible with life, its removal would, it was argued, also remove the likelihood of sudden, unexpected death. In the 1890s the German surgeon Rehn reported success in removing or fixing the thymus, thereby reviving the theory that it could obstruct the airway and strangle the child. In 1906 at the Surgical Congress, one surgeon advised complete thymectomy and recommended that the organ be drawn out, resected, or stitched to the breastbone. In 1908 an anaesthetist assured his readers that cases had been 'cured' by the operation. In the same year Osler's textbook stated, 'The possibility of an antemortem diagnosis, as well as of therapeutic measures, has been demonstrated beyond any doubt.' When surgery became the treatment of choice, however, the mortality was unacceptably high. In one series it was 33.3 per cent – and this was an operation done on apparently healthy children without symptoms and with few if any signs. Once this was generally known, few (or at least fewer) continued to recommend the treatment. The fashion for thymectomy died because it was dangerous. Another preventive treatment was required to fill the gap, and there was one available.

X-rays had been discovered in 1895. More and more uses were being found for them. Exposing animals to x-rays had shown that lymphoid tissue was more sensitive to x-rays than were other tissues and that it led to a diminution in their size. This seemed to be just what was needed to prevent death from status lymphaticus. In 1907 A Friedländer treated with x-rays a child diagnosed as having status lymphaticus. The thymus shrank. Soon irradiation was the treatment of choice where a large thymus was suspected, and thus the new fashion was born. Virtually every textbook of the period recommended x-ray treatment. There were even suggestions that all newborn babies should be irradiated as a preventive measure. Newspaper articles spread the idea among physicians and lay people that respiratory symptoms in children, especially breath-holding attacks, indicated abnormal enlargement of the thymus and required x-ray treatment. The fashion continued for half a century and has been called an 'epidemic'. It was even widely suggested that it was malpractice *not* to irradiate.

By 1910 it was known that exposure to x-rays could cause cancer and that there was a long induction period, but no one seems to have linked this with the irradiation of babies thought to have 'large' thymuses. The fashion continued unchecked.

In 1911 the diagnosis of status lymphaticus was recognised as an official cause of death in England and Wales. In that year it was held to be responsible for 121 deaths, nearly all of them children. Status lymphaticus was recorded as causing three deaths per million living persons.

Meanwhile, official efforts continued to be made to counteract the idea that anaesthetics were dangerous. In 1911, in addition to those classified as primary status lymphaticus, 25 deaths that occurred during anaesthesia were recorded as being 'related to the condition that led to the administration of an anaesthetic', nearly always chloroform. Chloroform deaths were still causing anxiety and general bemusement. The official attitude is reflected in the wording of the Registrar-General's Report: 'Apparently the status lymphaticus seldom causes death during the administration of ether. The operations during which these deaths occurred seem for the most part not to have been of a dangerous nature.' This line of thought influenced a change in registration practice regarding death under anaesthesia. '[I]t seems illogical to class deaths primarily to anaesthetics, since the primary cause must always be some condition which has occasioned the administration of an anaesthetic.' The Registrar-General had therefore decided to tabulate as a secondary classification all deaths where there was a mention of anaesthesia. There were 276 in England and Wales that year in patients aged from one to over 65 and fairly evenly spread between the sexes. Status lymphaticus was held to have caused 31 of these, all of them male. The Registrar-General did not explain the omission or absence of female deaths.

By this time irradiation of the thymus in children was becoming a standard preventive measure before surgery or anaesthesia, but more critical attitudes and appraisals were beginning to emerge. Pathologists were now actually weighing and measuring the thymus. Various and varying weights were published over the next fifty years. Nearly half a century later Sir Geoffrey Keynes found the need to write, 'It seems to be extraordinarily difficult to get at the truth concerning even the size of this enigmatic organ.'

The familiar label of status lymphaticus continued to be used. X-rays and occasionally surgery were still recommended for 'enlarged thymus', usually diagnosed by percussion and x-rays. Yet percussion of the chest of a small infant is an unreliable way of assessing the size of the underlying organs. So was x-ray, particularly when the standard of normality of x-rays of the chest was worked out on adults standing upright and holding their breath. A baby will not stand up and hold its breath, and its anatomy also differs from the adult and changes rapidly during the weeks after birth, as does the x-ray picture of heart and lungs. The big shadow in the middle of the chest varies in size according to respiration and heartbeat. It also varies according to the angle of the beam with which the radiograph is taken, which is different in babies and adults. It is therefore difficult to know exactly what you are looking at. It was to be many years, however, before the ability to assess the size of the thymus by this means was questioned and eventually rejected. Even the most distinguished authorities recommended the treatment.

A Swedish pathologist, J A Hammar, devoted many years to the study of the thymus, including the normal thymus. He produced much evidence to suggest that status lymphaticus was not a valid disease entity, and he denied the existence of 'thymus death'. In 1923 an extensive review criticised the lack of rigorous analysis in the literature, rejected the idea of thymic suffocation and argued that there was little firm evidence of status lymphaticus.

Yet still the fashion persisted. The conditions that created a need for the disease continued to exist. While pathologists were beginning to question the diagnosis, anaesthetists were increasingly certain of it. There is a marked difference in the literature of the two professions. A growing number of anaesthetists and others wrote on the subject of status lymphaticus, taking its existence for granted and stressing the importance of diagnosing the condition in advance and the difficulty of doing so. Some urged that a Royal Commission should be appointed to look into it. Others drew attention to the success of surgery or of 'cure' following 'application of x-rays to the throat'.

Status lymphaticus was diagnosed so widely and seemed to be such a problem that a committee was eventually appointed to enquire into it. In 1925 the members came out strongly against even the existence of the condition, but there were too few records to deduce any authoritative conclusions.

The following year, a committee of investigation was formed by the Medical Research Council and the Pathological Society of Great Britain and Ireland. It consisted largely of pathologists who had seen cases of status lymphaticus only in the mortuary. In a preliminary report they concluded that the normal thymus varied considerably in size and that in cases of sudden death there was no greater incidence of large thymuses than would be expected by chance. They insisted, 'There is no evidence to show that there is any connection between the presence of a large glandular thymus and death from unexpected or trivial causes.'

In 1927 an extensive analysis of deaths from status lymphaticus, announced as 'a critical examination of a curious phase of modern medical teaching', said that diagnosing in life was 'largely nonsense' and that, if thymic weight was the criterion, status lymphaticus and its associated conditions were 'mere verbalisms'. Such a diagnosis had 'no more value than affirmative evidence in cases of witchcraft' and 'ought to be abandoned'. The authors referred to 'an uncanny fourth dimension of medicine, where the familiar canons and methods of scientific criticism are becoming foolishness, where fact and hypothesis are habitually confounded and nothing is but what is not'.

The final report of the Medical Research Council Committee was not published until 1931. Based on 680 postmortem examinations, it established that the normal thymus may weigh as much as 70 or 80g up to the age of sixteen and may be substantial at any age, and that there was no significant deviation in size in any group of patients and no hypertrophy of other lymphoid tissue. In response the *Lancet* published an editorial called 'The end of status lymphaticus', in which it said:

It is simple humanity to search for some explanation which will satisfy the modern mind where the 'visitation of God' would once have been enough. Hence the doctrine of 'status lymphaticus' which, owing to our ignorance of the anatomy of the normal healthy human body, has survived longer than it should.

Nonetheless, fashions die hard when they are to the advantage of significant groups, so it is not surprising that many disagreed. There were protests in the medical journals. Some of the opposition came from clinicians, who objected that the evidence came only from the postmortem room and ignored the living. Some of the objections came from the postmortem room itself. As late as 1945 a pathologist published the angry statement, 'The now popular attitude that there is no such thing as Status... Lymphaticus can be quickly dissipated by autopsy studies in any Coroner's office where children are studied.'

Members of the public were also critical of the committee's findings. A typical letter in the *British Medical Journal* stated:

One would have thought that if any field of human endeavour was to escape the craze for settling things by committees that field was medicine... [T]he profession ought to look askance at the re-institution of medieval methods of arriving at the truth. A committee once decided that the earth does not move.

Among the influential objectors was Alan Moncrieff, Professor of Child Health at Great Ormond Street. He remained convinced that one could diagnose an enlarged thymus clinically and with x-rays and that, once diagnosed, it should be irradiated. At a meeting at the Royal Society of Medicine in 1937 he described twelve young children with symptoms 'which appeared to be associated with enlargement of the thymus gland as shown on x-ray examination of the thorax'. He pointed out that the MRC committee had been concerned with 'pathological material only', since they believed that the condition could not be diagnosed during life and the other evidence was also concerned with postmortem material. He said that it was now possible, radiologically, to obtain knowledge of the size of the thymus during life. Size could be varied by ˙treatment and symptoms disappear after treatment. He protested at the *Lancet* leader that had proclaimed the end of the condition. He showed x-rays of the chests of patients whom he had irradiated and stated that, in his opinion, 'syncope, dyspnoea and fits in young infants, associated with thymic enlargement, does not appear to have been recognized sufficiently in this country', insisting that, 'as soon as possible after an enlarged thymus has been provided by x-ray examination, in an infant displaying the alarming symptoms recorded above, the size of the thymus should be reduced by suitable radiation'. He said that he did not have the courage to withhold such treatment while trying out other forms of therapy.

Moncrieff was strongly criticised in the ensuing discussion. One critic doubted whether the wide variety of symptoms that he described could all be caused by thymic enlargement and also questioned his interpretation of x-rays, pointing out that the central shadow varied with respiration. Others were also critical, but Moncrieff was unmoved. One of his former house physicians told me that many years later he was still irradiating thymuses.

Meanwhile, chloroform had gone out of fashion as an anaesthetic, its dangers widely recognised. From its widespread use from the 1850s onwards, many patients had died while under chloroform, or shortly afterwards, and often from liver failure. It was now seldom used except in induction (mixed with ether) and in emergencies. Increasingly, reports indicated that symptoms attributed to status lymphaticus were due to other causes. Status lymphaticus was splitting up into different entities, and chloroform deaths were at last being attributed directly to the chloroform. From the late 1940s there were reports of 'cot death' as a separate condition and attention began to focus on that. The need for a diagnosis like status lymphaticus was therefore diminishing, and so the fashion began to come to an end. In 1939 the physician Henry Cohen wrote:

> The term 'status thymico-lymphaticus' is, on the present evidence, a meaningless term giving an air of profundity to what is a confession of ignorance, for it can mean only that 'this person has died suddenly from an unexplained or trivial cause'.

Pockets of resistance remained for a long time, however. In the same year, 1939, the eleventh edition of Savill's textbook of medicine still listed status lymphaticus as a cause of sudden death and said that x-ray treatment 'appears to be successful'.

Paediatricians remained divided. The American Emmett Holt Jr wrote in 1940:

> It is clear now that the supposed hyperplasia of the lymphatic structures and thymus in so-called status lymphaticus is physio-logical in young, well-nourished individuals... Satisfactory standards for the median and mean width of the supracardiac shadow and for the limits of the normal width at different ages have never been established. Moreover, supposedly pathologically wide supracardiac shadows have been found in from 25 to 50 per cent of healthy infants and children. The supracardiac shadow is a composite of the shadows of several structures [in the superior mediastinum].

In England, however, the royal paediatrician Wilfred Sheldon wrote in 1943 of 'gross enlargement of the thymus, with hypertrophy of the spleen and a general increase in lymphatic tissues'. He advised x-ray or radium treatment. He did not drop this advice until the eighth edition of his book, published in 1962.

Then, in 1949, an entirely new perspective arrived on the scene. It could have been a bombshell. Two American doctors reported the case of a five-year-old child whose thymus had been irradiated soon after birth. The child had developed cancer of the thyroid at the very point where the x-rays had entered its body.

The following year, the journal *Cancer* reported that of 28 patients under the age of eighteen with cancer of the thyroid, ten had had their thymuses irradiated in infancy. The authors showed that cancer of the thyroid, a rare disease in children, was a hundred times more common in those irradiated early in life than in those who had not been irradiated. Somewhat chillingly, they went on to recommend, instead of x-rays, 'an aggressive surgical attack on the thyroid glands and cervical nodes'.

The possible significance of the cancer evidence took some time to penetrate, however. Many anaesthetists and paediatricians were still stubbornly supporting the concept of status lymphaticus. A typical textbook, such as Letheby Tidy's *Synopsis of Medicine* (4th edn., 1925), still referred to 'the pale, flabby child with enlarged tonsils and adenoids and general enlargement of lymph glands and "night-crowing", in whom the diagnosis is established by x-ray of chest'. The author suggested that even if the condition was present, death could be avoided by a skilful anaesthetist. Most books continued to describe both the disease and its treatment in the old way, but one refreshing new textbook of medicine, *The Principles and Practice of Medicine*, edited by Sir Stanley Davidson and first published in 1952, did not even mention the thymus. Yet the following year, *Recent Advances in Anaesthesia* insisted that Moncrieff and others, in spite of attempts to discredit their work, 'have definitely established the existence of the syndrome.' Even a lot of science and the best opinions in the subject do not overturn ideas if they are part of people's mindsets and further their interests.

In 1954, nearly a quarter of a century after the judgment of the Medical Research Council that there was no such condition as status lymphaticus and despite increasingly serious warnings about the dangers of x-rays, the surgeon Geoffrey Keynes still found it necessary to point out that old beliefs die hard and that the 'disease' was still very much alive. As late as 1955, a book called *British Practice in Radiotherapy* stated: 'If the diagnosis of thymic hyperplasia has in such a case been established, x-ray therapy is the treatment of choice.'

By 1955 the high incidence of cancer in those who had been irradiated was widely known and discussed. It had been known that x-rays could cause cancer for over forty years. It may seem strange, therefore, that no one appears to have thought of the possibility of such cancer in irradiated children. Perhaps, like the chloroform deaths, these cases were still rare – but the treatment must have led to an enormous increase in a rare disease, especially since irradiation of the thymus was, for some paediatricians, a routine procedure for normal infants.

There may have been no immediate scare, but some took notice. The dangers of radical surgery were by now well known, and luckily the fashion did not revert to that. In 1955 a report in the *Journal of the American Medical Association* stated that in a series of thyroid cancer cases in children, all fifteen had been irradiated in childhood. Other reports followed. This was virtually the end of thymic irradiation and of status lymphaticus as a respectable medical diagnosis. By 1969 the same American journal was referring to it as a 'pesky medical misconception', which it has remained ever since.

The emphasis shifted towards interest in the thymus from the immunological point of view, and in the concept of sudden death in infancy as 'cot death', later known as Sudden Infant Death Syndrome (SIDS). Nonetheless, the belief that 'large thymuses' were dangerous was deeply embedded. Remarkably, at least one monograph supporting the concept was published as late as 1959 and the subject continued to be treated seriously in widely used textbooks. In 1976 evidence was produced that the thymus in cases of cot death was actually smaller than the average size in a control group, yet it continued to be blamed by some for sudden death in infancy. Even today references to it still appear, especially in medical books written for popular consumption.

Status lymphaticus is a telling example of how a medical fashion can grow from a medical 'need' – how it forms, flourishes and eventually fades. It is also an example of a fashion that had entirely unforeseen, long-term consequences – in the effects of the irradiation from x-rays of the thymus. It was a disease invented to provide an explanation and an excuse for the occasional unexpected deaths that occurred under chloroform, and therefore its existence was very much in the interests of anaesthetists and surgeons. It also explained other mysterious deaths which had to be accounted for to the Registrar-General. It was widely accepted and was described in all the textbooks, then led to controversy and harm to patients, and was finally deemed never to have existed. The sequence was very slow, however, and because of the vested interests which came into play, much of the evidence that accumulated against it and its treatments was ignored for a long time. When people are strongly motivated or have fixed beliefs, they are not deflected by evidence and they defend their positions strongly. Eventually the old guard retires and others take their places. Gradually the deaths that had come to be attributed to status lymphaticus acquired different and separate causes, including cot death, SIDS, anaphylactic shock, overwhelming infection and myocarditis.

Surgery

Surgery was becoming fashionable even before anaesthesia was widely introduced in 1847. This may seem strange, because it is often assumed that the development of surgery was a result of anaesthesia rather than a cause. Yet the practice of surgery, along with the *idea* of surgery as an effective form of treatment for conditions that were not necessarily visible, began to develop some time beforehand. Enthusiasm for it was detected a century earlier. In 1750 a London surgeon, Samuel Sharp, wrote: 'Perhaps there never was a Period of Time in which any Art was more cultivated than Surgery has been for the last thirty years.' In 1841 a contributor to the *Lancet* wrote:

> The whole history of surgery will scarcely, perhaps, exhibit such an extraordinary number of new operations within the same period of time as the last twelve months have produced. A perfect mania for operating has existed ever since the first operation for squinting was declared to be successful...

Surgery, like most branches of medicine, has experienced many fashions. These have developed, run their course, intertwined and influenced each other, and then declined or changed, often leading to other fashions. A few, including thorough anatomical knowledge, anaesthesia and asepsis, have remained and are traditions in our time.

It is often accepted as common knowledge that surgery was primitive and in a state of stagnation until the discovery and adoption of anaesthesia in the late 1840s and of antisepsis/asepsis twenty to fifty years later, and that only after that did surgical methods of treatment become prominent. Yet to some extent it was the other way round. It seems that anaesthesia and antisepsis were introduced *because* surgery was becoming a fashionable form of treatment. If it was to advance, it needed to solve the problems of pain, bleeding and infection.

Surgery, the treatment of local lesions, suited the new theory that disease was due to local abnormalities rather than humours that affected the whole body. Surgery concerned itself with the solid parts of the body, 'the anatomical method of therapy'. The old humoralism, by contrast, had assumed disease to be an imbalance of the body fluids. The study of anatomy in relation to disease became known as pathological anatomy and was the basis of new thought in medicine. As a result, surgery came into greater prominence, developed rapidly and became increasingly fashionable.

As early as the seventeenth century a few outstanding doctors had been moving towards the idea of dissecting bodies in order to discover and analyse their diseases rather than for other purposes. The real changes, however, occurred during the eighteenth century, when the idea that society was in a state of progress became widespread. As in other fields, surgeons had been praising and labelling advances in their field for two hundred years, but during the eighteenth century they made considerable and real advances. New attitudes developed not only towards the body, but also towards its dissection and study. When Samuel Sharp noted the increase in surgery in the mid-eighteenth century, he was referring to the changed attitudes and skills that had developed along with the interest in pathological anatomy. Anatomy and pathology had previously been quite separate areas of study. In the present context one might argue that bringing them together in pathological anatomy was an early 'scientific fashion', part of the fashion for acquiring new knowledge, for regarding the body as a machine and disease as faults in the machine. Ever since then, these ideas have remained as part of the culture of Western medicine and are more appropriately regarded as traditions rather than fashions. Anatomy and the dissection of corpses has continued as an essential part of the culture of medical professionalism, patient care and medical education.

An interesting fashion that developed among surgeons after surgery became safer and easier was the tendency to remove organs whose function was not known and which were clearly not vital to life, and also to remove anything thought to be 'enlarged'. This was true even when the organ had not been measured and no one had worked out its average size, let alone the normal variation. The literature of surgery in the late nineteenth century reveals the fascination that some surgeons had with removing parts of the body – 'extirpation', as they called it. There was much discussion about vestigial organs that were thought to have become redundant and even dangerous during the evolutionary process, and organs whose function was unknown but whose removal seemed to cause no obvious disadvantage. Many thought that these structures were better removed, and this belief grew as surgery became safer. At one time or another tonsils, uvula, ovaries, foreskin, appendix, thymus and colon were all 'extirpated' in accordance with this theory. The fashion for this mindset persisted until the mid-twentieth century. As surgery became more sophisticated and specialised, the fashion gradually changed from the removal of organs, which was seen to be unnecessary and dangerous, to the manipulation of organs, such as the operation of nephropexy (see page 167).

Tenotomy

The early nineteenth century produced many distinguished surgeons, particularly in France, Britain and Germany. They attracted students from far and wide, including from the United States. One of these surgeons, the German J F Dieffenbach (1792–1847), created a widespread surgical fashion for cutting muscles and tendons in order to correct deformity, also known as *Muskelschnitt* and *Sehnendurchschneidung*. The technique became particularly popular in Germany, and it has been said that it preoccupied German surgeons for more than a generation.

Dieffenbach believed that cutting tight muscles or their tendons would correct some deformities by straightening the opposing part of the body. The principle was not new. In 1784 Ottoker Lorenz, a Frankfurt surgeon, had divided the Achilles tendon in a case of clubfoot, and it had been practised by others ever since. In 1822 the sterno-mastoid, the large muscle in the neck, had been cut in order to correct the deformity of torticollis (wry-neck). During the years that followed, another German surgeon, Louis Stromeyer (1804–76), established the operations of cutting tendons and muscles as permanent procedures in the surgical repertoire.

The principle of dividing muscles and tendons had many possible applications, because the idea of too-tight muscles could be seen as the basis of many deformities. Several popular fashions developed from it, the most famous and spectacular being promulgated by Dieffenbach. In 1839 he invented two operations that had very different histories. One was a treatment for squinting and the other a treament for stammering. Both were based on the same principle, but were to have very different outcomes. The operation for dividing eye muscles in cases of squinting became standard practice, and is still the principle behind operations for squint. In Dieffenbach's hands the procedure was successful. In the hands of others it was less so, but it still became the basis of future treatment for this condition and one of the most famous operations in the history of surgery. In 1839 the *Lancet* referred to it as 'this beautiful and simple operation'. The operation was widely praised in the medical press and was soon widely taken up.

Dieffenbach's other operation divided the muscles of the tongue in cases of stammering. He assumed that stammering was a mechanical problem of articulation rather than a functional disorder of speech. The operation, popular at first, was a disaster. The only modern historian who has written on the subject said that it 'will never be accorded a place among the epics of medical history' and can 'never be regarded as one of the major themes in the development of surgery in the nineteenth century'. Yet it was based on what turned out to be a generally successful idea in surgery. Perhaps it is best regarded, not as an aberration but as part of a great innovatory surgical trend in the nineteenth century, albeit an unsuccessful part.

The theory behind Dieffenbach's operation accorded with the general custom of the time of attributing disease to anatomical structural changes – a theory which most people accepted, although many physicians had reservations about its most extreme applications. Since 1823 the idea had been mooted, and in 1831 the famous physiologist and physician Marshall Hall (1790–1857) had expressed a belief that stammering was a disease of articulation and not of brain function. Dieffenbach took up the idea and devised an operation to solve the problem. Many were unconvinced by the theory and, unlike the eye operation, the surgery for stammering was not welcomed with acclaim. Many, indeed, regarded it with suspicion, including the *Lancet*, which stated that the operation for stammering was 'both severe and dangerous to life' and based on nonsense.

The hostility did not stem from opposition to the fashionable principle of dividing muscles in cases of deformity, but from an awareness of the serious dangers of operating on the tongue (and this was before the days of anaesthesia). Dieffenbach himself eventually realised this from results in his own clinic, and the operation became obsolete. Cutting the muscles of the tongue as a treatment for stammering turned to be a fashion that was both useless and harmful.

Other, less dangerous, operations founded on the same principle lasted longer and were received with greater enthusiasm. Dieffenbach went on to extend his ideas of tenotomy to clubfoot, or strephopodia as it is sometimes called. The idea was to divide the taut tendon in order to balance it against the tendons on the other side. The operation increased in popularity after the discovery of anaesthesia. There is a brilliant and horrendous description of one (done without anaesthetic) that went wrong in rural France in Flaubert's *Madame Bovary*, published in 1857. Hippolyte the ostler had a clubfoot that was splendidly serviceable, but after the operation it went septic and the leg had to be amputated (also without an anaesthetic). The story is fictional, but it has a realistic ring!

Thus it was that of two related fashions, both originating from one gifted surgeon, one was a disaster and the other became a permanent surgical custom.

Thalidomide

Thalidomide is an effective sedative drug that was first synthesised in 1953 and became fashionable in the late 1950s and early 1960s. It caused one of the most dramatic tragedies in the history of medicine, one of the biggest medical scandals of all time. It was prescribed, with great success, for many conditions, including morning sickness in pregnancy. Then it was shown to produce terrible deformities in unborn babies, mostly to their limbs and hearts. Its common and most dramatic product was *phocomelia*, or limbs like seal's flippers. These deformities were particularly common in Germany, where the drug had been available without prescription, but there were also hundreds of cases in Britain and other countries, where it had become a popular prescription drug.

Thalidomide had been widely praised, advertised and prescribed on the grounds that it was highly effective and almost impossible to use for suicide. There seemed to be no reason to doubt its safety. It had not been tested on unborn children or even on pregnant animals, but then again, there had been no demand for such tests. The tragedy was unlike anything that had gone before. It was widely believed at the time that the human placenta was impervious to poisons except in such doses as killed the mother. This was a fashionable belief without evidence to support it. Indeed, there was already evidence that it was untrue and that foetuses could be deformed by external influences, including poisoning and therapeutic drugs, infection, x-rays and malnutrition. One pre-thalidomide review of evidence of the effects of drugs on the foetus contained 354 references, most of them referring to damage and many of them published in influential and widely read journals. Some of this evidence, particularly in relation to syphilis and rubella, had been accepted and acted upon by the medical profession (e.g. by Wassermann tests for pregnant women and rubella parties for pre-pubertal girls), but most of it had been ignored because the idea was unfashionable.

Thalidomide was soon found to cause peripheral neuritis (inflammation and loss of function in the body nerves), but little notice was taken of this also. Antenatal care did not include advice about drugs. Testing of new drugs on pregnant animals was perfunctory or non-existent. Editors of general medical journals showed little interest in congenital malformations, and the absence of comment and information that was easily available to most doctors was not conducive to new ways of thinking.

Why did the medical profession ignore the extensive existing evidence that damaging substances could cross the placenta? There is no evidence that, before the tragedy, the drug companies were trying to keep such information away from public gaze. They had no reason to develop tests on pregnant animals when the medical profession itself thought them unnecessary. It is useful to look at it as part of a mindset or a shared view of reality that controls, organises and limits perception and understanding. We all tend to ignore anything that does not fit our theories and beliefs, so that it tends to be downgraded until circumstances change or something happens that makes it impossible to ignore it any more. The fashionable belief was that the placenta was impermeable to harmful substances, and thus evidence to the contrary was ignored until something occurred that was so startling, anomalous and public that it could be ignored no longer. Then, and only then, was the belief challenged and changed.

To some extent this rearrangement of outlook involved a return to past theories and beliefs – which raises the question of why they had ever been abandoned. The idea that maternal impressions can affect an unborn child for better or worse is an old one. Interest in 'monsters' (grossly deformed infants) as they were called, goes back at least to ancient Egypt. For many centuries they were seen as warnings or divine omens and were often confused with mythological beings. It was an ancient Jewish custom to put a beautiful child at the door of public baths to help women to 'have children as fine as he'. It is said that in ancient Carthage alcohol was forbidden to a bridal couple in case a conceptus was damaged by it. Later monsters became objects of interest, to be collected and described. Most museums of pathology still possess a collection of them.

In the eighteenth century there was much interest in maternal impressions. In the mid-nineteenth century it was believed in the English-speaking world that heredity could be altered by external circumstances at any point between conception and weaning. Physicians warned against sexual intercourse under the influence of drugs or alcohol, as they believed that these could affect the constitution of a child. In 1870, however, the medical profession was criticised for its 'prevalent belief' in the ability of maternal impressions to cause any degree of malformation.

In the late nineteenth century the belief in the effect of material impressions was falling into disrepute for being linked with magic and 'unscientific' thinking. This connection may be important in the way the idea became unfashionable. As medicine became more scientific, so 'magic' came into contempt. The placenta was steeped in myth and mystery, however, and no one working with humans thought to analyse the evidence. Apart from a few people who worked with it 'scientifically', it seems to have remained in a kind of quasi-magical limbo and vulnerable to the social fantasies of the time.

Belief in the placenta as a perfect barrier against damaging influences in the environment was reinforced by the Victorian tendency to put 'woman' on a pedestal, which led to idealisation of the womb as well as of the woman. Women's reproductive organs were regarded as different and special, and also as the source of all women's symptoms and ills not visibly due to something else. Only a few practising doctors disagreed. One of these was F W Ballantyne (1861–1923), a teratologist (specialist in foetal abnormalities) and lecturer in antenatal pathology in Edinburgh, who initiated many advances in antenatal care. In 1904 he listed 'varieties of foetal morbid states', including transmitted diseases and toxicological states such as lead poisoning, alcoholism and morphine poisoning. Few took notice. Typically, as late as 1937, Professor F J Browne in his popular textbook *Antenatal and Postnatal Care* discussed the diagnosis of foetal abnormalities but not their causes. In 1941, when rubella (or German measles) was first shown to damage unborn babies, the peculiarity of the infection was emphasised but it was not taken as a general warning about the vulnerability of foetuses. Today one can still find examples of residual idealisation of the womb. For example, in 1999 an article on foetal surgery in *The Sunday Times* declared, 'The womb is the perfect operating theatre and an ideal convalescent home.'

Another possible reason why little notice was taken of environmental dangers in pregnancy was that foetuses, stillbirths and newborn babies had been regarded as expendable, or at least as not very important. Few doctors were interested in them for their own sake. Infant mortality was high, and babies created danger for their mothers at a time when maternal mortality was also high. Nineteenth-century accounts of obstetric cases seldom mention whether or not the infant survived, clearly regarding it as a trivial matter. A deformed foetus was likely to arouse even less interest unless it had rare abnormalities, in which case it might be described in a journal or preserved in a pot. By the 1930s, however, the maternal morality rate was falling, birth control was spreading, families were smaller and there was greater interest in infants and their survival. Also, decline in mortality from infection and improved antenatal care meant that congenital defects became more prominent as a cause of morbidity and mortality, which at least provided a reason for studying them. The British Perinatal Mortality Survey of 1958 brought foetuses into prominence and provided a background and a context for future foetal studies.

Confusion reigned for a long time, however. Scientific work on mammalian foetuses, which began seriously only in the 1930s, was hampered by the enormous variability between animal species. What was highly teratogenic (inducing abnormalities) to one species often had little or no effect on another, which complicated or invalidated many tests. Moreover, teratologists had a different attitude in that they were trying to *produce* foetal malformation as part of their experiments, and their publications frequently reveal their understandable enthusiasm for highly teratogenic substances. One referred to thalidomide as '*an almost perfect example…*' (my italics). Another wrote, 'We *succeeded* in inducing abnormalities…' and 'we *failed to produce* endemic cretinism but *found something much better* in the skeletal malformations induced by riboflavin deficiency'. Teratologists published their findings in journals with limited, specialist readership, and these were not reported in general medical journals. The evidence did not fit current beliefs, so was overlooked or discounted.

Even a brief analysis of the historical context of the thalidomide disaster suggests that it occurred largely because human teratology was unfashionable among clinicians, who therefore had no reason or motivation to take it seriously. It was an attitude of mind that idealised the placenta and ignored most of the existing evidence of foetal damage through environmental influences.

Thalidomide changed the way in which the medical profession and the lay public regarded drugs taken in pregnancy. It is now fashionable to avoid them altogether when possible. Thalidomide also played a part in breaking down the paradoxical idealisation and denigration of women that has been so prominent in Western medical history. It is, however, also true to say that in some ways it was a useful and effective drug. Recently it has been used again in some parts of the world in the treatment of leprosy – with the inevitable result that 'thalidomide babies' are once again being born.

Tongue-tie

In the days before anaesthetics, surgeons and physicians carried lancets in their pockets and quite often performed small operations spontaneously. One popular little operation was to slit the frenum (the fold of membrane under the tongue) to cure 'tongue-tie', a condition in which the infant appeared to be unable to stick out its tongue and which, if untreated, was said to interfere with the development of speech.

The condition was mentioned by the sixteenth-century surgeon Ambroise Paré, who wrote of 'disjoyning those things which are continued...by the dissection of the ligament of the tongue, which hinders children from sucking and speaking'. By the nineteenth century it was established practice to cut the frenum when it was thought that a child was tongue-tied. Since an infant will not put out its tongue on request, however, the diagnosis was difficult and often wrong. In 1890 Quain's dictionary advised the doctor 'to snip the fraenum with a blunt-pointed pair of scissors', but he also wrote, 'Mothers often suppose that their children are tongue-tied when, in truth, they are only backward.' It was only slowly realised that the condition was usually a variation of the normal. In 1911 the surgeon Edmund Owen wrote that it is often noticeable at birth, but 'will probably right itself as the front part of the tongue takes on its natural growth'.

The fashion has long passed, and the operation is now rarely done. The diagnosis and operation for tongue-tie has joined the long list of outmoded surgical fashions that have played so prominent a part in the development of modern medicine.

Tonsils and adenoids

One of the most popular medical fashions of the twentieth century among both doctors and parents was the belief that the tonsils were responsible for colds in children and that they were better removed through the operation of tonsillectomy. A straw poll at a recent academic meeting revealed that about two-thirds of an audience of mixed ages and nationalities had lost their tonsils during childhood. Many of the operations had been done at home, often at the same time as similar operations on siblings. Nowadays, however, routine tonsillectomy has become unpopular with most surgeons, who prefer to perform the operation only when there are strong indications.

The tonsils are collections of lymphatic material lying in the back of the throat. Adenoids, of similar material, lie further back, behind the soft palate. Both organs have featured in some of the most popular fashions in medicine. The history of tonsillectomy is a good example of the way in which a new discovery or treatment that seems to be successful and part of medical progress can become fashionable with the public as well as with doctors, then greatly exaggerated, then deprecated, finally emerging with a firm place in the medical repertoire but with considerably diminished popularity and prestige.

Children have large tonsils but, since knowledge of children's anatomy and its differences from adult anatomy had not been studied, for centuries the large size was believed to be abnormal. Moreover, the tonsils often become infected as the child builds up immunity to surrounding diseases. It used to be thought that large tonsils in themselves were an indication for surgery, and the custom of removing children's tonsils became increasingly common during the nineteenth century. This continued on a large scale until the middle of the twentieth century. In some sections of society, it became virtually a rite of passage. Its popularity gradually declined and it was performed less and less often and, increasingly, only after serious consideration.

Tonsillectomy is an old operation. It was known to the ancients and has been performed in one way or another ever since, usually for serious infection, especially abscesses in the throat. For centuries the operation was done for severe infection or quinsy, either with a knife or with the fingers. In AD 10 Celsus wrote a clear description of the operation. In AD 750 Paul of Aegina gave precise instructions about it. Fabricius of Padua (1537–1619), who taught William Harvey (1578–1657), believed that the operation was 'neither easy nor altogether safe'. As surgery and surgical instruments became more sophisticated, cutting out the tonsils became easier and was done more frequently, but still only for serious cases of infection and swelling.

By the late eighteenth century, new ideas about diseases as lesions, located anatomically, together with other influences such as the development of hospitals, the invention of new surgical instruments and improved education in anatomy, were changing the principles and practice of surgery. By the middle of the nineteenth century surgery was well established on a new course. Anaesthesia was gaining acceptance, although asepsis was still some years in the future. The idea was gaining ground that tonsils were dangerous when they were large, in which case they should be removed. Since all children have large tonsils and tonsils are easy for even an inexperienced doctor to reach, one can see how the fashion for tonsillectomy developed.

The knife was used in ancient times to excise ulcerated tonsils. In a development of this, the first Professor of Surgery at the University of Pennsylvania, an innovative surgeon called Philip Syng Physick (1768–1837), invented an instrument called a guillotine for cutting off the tonsils. This was refined and improved by the American William B Fahnestock. For the next eighty years, the guillotine was the basic instrument used for tonsillectomy.

In 1853 James Syme (1799–1870), Professor of Clinical Surgery at the University of Edinburgh, addressed the Edinburgh Medico-Chirugical Society 'On the Improvements which have been Introduced into the Practice of Surgery in Great Britain within the last Thirty Years'. These thirty years covered his own surgical experience and during that time he had been responsible for many of those 'improvements' himself. Syme was a former pupil of Robert Liston, who performed the first operation under anaesthetic in Britain. He was also the future father-in-law of Joseph Lister, who introduced antisepsis. Syme held the Edinburgh chair for 37 years and was a distinguished surgeon and innovator.

When Syme's address turned to the subject of the tonsils, he became enthusiastic. Enlargement of the tonsils, he said, was a problem for which, thirty years previously, 'the practice of surgery in Great Britain did not afford any effectual remedy'. Now Edinburgh had introduced 'removal by the knife', an operation which, 'through the influence of gentlemen educated here, is now widely extended... The operation, when properly performed, in circumstance really requiring it, affords, with perfect safety, such an amount of speedy and permanent relief, as justly to merit the title of a substantial improvement.'

Syme was also aware of possible harm and abuse, however. He referred to 'a certain degree of discredit which it has acquired, from the proceedings of those specialists who profess to cure cases of deafness usually reputed incurable; and among other means for this purpose, are alleged to cut tonsils in no wise redundant, or in any respect warranting interference.' This too was to become a theme running through the history of tonsillectomy.

In Syme's view, therefore, tonsillectomy for enlarged tonsils had become an established operation which, in the right hands, was respectable and safe, but which less scrupulous operators were bringing into disrepute. The next hundred years were to see it develop as part of the new surgery until it became, in some circles, almost universal.

It used to be thought that tonsils were an aid to digestion, helping the food slip down. A typical description of their normal function was that they secreted mucus 'to lubricate the food in its passage to the stomach'. Other, sometimes bizarre, functions were also suggested, such as that the tonsils act in utero to prevent the foetus from swallowing amniotic fluid, or that they absorb some of the products of salivary digestion. The theories became increasingly complicated. One writer in the *Lancet* thought that the tonsil in the back of the throat was meant to absorb the snot and tears of someone lying down, while the tonsil behind the tongue did the same for someone standing up, as the uvula drips onto it in that position. Together they acted as a kind of 'sewage farm' for the contaminated secretions of the nose and mouth. Another writer believed that mouth fluids accumulate in the crypts of the tonsils and are absorbed. During the nineteenth century the tonsils came to be seen as dangerous organs, vestiges of evolution or creation, that often became infected and were better removed.

We now believe that lymphatic tissue is important in the immune system and that the tonsils are more protective than infective, especially in childhood. Like other lymphatic structures, they tend to be large in small children and diminish in size as the child grows. At the same time, small children tend to get infections of the nose and throat while they build up immunity. This has confused the issue and a powerful myth persists to this day that tonsils are potentially dangerous and actually cause infections.

It is understandable that tonsils came to be seen as potentially dangerous. The Industrial Revolution brought urbanisation, over-crowding, polluted air and child labour under generally poor conditions, which led to an increase in infection. A serious problem before the days of antibiotics was quinsy, a severe infection of the throat with abscess. Quinsy was life-threatening not only because the infection could spread and lead to septicaemia, but also because it could block the airway and cause death by suffocation. This danger had been recognised since antiquity. Suffocation is both dramatic and terrifying, a stark demonstration of a doctor's failure to help his patient. Gradually the idea developed that large tonsils were in themselves potentially dangerous and sufficient reason to operate. It came to be believed that they, like quinsy, could obstruct the airway and suffocate the patient. The operation of tonsillectomy was mostly done because of recurrent infection (such as quinsy) or because the tonsils were enlarged, or were thought to be so. The idea was not totally new; in 1509 Ambroise Paré had advised tracheotomy (making a hole in the trachea or windpipe) where there was serious enlargement.

James Yearsley (1805–69) was a London surgeon with a royal appointment and a great interest in promoting surgery of the tonsils. (He was not, incidentally, accepted by the medical 'establishment', the powerful doctors who controlled the profession in London.) In 1842 he published a book that emphasised the importance of removing enlarged tonsils. He maintained:

The attention of the medical profession has never been sufficiently directed to the subject of morbid conditions of the throat...nor has it been shown how closely the health and strength, and, consequently, the growth of young persons, are dependent on a normal state of the throat.

As the belief grew that large tonsils were in themselves an indication for surgery, the true indications for operating became somewhat obscured. In 1851 Bransby Cooper, senior surgeon at Guy's, wrote (apparently of adult tonsils) that 'the most common affection of the tonsil requiring surgical treatment is chronic enlargement which sometimes goes to so great an extent as to interfere materially with breathing, speech and deglutition'. In 1853 James Syme wrote:

> Enlargement of the tonsils occurs very frequently at an early period of life, impeding respiration, especially during sleep, rendering the voice husky, causing a disposition to sore throat, and occasionally producing a degree of *deafness*...

In the same year, James Yearsley wrote to the *Medical Times and Gazette* about 'the improvement of the general health which almost invariably follows excision of enlarged tonsils'. Robert Liston asserted, 'Sudden death from enlarged tonsils has been known to happen.' The London surgeon Sir William Fergusson (1808–77) wrote of 'permanent enlargement' of the tonsils which 'gives rise to difficulty of swallowing, sometimes even of breathing, change of voice, hoarseness, *deafness*, and other ailments'. Fergusson was an advocate of conservative surgery and he recommended that 'in the event of constitutional remedies and applications having been proved of no service, either as regards the state of the mucous membrane or tonsils, then a portion of one or both glands should be removed'. In 1874 another surgeon wrote that enlarged tonsils cause 'cup-shaped depressions in the chest', relieved by tonsillectomy. He explained it as 'permitting a freer influx of air than before and so does away with the depression'. Charles West of Great Ormond Street distinguished between children and adults. He wrote that hypertrophy (overgrowth) of the tonsils in an adult 'is little more than an inconvenience', but in a child it 'is not infrequently the cause of more serious evils'. He thought that enlarged tonsils 'maintain a condition most unfavourable to the arrest of tubercular disease in the chest', and thought that they should be excised immediately if there was cough 'or any other symptom warranting a suspicion of phthisical disease of the chest.'

Here one is reminded again of the ever-present danger of infection before the days of antibiotics and, in this case, of the constant menace of a specific and dangerous infection, tuberculosis. Fears associated with this awareness underlay much medical thinking of the time. Urban growth was increasing the dangers of infection, and improving medical knowledge was increasing awareness of diseases connected to infection, including rheumatic fever, endocarditis, nephritis and arthritis. Much of the contemporary literature emphasised the close relationship between large, and so presumably infected, tonsils and surgical conditions such as chronic cholecystitis, peptic ulcer and appendicitis. It was generally assumed that tonsils were better out than in. It was thought that little harm could result from removing 'useless' organs.

One of the surgical giants of the period, W H A Jacobson of University College Hospital, was very much geared to the severely abnormal rather than to the fashionable treatment of the moment. In his textbook he gave his chapter 'Operation on the Tonsil' the subtitle 'Removal of new growths of the tonsil' and dealt only with that subject. Elsewhere he discussed 'Removal of enlarged tonsils', saying, 'This is so minor and usually so uncomplicated an operation that I only allude to it here to urge my readers to give a trial to enucleation. It removes the entire tonsil and is adapted to all cases.' This is an implied criticism of the 'guillotine' method then in fashion (in which part of the tonsil was cut off, leaving the rest behind) and it anticipates the method of dissection (removing the whole tonsil) which became fashionable in the twentieth century.

In spite of all this evidence of surgery, some contemporaries seemed to think that tonsillectomy was uncommon before the 1890s. The London surgeon T F Layton thought it was then done only for a large tonsil with the object of removing the redundant lymphatic tissue. Another wrote in the year 1890:

There is probably no disease with which the laryngologist has to deal more frequently than enlarged or hypertrophied tonsils and consequently a successful method of their treatment, I trust, will prove of interest to all.

J W Haward, assistant surgeon at Great Ormond Street, wrote in 1883 of 'distressing nightmare in children clearly referable to the condition of the tonsils'. In 1892 William Osler warned of the dangers of enlarged tonsils, which, he wrote, make children prone to colds, recurrent attacks of follicular disease, diphtheria and scarlet fever. 'If the tonsils are large and the general state is evidently influenced by them, they should be at once removed.' However, fifteen years later, in *Modern Medicine*, which he edited, a contributor wrote:

> The faucial tonsils are really a large pair of lymphatic glands, the functions of which are but imperfectly understood. As with other lymph glands they probably protect the organism from infections of various kinds by acting as filters, and by in some way lessening the toxicity of microörganisms which come within their sphere of activity.

Some surgeons felt the dangers of the tonsil so strongly that they believed that its mere existence was a ground for its removal. In 1892 an American surgeon, F H Bosworth, published an article entitled 'The Existence of a Tonsil should be Regarded as a Disease', in which he wrote, 'There is no tonsil in the healthy throat. The existence of a tonsil should be regarded as a disease to be dealt with summarily and promptly … What tonsil should be cut out? All tonsils should be cut out.' This was a common American attitude, more extreme than the English.

Although the enthusiasm for tonsillectomy was strongest in the English-speaking world, it was not confined to it. In 1854 the Parisian surgeon E Chassaignac wrote of people being 'attacked with obstinate hypertrophied tonsils', making them 'pale, sick and delicate'. He warned of 'a thing which very obviously is not cured – namely, *the deep-seated injuries sustained by the condition*'. He even cited a case of one-sided development of the breast that was cured by tonsillectomy! There was also enthusiasm for tonsillectomy in German-speaking countries. The surgeon Tenzer wrote, 'The faucal tonsil may be unhesitatingly sacrificed when necessary.' According to him, extensive investigation among children had 'failed to discover disadvantages of any kind whatever, as sequelae to the operation'.

During the last decade of the nineteenth century voices began to be raised in favour of the idea that the tonsils were protective rather than destructive and might even be an important contribution to children's development. At a meeting of the British Laryngological Association in November 1890 it was said:

Many and extraordinary are the notions entertained, not only by members of this profession but by the public at large, as to the nature and functions of these structures. Loud and frequent are the objections encountered daily by surgeons on proposing to partially remove the parts when diseased. Interference with growth, loss of sexual power, consumption and laryngeal troubles are only a few of the mildest of consequences that are said to follow their interference.

Another objector wrote in 1891: 'We should have been spared much vain theorizing on this subject if writers on the human tonsil had examined the same organ in other animals...' He went on to say that this study 'completely negatives the idea that this structure is a functionless survival of some pre-existing organ'. He discussed enlarged tonsils and asked why children's are bigger than those of adults, suggesting that they were protective and that the obstruction to respiration that was thought to be due to enlarged tonsils might be caused by 'constitutional delicacy' rather than alteration of the shape of the pharynx.

Towards the end of the century there were several notable changes in outlook. In 1897 W L Ballenger, Professor of Otology, Rhinilogy and Laryngology at the University of Illinois, grew disenchanted with the custom of removing only part of the tonsil and became convinced that this was not a useful therapeutic measure. Using scalpel and forceps, he began to remove the whole tonsil – and thereby began a new trend. Later, in 1908, George Waugh of Great Ormond Street introduced his blunt dissection method of enucleation which became a landmark in the history of tonsillectomy. One of his colleagues remarked that 'unfortunately' it made the operation easier to do and too much tissue was removed. There began a long dispute about the relative merits of guillotining the tonsils and enucleating them at their roots. The results of enucleation seemed to be good, and the guillotine fell into disrepute.

Another landmark had little immediate influence. In 1898 Jonathan Wright's *The Nose and Throat in Medical History* recognised the psychological importance of the nose and throat. Others began to see tonsillectomy as protective against rheumatic fever, and even that removal of tonsils would cure an attack of rheumatic fever and prevent recurrences. Still others began to suspect that the operation increased susceptibility to poliomyelitis, which was becoming a problem. The hypothesis was gaining ground among a minority that the tonsils protect against infection rather than increase it.

Thus fashions began to conflict. In the second decade of the twentieth century a rival treatment to tonsillectomy was devised and briefly became fashionable: irradiation. In 1914, in a series of animal experiments, it was found that suitable exposure to x-rays could cause a complete disappearance of the tonsils and virtually all lymphoid tissue without causing detectable injury to other tissues or organs. This suggested that x-ray might be used with success in the treatment of large tonsils and other lymphatic organs. The *Lancet* approved. In an editorial it announced:

> The cure thus brought about is apparently permanent, and the treatment may safely be applied to the ordinary chronic septic tonsil... It is satisfactory to learn of a method of treatment which appears to have considerable advantages over the usual surgical procedures.

However, this new potential fashion did not become popular. Many doctors continued to believe in surgery and insisted that tonsillectomy was a cure for many conditions, including repeated vomiting. There were arguments for and against complete tonsillectomy, and an argument about whether children with nothing wrong other than large tonsils should have '-otomy' (cutting into) or '-ectomy' (complete removal). The rivalry between those who cut and those who delved continued unabated. In 1921 there was a debate about it at the Royal Society of Medicine.

In the same year, the ongoing popularity of tonsillectomy was demonstrated by the fact that more than 13 per cent of schoolchildren in London had been operated on before they left school at fourteen. One surgeon commented, 'During the last few years the practice has sprung up of systematically enucleating all tonsils which were found to be enlarged, quite irrespective of the cause of such enlargement.' The argument shifted from whether all enlarged tonsils should be removed to whether *all* tonsils should be removed.

It may not have caught on in a big way, but irradiation of the tonsils remained popular among some doctors for many years. It was already known that irradiation could lead to cancer and also to burns (regarded as virtually routine by some laryngologists), baldness, sterility, atrophy of any or all of the glands of internal secretion, arteriosclerosis and permanent gastric injury. Yet in 1923 it was suggested that the 'good results' of irradiation were tonic effects of x-ray. As late as 1930 a New York physician was still extolling its virtues in the *Journal of the American Medical Association*, saying that fears of complications from x-rays 'have been largely allayed in the United States' and deploring the fact that 'there remain those who still ascribe fever, bronchitis and vomiting to any dose of x-rays over a period of days if not weeks, following any irradiation, however small.'

Meanwhile, the theory of focal infection was gaining ground and this led to a great increase in publications advocating removal of the tonsils, which were still widely thought to be a breeding ground for bacteria. In 1915 the *Archives of Pediatrics* intoned:

> It would seem that everyone must be aware of the deleterious effect of hypertrophied adenoids and tonsils... The medical profession is to blame that children come to school age with offending adenoids and tonsils. Some of these children will be deformed for life. They will always show...marks of an injury which ought to have been prevented [by removal of their adenoids and tonsils].

Some surgeons believed that it was better to sacrifice many innocent tonsils rather than allow one guilty one to escape. A Hunterian lecturer to the Royal College of Physicians emphasised that 'extirpation of the organ, so far as can be discovered, causes no defect in the economy'.

Parents became, and have remained, strong supporters of the operation. Many of them seem to have developed the idea that tonsillectomy was good for their children. One New York paediatrician wrote that it had 'aroused the mind of [the] thinking parents to the benefits', so that 'we often now find the parents bringing the child to us to have his tonsils removed'. The operation, 'far from being harmful, is a long step in advance in prophylaxis and preventative medicine'.

New indications were found for the operation, for instance as a cure for diphtheria carriers and as a protection against endocarditis. A London surgeon began a paper by announcing, 'The number of tonsil and adenoid operations to my credit...now exceeds the respectable total of 5,000.' He added, 'To effect a cure, the operation must be radical.' Enthusiasm for the most extensive operations was widespread among surgeons. Children, like women, have often been the object of medical enthusiasm and experiment.

Like many other medical and physiological conditions, large tonsils were labelled 'a disease of modern times'. Primitive humans 'did not suffer from enlarged tonsils and adenoids'. The 'disease' was also thought to be 'essentially British' and possibly due to artificial feeding in infancy. A typical statement comes from Harper, a surgeon working in Glasgow in 1920:

> The [tonsil] is a source of grave potential danger to the child... [and] also to the adult. Its early and complete removal must be insisted upon should there be any reason to suspect that its presence is having an ill effect on the well-being of the individual.

The ear, nose and throat (ENT) surgeon to University College Hospital and the Evelina Children's Hospital gave 33 indications for removing the tonsils and added that the operation often relieved the symptoms of other diseases as well, among them epilepsy, bed-wetting, laryngismus and night terrors.

The 1930s were a peak time for tonsillectomies. Hospitals provided a service for the working class, while the family doctors of the middle classes usually did the operation themselves, often on several children in a family at the same time, on the kitchen or nursery table. The higher the social class, the more likely it was to be done. In 1937 83 per cent of the boys at Eton had had their tonsils removed. Lower down the social scale, the operation was also becoming popular. During the twenty years before the National Health Service came into being the operation was performed upon more than one and a half million children attending public elementary schools in England and Wales, and the *British Medical Journal* expressed surprise that doctors had 'not reached definite conclusions' about the value of the operation. After the foundation of the NHS in 1948, it was nearly always done in hospital. In 1958 40 per cent of entrants to the Royal Air Force had had their tonsils out and tonsillectomy was the commonest operation done under the NHS. Between one-sixth and a quarter of all children admitted to hospital came for tonsillectomy. The commonest indication for the operation at this time was always infection, or the presence of inflammation or pus, but size was also often regarded as an indication. Size became an increasing source of argument. In one series of 4,500 children, 31 per cent had been referred only because of the size of their tonsils. This was despite the fact that many leading authorities were by now united in the belief that size alone was of no importance.

There were also curious variations from place to place. It might be thought that more children would have their tonsils out in the smoky industrial north than in the sunny, rural south, but this was not so. The seaside resort of Margate had eight times the tonsillectomy rate of neighbouring Ramsgate. The leafy London suburb of Enfield had twenty times the rate of less prosperous Hornsey. Children in Rutland were nineteen times more likely to have their tonsils removed than those in neighbouring Cambridgeshire, and 27 times more likely than children in Birkenhead. In Kent the incidence varied from 45 per cent in Bexhill to one per cent in Deal. In the United States there were comparable figures and variations between districts.

It seems that these differences could be explained not by generally accepted need, but largely by the attitudes and practices of the local doctors. A few school medical officers made concerted efforts to reduce the number of tonsillectomies performed in their districts. A Dr Ash reduced the number of operations in Derbyshire from nearly 3,000 in 1928 to only 156 in 1934.

The man who worked out and publicised many of these figures was a Medical Officer of Health called J A Glover, who became something of a crusader against the operation and described it as 'one of the major phenomena of modern surgery'. He expressed astonishment 'to find how recent is the great vogue of the operation'. He quoted the distinguished nineteenth-century physician Sir James Goodhart, who had noted in 1885 that parents were reluctant to have their children tonsillectomised. Glover compared this with their eagerness for the operation in 1938. He produced evidence that the incidence of the operation in well-to-do families was three times that in poorer families, and that there had been 'a rapid rise in vogue of the operation' at the beginning of the twentieth century which slackened during World War I, then rose again to a high tide in 1931. He gave figures for various hospitals.

Glover also discussed the physiology of children's tonsils, pointing out that these tended to enlarge between the ages of four and six, a popular age for removing them, but that they receded later as the child became less prone to infections – and this was just the age when the success of the operation was measured by the reduced number of infections. In other words, at least some of the apparent success of the operation was due to physiological changes which normally take place at this stage in a child's life. He deplored 'the many – parents or practitioners – to whom enlargement at any age seems always pathological'. He asked, and was not the first to do so, why it had been debased into 'so widespread an attack upon a normal structure of the body.'

Why indeed? How and why did this operation become so popular with both doctors and parents? What were the likely causes of the enormous rise in the incidence of tonsillectomy between the late nineteenth and mid-twentieth centuries?

The development of the medical profession and the medicalisation of society, against a background of increasing secularisation, undoubtedly played a significant part. Faith in medicine goes with the desire that the doctor should *do* something, even when there is really nothing to be done, so it is not surprising that this new faith in doctors and their medicine was particularly conspicuous in surgery after it became relatively safe – especially surgery in areas of the body that were relatively easy to reach and safe to remove, and performed on patients who were easy to persuade and control. Women and children were ideal subjects.

Another interesting line of investigation is the personalities of the surgeons, some of whom liked to remove as much as possible, some of whom aimed to conserve as much as possible. This dichotomy continues today, and often influences general practitioners' choice of surgeon for their patients. The history of 'heroic' versus 'conservative' surgery has yet to be written, however.

In the early nineteenth century, a New York physician called Horace Green became a crusader for tonsillectomy. In 1846 he published a book called *Diseases of the Air Passages*. It strongly reinforced the views of the London surgeon James Yearsley, who had already written a book emphasising the importance of removing enlarged tonsils. He referred to 'the improvement of the general health which almost invariably follows excision of enlarged tonsils'. Some supporters even thought that there was a connection between the tonsils and the ovaries and that both were best removed. A physician to the Royal Edinburgh Hospital for Sick Children, M P James, wrote that disease of the tonsils often formed 'the starting-point of other and more serious ailments'. The following year he wrote: 'Hypertrophy of the tonsils in children gives rise to a variety of conditions, in themselves more or less indicative of distress and even danger.' Then came an extreme article entitled 'The existence of a tonsil should be regarded as a disease'.

Paradoxically, some of the more extreme warnings about tonsillar danger now seem more rational than they have done at times in the past. For instance, an assistant surgeon at Great Ormond Street wrote in the *British Medical Journal* 'On enlargement of the tonsils as a cause of nightmare', and the *Lancet* published an article called 'Night terror and screaming in a child cured by removal of the tonsils'. These might seem to be among the more absurd claims of the eager tonsillectomists, but the recent discovery of sleep apnoea and its frequent cure by tonsillectomy suggests another possible explanation.

Those making the most extreme claims were not all fringe doctors trying to be important or to make a living. They included many professional heavyweights, though there were others who opposed the wholesale removal of tonsils even if they recommended other drastic forms of intervention. One of these was John Erichsen (1818–96), Professor of Surgery at University College Hospital, whose *Science and Art of Surgery* was published in 1853 and went through ten editions. He recommended that inflamed tonsils should be treated by the 'application of leeches under the jaw, of fomentations, the inhalation of the steam of hot water, and low diet'. Like others, however, he believed in the evil of enlarged tonsils. During the 1880s there was a theory that tonsillectomy had an adverse effect on the reproductive system, an idea which the supporters of the operation were quick to attack.

At this time the function of the tonsils as part of the immune system had not yet been suggested. It was widely believed that they merely lubricated the digestive tract and that as long as a small piece was left behind, this would continue to happen. In 1888 Sir James Goodhart, Physician to Guy's and Great Ormond Street, wrote, 'It is comparatively seldom that an operation is necessary and fortunately so, for parents manifest great reluctance to it. Children grow out of it...' This could be a statement of the modern official attitude, but it did not halt the growing fashion for tonsillectomy.

When the new idea of irradiation came into the discussion (see page 220), a *Lancet* editorial remarked that chronic enlargement of the tonsils 'has been the subject of active interference rather than pathological study' and recommended irradiation as an alternative. This had been found to shrink the tonsils. It was not widely taken up, however, and, as we have seen, the argument moved on to whether children with large tonsils and no infection or symptoms should have the tonsils partially or wholly removed.

Meanwhile, the fashion for tonsillectomy became so strong that admission as a cadet to West Point was refused until the tonsils were removed. In 1923, 48,000 elementary schoolchildren in England and Wales had their tonsils out and Sir George Newman, Chief Medical Officer to the Ministry of Health, issued the first of many warnings against premature resort to the operation. He repeated these warnings every year and was endorsed by a memorandum from the Section of Laryngology of the Royal Society of Medicine. Warnings were also coming from America, in articles with titles such as 'An enquiry into the status of tonsillectomy today: promiscuous removal distinctly to be condemned'.

So what about the patients in all this? And what part did parents play? Some parents, particularly middle-class and ambitious parents, were now even keener on the operation than were the doctors. They were developing great confidence in the procedure and total trust in doctors. They were pushing their children forward for the operation. An interesting comment was made in an article published in 1924, when the surgeon G H Lansdown wrote:

> I can imagine no greater compliment can be paid to anyone than that which our patients pay us, when, on our advice, they lie down on an operating table and allow us to render them unconscious and do whatever we think fit.

From then on there was much comment in the medical literature that pressure from parents was the most important cause of operation being done, and that this had become the commonest 'indication'. The parents were pushing the doctors and, while some surgeons resisted, others were willing, even eager, to oblige.

This was a time when infant and child mortality was falling. For the first time in history it was possible to have reasonable confidence in the survival of one's children. It seems likely that this influenced changes in attitudes to children that were discernible from the late nineteenth century onwards. For the first time ideas developed about children's rights, children as individuals, as people. At first the changing law had concerned itself largely with the rights of children outside the family and had not entered the home or questioned the power of the pater-familias, but gentler feelings were becoming apparent, along with a wider understanding of children and sympathy for them. This can be seen, for instance, in the contemporary manuals of child-rearing. These changes had accelerated other changes, including the involvement of children with doctors.

From the mid-nineteenth century children began to be seen as a desirable part of a medical practice, and they made up to one-third of an average Victorian practice. This was probably from necessity rather than choice: doctors competed fiercely for business. Moreover, in 1851, 40 per cent of the population was aged fourteen or less, compared with 22 per cent a century later. Doctors had to treat whole families, and parents wanted their children to share in the new scientific medicine.

How far were the doctors out for money? Of course they were paid to take out tonsils, and their practices were increased by so doing. Those who operated in public hospitals also gained power, prestige and that great symbol of medical power, beds. Tonsillectomy became the operation done most frequently. These considerations must have played a part. They are surely relevant in the tendency towards intervention that has always been such a feature of scientific medicine, although they do not wholly explain it.

As time passed, the opponents of routine operation gained power and influence. Some studies found minor advantages from the operation in younger age groups and over a short time, but by then much more had been learned about the natural course of development of the tonsils. Large tonsils and frequent upper respiratory infections were found to be the norm in small children, whereas there was shrinkage of the tonsils and fewer infections in older children, who might thus seem to have benefited from the operation. Enlarged tonsils, even with symptoms, diminished spontaneously in 90 per cent of cases.

Nonetheless, in 1931 more than 110,000 elementary schoolchildren in England and Wales had their tonsils out. There were so many protests about this that the number fell for a few years, but rose again after 1936. One study found that in the lower forms of elementary schools, children with large tonsils who had not been operated on were better grown than those with 'normal' tonsils.

Meanwhile, in 1934, the American Child Health Association published a study in which they described how they examined a thousand children in New York, 611 of whom had already had their tonsils removed. The remaining 389 were then examined by other physicians, who selected half of them for tonsillectomy. Another group of doctors was asked to examine the remaining children, and these judged 99 of them to be in need of tonsillectomy. Still another group of doctors was then employed to examine the remaining children, and they recommended nearly half of them for operation. In the end only sixty children from the original thousand were thought not to need tonsillectomy, and by this time they had run out of doctors to examine them. Later this study caught the attention of Eliot Freidson, one of the pioneers of the sociology of medicine. He commented that it was like the teacher who fails a certain number of pupils regardless of the overall quality of the class and that it demonstrated the tendency of medics to impute or diagnose illness rather than health.

In America in 1942, a further study of five thousand children concluded:

It is at once apparent that tonsillectomy does not remove from children many or, in fact, any of the normal hazards of childhood. All of the complaints and infections incident to school life are occurring in children who have been operated on as well as those who have not. There are a few diseases that occur a little less frequently in the tonsillectomized children, but the difference is not significant.

Doctors, at least those who specialised in children, were turning against tonsillectomy. They were now emphasising the importance of tonsils in the defence mechanisms of the body. The psychological effects of operating on small children were also beginning to be realised. Here is a quote from a 1934 article by K M Menninger, the first publication on this subject:

Certainly there is nothing in the practice of medicine so barbarous and so fraught with psychological danger as the prevalent custom of taking a child into a strange white room, surrounding him with white-garbed strangers, exhibiting queer paraphernalia and glittering knives, and at the height of his consternation, pressing an ether cone over his face and telling him to breathe deeply. The anxiety stimulated by such horrors is probably never surpassed in the child's subsequent life.

Despite such arguments, in 1937 in a British series of 4,500 children, 31 per cent were sent to hospital merely because of the size of their tonsils. In 1938 in one London district the proportion of children undergoing tonsillectomy rose from two to 25 per cent, coinciding with the appointment of a new medical officer.

In the same year an author writing by invitation in the *British Medical Journal* wrote: 'There is a tendency towards the view that it can do no harm and always does good by freeing the patient from a focus of sepsis...' Also in 1938, a Medical Research Council report concluded: 'There is a tendency for the operation to be performed as a routine prophylactic ritual for no particular reason and with no particular result.'

Meanwhile, there was growing consciousness of the suffering of children when they were in pain, in strange surroundings and separated from their mothers. It was several decades since Freud had made his observations on the unconscious. He was not concerned directly with children, but in 1942 his pupil Helene Deutsch wrote, 'I have noted that operations performed in childhood leave indelible traces on the psychic life of the individual.' In 1944 the paediatrician D M Levy presented an influential paper to the American Psychiatric Association on the psychic trauma of operations on children, especially when the children were very young.

It was around this time that paediatricians began to insist that they, rather than social workers, surgeons or parents, should screen children referred for tonsillectomy. This may have been a bid for power in a growing speciality, but it did at last produce some sanity in the race for maximum tonsillectomy.

Convincing evidence was also accumulating that the tonsil played a positive role in the defence against infection. A 1943 *Lancet* editorial said:

It now seems probable that the tonsil, by trapping pathogenic bacteria, not only may act as a front line guard against infection, but may also contribute to the production of antibodies specific against the invading micro-organisms. Enlargement of lymph glands in response to infection is commonplace.

By 1947, the medical doubts about routine tonsillectomy had reached the public. The magazine *Woman's Home Companion* described the doubts about the operation under the title 'Unnecessary Operations'. Meanwhile, the medical controversies continued. Between 1947 and 1956 the *Quarterly Cumulative Index Medicus* listed more than 1,200 papers on the subject of tonsils – but, surprisingly, no controlled trials of tonsillectomy were begun until 1962.

In 1948 there was a large increase in the number of tonsillectomies done in England. It was the year the NHS was founded, and many doctors were competing for beds and power and trying to demonstrate the needs of their particular speciality. J Glover, the veteran campaigner for the tonsil, asked, 'Why have its probable function in childhood and its tendency to involution alike been so often overlooked in this wholesale and hasty resort to symptomatic treatment in its crudest form?'

Still no controlled trials were done, but pertinent questions were being asked. In 1957 Dr John Fry, an influential GP and medical politician in south London, published a powerful article in the *British Medical Journal* called 'Are all Ts and As really necessary?' He pointed out that much unscientific medicine was practised on young children and asked, 'Why has the present century seen such a savage attack on these normally present and easily accessible structures?' He referred to tonsillectomy as 'a major medical phenomenon of the century', referring to the cost to the Health Service (almost £3 million, a large sum in those days) as 'a ridiculous sum spent on a mass ritual which has never been proved to be scientifically necessary' and with many possible dangers. The Registrar-General had shown that during the previous five years 190 children had died from the operation. Fry asked, 'In how many of these was the operation really necessary?' He listed the complications of the operation and said that enlargement was 'physiological and natural' and 'common to all lympathic structures in children between 3 and 8, and which undergo spontaneous decrease in size after this period'. He demolished the accepted indications. He said that local variations depended on local medical opinion. He thought the class differences were due to 'parental pressure and anxieties' and said that the major factor responsible for the high rate of tonsillectomy was 'the very nature of the conditions for which it is undertaken'. Coughs and colds, he said, are not dangerous but are irritating, trying and demoralising, persistent and recurrent. They produce worrying signs and symptoms and little response to treatment. The family becomes more anxious, teachers remark on lack of progress. So the GP sends the child to the ENT surgeon, possibly with the suggestion that a tonsillectomy is done. The surgeon takes the line of least resistance and operates. There is no benefit, but eventually the child grows out of the problem. Fry suggested that the whole procedure was 'a desperate attempt to treat a normal phase of child development'. In other words, it was a form of medicalisation.

Fry's article made a strong impact on the medical profession and it is interesting to speculate about why that was. He was 'only' a GP at a time when GPs were despised by some senior doctors. Indeed, the powerful Lord Moran had described them as doctors who 'fell off the ladder to success'. Fry's original research was not spectacular and consisted of looking at the records of his own practice. Yet the article was clearly written in a simple, outspoken style that was unusual in professional journals of the time. Also, Fry was an effective medical politician. A powerful force promoting the new Royal College of General Practitioners, he sat on many important committees and had a forceful personality. He was widely regarded as a member of the medical establishment.

There were still doctors who thought the operation was 'valuable'. Others were becoming aware of social factors and were pointing out that, at least in America, it was the insurance companies and those with financial interests who were trying to keep alive the idea of the benefits of tonsillectomy. Medical insurance thrives on extensive or routine surgery, through which the perils of not being insured are made apparent and so new customers are attracted. In Britain it was more a question of the control of hospital beds.

It was also becoming recognised that the main problem in controlling the number of operations was parental pressure. In 1961 Professor R S Illingworth of Sheffield told the Royal Society of Medicine, 'It is altogether wrong to perform an operation on a child because the parents want it.'

Furthermore, there was increasing laboratory evidence that the tonsil produced antibodies and played an important part in the defences against disease. In the next five years several useful, if flawed, studies were published. One of them, for instance, found slight benefits from the operation, but the patients were given prophylactic penicillin while the controls were not, which rather invalidated the results.

During recent years there have been fewer tonsillectomies and more effort has been made to pick the few children who will genuinely benefit. Yet even now, in the twenty-first century, two surgeons have been overheard discussing what they called their 'hit rates', by which they meant the number of parents they could persuade to have their children tonsillectomised. This is almost certainly a result of the encouragement of private medicine in recent years.

In conclusion, then, what do we learn from this story and what further questions might we ask? It reveals very clearly the complexity and variation that can be involved as medical fashions wax and wane. It reveals some of the aspects of the history of medicine that are often ignored, including the enthusiasms of doctors, patients or parents, how and why they wax and wane, and the complicated pressures that influence them. It suggests that nine out of ten operations were probably not beneficial, and reminds us that some of them were fatal. We might usefully look at the history of other popular surgical operations in the same light. How far have they become fashionable because of their accessibility, or because of compliance to the patients' demands, or by the ease with which doctors could perform them? And who is on the receiving end? Most of these popular operations were performed on women or children. Has there ever been an operation, popular among patients, that was done primarily or frequently on men?

Uvula

The uvula is the finger-like projection of soft tissue attached to the soft palate that hangs down at the back of the mouth. It is even more accessible to the surgeon's knife than the tonsils. Like them, it was also known and sometimes removed in antiquity. The modern operation of tonsillectomy developed from ideas about the uvula. A Hippocratic text mentions that, 'of infants those that have a cough during sucking usually have the uvula enlarged'. Before the days of antibiotics, when there was no quick or reliable way to control infection, the uvula was often infected, though this is rare today. 'Elongated uvula' is not even mentioned in modern textbooks and few modern doctors have encountered it, but when infection was common and virtually untreatable, chronic swelling was not uncommon. This is likely to have encouraged the increasing tendency to remove the tonsils if they became infected or were enlarged.

Surgery developed rapidly during the decade before the introduction of anaesthesia and surgeons were already looking for new reasons to operate. In 1841, for instance, at a meeting of the Westminster Medical Society, a Mr Robins advised that every stammerer should have his uvula removed. In 1842 James Yearsley, the London surgeon who later tried so hard to promote the operation of tonsillectomy, gave as an argument in favour of removing the uvula, 'the impunity with which the uvula may be removed; its loss entailing neither present nor subsequent inconvenience'. Discussing elongation of the uvula, Yearsley asserted that 'few persons in our humid climate, pass through life without experiencing annoyance from this troublesome affliction.' This was echoed by his American colleague, Horace Green:

Elongation and enlargement of the uvula is a frequent con-
comitant, of follicular disease of the throat... On some occasions
...great inconvenience...and, even in some instances...to
endanger the life of the individual...where hypertrophy actually
exists, and the uvula itself is both thickened and elongated,
excision will prove the only, effectual remedy. So simple is this
operation, and so entirely unattended with subsequent danger or
inconvenience, that the removal of the uvula should not be
omitted, or delayed, in cases of follicular disease.

These two surgeons were influential in promoting the fashion for
operating on the uvula. During the nineteenth century, uvula and tonsils
were often discussed together, with articles being written under such
titles as 'Ought the tonsils or uvula to be excised in the treatment of
deafness?' and 'On the treatment of enlarged tonsils and elongated
uvula by excision and by local applications'. Yearsley stated that he had
removed the uvula many times 'with such a result as might be
anticipated'. He asked, 'Why should not excision be performed more
frequently?' and lamented the 'distaste...in rural districts' for surgery.

In the second half of the nineteenth century, writers of general
medical textbooks wrote less often about the uvula than about the
tonsils, but textbooks of surgery, particularly throat surgery, included
disorders of the uvula. In 1900 the popular *Manual of Surgery* discussed
its elongation:

At first it merely lasts for a time, and by the use of astringents
disappears; but later on the elongation becomes chronic, and
causes great irritation of the back of the tongue and fauces,
resulting in a troublesome throat-cough and even vomiting. Under
such circumstances it should be removed.

Discussing 'sensitive' – as opposed to 'robust' – patients, the leading
American ENT professor W L Ballenger wrote in his book *Diseases of
the Nose, Throat and Ear: Medical and Surgical* (1908):

Nausea and vomiting, especially early in the morning, are sometimes complained of. Patients have applied to me for the relief of
the persistent hacking cough, fearing tuberculosis had set in. An
examination of the lungs failed to reveal disease in that region,

whereas an examination of the throat showed the presence of a long pendulous uvula. The amputation of the lower relaxed portion of the uvula immediately stopped all symptoms.

There was also some awareness of psychological aspects of uvula disorder. Again, those involved were usually women. William Lamb, Honorary Surgeon to the Birmingham Ear and Throat Hospital, in his *Practical Guide to the Diseases of the Throat, Nose and Ear* (1909), mentioned how there can be great changes without complaint, yet:

> It is a familiar experience that many patients, especially women of nervous temperament, complain of acute throat discomforts of various sorts, although the closest scrutiny may fail to detect any considerable local change. In such cases active local treatment is likely to do harm by focussing the patient's interest on a part which is already receiving too much attention.

The fashion for removing the uvula died completely. Modern surgeons seldom operate on it. A search of modern surgical texts found that its enlargement is not even mentioned and an enquiry among ENT surgeons and anaesthetists revealed little or no experience of operations on the uvula. One of them, a retired anaesthetist, thought he had anaesthetised just one or two uvulectomies in his career, and a retired ENT surgeon had seen many long uvulae but had never seen the need to excise one. This may be largely due to the relative conquest of infection during our time – which merely raises another question: why did operations on the uvula cease, while those on tonsils increased? Medical fashion is a weird and wonderful subject, full of fascination!

Conclusion

Modern Western medicine benefits us all, prolonging our lives and increasing our comfort, well-being and fitness. I have argued, however, that it has influenced us to an unrealistic degree with its 'progress', its 'breakthroughs' and its 'miracles'. The result has been that, when its disadvantages become evident, its mistakes are revealed and its villains are exposed, some of the differences between doctors and patients can no longer be concealed. Then follows an outcry, with distrust and hostility that affects both doctors and patients. Without denigrating the idea of progress, and believing that much progress has indeed been made, I have tried to show that there are other aspects of medicine that need to be understood in order to arrive at a balanced view.

There are many questions we need to ask. What determines and influences medical fashion? Why is a successful or apparently successful treatment so often applied so extensively and so wrongly? We might also consider the attitudes of people (e.g. patients and parents) towards doctors. What has given them so much confidence in medical practitioners, and how far have they dictated the terms? What made them, and their doctors, so enthusiastic for local intervention and treatment? Why is there a tendency in doctors, patients and parents to ignore evidence, however strong, that is contrary to their views? When and how does any evidence, as opposed to feelings, influence medical practice? How far is the practice of medicine and surgery a pastime, a ritual or a game that adapts itself to changing conditions, demands and possibilities? These are huge questions, demanding much careful thought and investigation in the future if we are ever to come to any profound conclusions. We would, however, surely benefit from examining them and acting on our conclusions.

Of all the various aspects of medicine, one of the most important to understand is how medicine 'progresses' through fashions and how the process of fashion is essential to progress. Taking that point of view, and casting our sights backwards into the fascinating history of medicine, we can come to a different and, I suggest, healthier understanding of the subject.

Further Reading

Ackerknecht, Erwin H, *A Short History of Medicine*, New York, Ronald Press Company, 1955.

Berrios, G E, & Porter, Roy, eds., *A History of Clinical Psychiatry: The Origins and History of Psychiatric Disorders*, London, Athlone, 1995.

Bynum, W F, & Porter, R, eds., *Companion Encyclopaedia of the History of Medicine*, 2 vols., London, Routledge, 1993.

Bynum, W F, & Porter R, *Medicine and the Five Senses*, Cambridge University Press, 1993.

Dally, Ann, *Women Under the Knife: A History of Surgery*, London, Hutchinson Radius, 1991.

Dally, Ann, *Fantasy Surgery, 1880–1930*, Amsterdam & Atlanta, GA, Rodopi, 1996.

De Moulin, Daniel, *A History of Surgery*, Dordrecht, Martinus Nijhoff, 1988.

Dubos, Rene, *The Mirage of Health*, New York, Harper, 1959.

Foucault, M, *The Birth of the Clinic*, trans. A M Sheridan Smith, London, Tavistock, 1973.

Garrison Fielding, G, *An Introduction to the History of Medicine*, 4th edn., Philadelphia & London, Saunders, 1929.

Hunter, Richard, & McAlpine, Ida, *Three Hundred Years of Psychiatry*, Oxford, Oxford University Press, 1963.

Keele, K, *Anatomies of Pain*, Oxford, Blackwell Scientific Publications, 1957.

Kiple, K F, *The Cambridge World History of Human Diseases*, Cambridge, Cambridge University Press, 1993.

McGrew, Roderick E, *Encyclopedia of Medical History*, New York, McGraw-Hill, 1985.

Manuel, Diana E, *Marshall Hall (1790–1857): Science and Medicine in Early Victorian Society*, Amsterdam, Rodopi, 1996.

Morton, Leslie, *A Medical Bibliography (Garrison and Morton): An*

Annotated Checklist of Texts Illustrating the History of Medicine, Aldershot, Hants, Gower, 1983.

Porter R, ed., *The Cambridge Illustrated History Of Medicine*, Cambridge, Cambridge University Press, 1996.

Porter, Roy, *A Social History of Madness*, London, Weidenfeld & Nicolson, 1987.

Porter, Roy, & Porter, Dorothy, *Patient's Progress: Doctor's and Doctoring in Eighteenth-Century England*, Cambridge, Polity Press, 1989.

Quain, R, ed. (1882), *A Dictionary of Medicine: Including General Pathology, General Therapeutics, Hygiene, and the Diseases Peculiar to Women and Children*, 2 vols., London, ii, 1789. New revised edn., 1894, London.

Reiser, Stanley Joel, *Medicine and the Reign of Technology*, Cambridge, Cambridge University Press, 1981.

Rosenberg, Charles E, & Goulden, Janet, eds., *Framing Disease: Studies in Cultural History*, New Brunswick, NJ, Rutgers University Press, 1992.

Scull, Andrew, *The Most Solitary of Afflictions: Madness and Society in Britain, 1700–1900*, New Haven & London, Yale University Press, 1993.

Shryock, Richard H, *The Development of Modern Medicine: An Interpretation of the Social and Scientific Factors*, 2nd edn., New York, Alfred A Knopf, 1947.

Singer, Charles, & Underwood, E A, *A Short History of Medicine*, Oxford, Clarendon Press, 1962.

Smith, F B, *The People's Health, 1830–1910*, London, Croom Helm, 1979.

Sontag, Susan, *Illness As Metaphor*, New York, Farrar, Straus & Giroux, 1978.

Wohl, Antony S, *Endangered Lives: Public Health in Victorian Britain*, London, Dent; Cambridge, Harvard Univesity Press, 1983.